# Fire in the Dark

# Rochester Studies in Philosophy
Senior Editor: Wade L. Robison
Rochester Institute of Technology
ISSN: 1529-188X

*The Scottish Enlightenment: Essays in Reinterpretation*
Edited by Paul Wood

*Kant's Legacy: Essays in Honor of Lewis White Beck*
Edited by Predrag Cicovacki

*Plato's Erotic Thought: The Tree of the Unknown*
Alfred Geier

*Leibniz on Purely Extrinsic Denominations*
Dennis Plaisted

*Rationality and Happiness: From the Ancients to
the Early Medievals*
Edited by Jiyuan Yu and Jorge J.E. Gracia

*History of Reasonableness: A Testimony and Authority
in the Art of Thinking*
Rick Kennedy

*State of Nature or Eden?
Thomas Hobbes and His Contemporaries on the Natural
Condition of Human Beings*
Helen Thornton

*Fire in the Dark: Essays on Pascal's Pensées and
Provinciales*
Charles Natoli

# Fire in the Dark

## Essays on Pascal's *Pensées* and *Provinciales*

Charles M. Natoli

Ⓡ THE UNIVERSITY OF ROCHESTER PRESS

First published 2005

University of Rochester Press
668 Mt. Hope Avenue
Rochester, NY 14620, USA
www.urpress.com
and of Boydell & Brewer Limited
PO Box 9
Woodbridge, Suffolk IP12 3DF, UK
www.boydellandbrewer.com

ISBN: 1–58046–187–5


**Library of Congress Cataloging-in-Publication Data**

Natoli, Charles M., 1949-
 Fire in the dark : essays on Pascal's Pensées and Provinciales / Charles
M. Natoli.
  p. cm. – (Rochester studies in philosophy, ISSN 1529-188X)
 Includes bibliographical references and index.
 ISBN 1-58046-187-5 (hardcover : alk. paper)
 1. Pascal, Blaise, 1623-1662. Pensées. 2. Apologetics–History–17th
century. 3. Pascal, Blaise, 1623-1662. Provinciales. 4. Christian
ethics–History–17th century.  I. Title. II. Series.
 B1901.P43N38 2005
 230′.2–dc22
                                        2004025541


A catalogue record for this title
is available from the British Library.

This publication is printed on Acid Free Paper.
Printed in the United States of America.

*The journey to Hades.*— I, too, have been in the underworld, like Odysseus, and shall be there often yet; and not only rams have I sacrificed to be able to speak with a few of the dead, but I have not spared my own blood. Four pairs it was who did not deny themselves to my sacrifice: Epicurus and Montaigne, Goethe and Spinoza, Plato and Rousseau, Pascal and Schopenhauer. With these I must come to terms when I have long wondered alone; they may call me right and wrong; to them will I listen when in the process they call each other right and wrong. Whatsoever I say, resolve, or think up for myself and others—on these eight I fix my eyes and see theirs fixed on me.

May the living forgive me that occasionally *they* appear to me as shades, so pale and somber, so restless and, alas, so lusting for life—while those men then seem so alive to me as if now, *after* death, they could never again grow weary of life.

Nietzsche, *Human All Too Human*, II 408.
(Walter Kaufmann, trans., *Basic Writings of Nietzsche*
[New York: Random House, 1968])

nisi ingratissimi sumus, illi clarissimi sacrarum opinionum conditores nobis nati sunt, nobis vitam praeparaverunt. ad res pulcherrimas ex tenebris ad lucem erutas alieno labore deducimur. . . .

Unless we are utterly thankless, those glorious fashioners of blessed thoughts have been born for us; they have made life ready for us to live. By others' toils we are led to things finest and fairest, delved out from the darkness into the light. . . .

Seneca, *De brevitate vitae*, 14.1

# CONTENTS

# To the Reader

In the vast field of criticism on which we are entering, innu-
merable reapers have already put their sickles; yet the harvest
is so abundant that the negligent search of a straggling gleaner
may be rewarded with a sheaf.

Macaulay, "Milton"

Save for the first and the last, the eight essays in this volume have all
appeared elsewhere. Two of those previously published appeared in
English, and four in French; the latter are now translated into English. All
six of these appear here with significant revisions; in the case of "Pascal on
Proof," there are considerable additions as well. A bit of overlap has been
tolerated so that each can remain self-contained.

The present writer is not, alas, Macaulay in his masterful vein, sum-
moning shades before the authorial throne for final, definitive judgment,
and pronouncing the same in language worthy of Rhadamanthus or One
higher still. In keeping with the term's root, primordial sense, the "essays"
that follow are neither more nor less than trials or attempts. They are but
reflections of an aspiration to read with some understanding an author who
can not only richly repay the endeavor but transfigure it.

Even taken *en bloc*, the essays that follow are not an introduction to
Pascal, nor even to the *Pensées* or the *Provinciales*, save perhaps as a "leading in" to a Thebes through one of its hundred gates. Nor are they offered
as mere woof and warp from the ever-busy looms of academic cottage
industry—nor again, to vary the metaphor, and to traipse still further along
the *via negativa*, as just more grist for its slow and exceedingly fine mills.
Though they have a share in these things, these studies are as much readings and reflections as anything else.

They were undertaken out of a conviction that, as Montaigne says, "Le
guain de nostre estude, c'est en estre devenu meilleur et plus sage" (The
gain from our study is to have become better and wiser, I 26). And so, they
are presented in the hope—that fond deluder, of all evils deepest in
Pandora's Box—that they may be of some interest and profit, not only to
Pascalian and seventeenth-century scholars, but to citizens of what an
earlier day called the Republic of Letters. Or, as L. P. Wilkinson delightfully
puts it in the introduction to his notable *Golden Latin Artistry*, "to the

undergraduate, the schoolmaster, the sixth-form boy, the civil servant on Sunday, the country parson on Monday—even perhaps to the don who has specialized in other departments . . ." For even though the essays discuss particular texts, and hence at times may fall short of full transparency for readers largely unacquainted with them, they broach wide topics that are well able to spark the interest of thinking people.

About eighty percent of the matter in Pascal's fragmentary, posthumous *Pensées* consists of material destined for a never to be completed Apology for the Christian religion. In part of his argument, Pascal would convince an unbelieving reader that Christianity is uniquely able to shed light on the riddles and uncertainties of the human condition. The first of this volume's three essays on the *Pensées* poses the question of whether God, as understood by Pascal, is Himself too mysterious, especially in the matter of his justice, really to illumine what Pascal would use Him to explain. If so, why should an unbeliever exchange his present darkness for Christian darkness?

The second of these essays is a burrowing into what certainty and proof really amount to in a world where, if Pascal is right, if we speak but according to our natural lights, the truth is that Pyrrhonist skepticism is true. (In which case, small wonder that having asked "What is truth?" jesting Pilate did not stay for an answer.) The third probes the question of whether, for Pascal, in the last analysis the Hidden God of Christianity is not more deeply cloaked by speech than revealed by it.

The three studies dedicated to the *Provinciales* are largely connected with the moral question of how good is good enough for beings such as we to aspire to and to attain. May we, like Chaucer's Wife of Bath, have the world in our time while yet accounting ourselves in good standing among the good? Is it enough, like her, to dismiss not only sexual restraint but other Evangelical rigors as counsels of perfection for a handful of saintly enthusiasts? May we thus well content ourselves, like the Tibetan monks in James Hilton's *Lost Horizon*, with being "moderately chaste" and "moderately truthful"? (The words are the High Lama's—an ex-Jesuit!) Or, if we aspire to a proper goodness, and one really consistent with the Gospel, is it St. Theresa or bust? Though Pascal and his contemporaries weigh the matter in Christian terms, "How good is good enough" is obviously a moral question that all must face. Livy's Romans confront it head-on in the aftermath of the debacle at the Caudine Forks (IX viii–x), dividing themselves into rigorists and laxists, Jansenists and Jesuits *avant la lettre*[1] over what oath-keeping required of a trapped Roman army that

---

[1] Afterwords, the Samnite Pontius, in a flood of "Jansenist" eloquence and indignation almost worthy of the narrator's outburst in the tenth *Provinciale*, scathes the "Jesuitical" Romans for their legalisms, tricks and frauds which make a mock of the gods. Livy, IX xi.

secured its release by swearing to the state's disadvantage. And no Jesuit was ever as urbanely indulgent as Cicero in the *Pro Caelio* (xx): surely neither the prosecution nor anyone else would be so unreasonable as to reproach a young man for consorting with whores![2]

Another universal question emergent in the *Provinciales*, though again it is posed specifically within the Christian framework, concerns the weight with which the hand of the past is to weigh on the present. If the teaching of the past is to be authoritative for Christians, or for that matter for anyone, why may not our time, tomorrow's past, have the world in *its* time by supplying new authoritative pronouncements of its own? Our time's answer can be inferred from one of its most interesting innovations, to wit, the judgment that "innovation" and its cognates are no longer terms of reproach! The contrast to the stand fast, *stare decisis* mindset of more self-effacing eras is no less stark than momentous.

The first four Letters of the *Provinciales* were written to defend the Port-Royalist theologian Antoine Arnauld from the threat of expulsion from the theological faculty of the Sorbonne. At issue was Arnauld's championing of the Augustinian doctrine of irresistible ("efficacious") grace as being alone sufficient to save the souls of fallen mankind. After the failure to avert Arnauld's expulsion, the Letters turned to an attack on the laxity of the moral teachings of its prime instigators, the Jesuits, and followed with an assault on their policies and methods.

The Society of Jesus was, in fact, the arch-adversary of the more severe and conservative (if not reactionary) Augustinians. Their struggle embroiled French society from cloister to throne. The Augustinian group, or movement, most notably included the religious and Solitaries resident at the

---

[2] The pagan Romans, like Augustine later, were convinced that if prostitutes were not available, the world would be torn apart by lust, i.e., that married women and virgins would be seduced and attacked in their stead. But presupposing, unlike the saint in this context, that "ought implies can," by and large they concluded that affairs with whores were not only inevitable but permissible, especially for young men. "Verum si quis est qui etiam meretriciis amoribus interdictum iuventuti putet, est ille quidem valde severus" (*Pro Caelio*, xx). In fact, such amours are even praiseworthy, since the choice, after all, is between "expugnare pudicitiam" and "explere libidinem" (ibid.). Hence the famous anecdote in which Cato, a byword for old-time severity, praises a man he sees exiting a bordello (though the frequency of his visits later provokes Cato to remark that he had praised the fellow for visiting the *lupanar*, not for living there). The stricter virtue of the most severe among the worthies of old is dismissed by Cicero as belonging more properly to "divinis" than "bonis" (xvii). But our age, he continues, has repudiated such severity. And so "detur aliquid ætati; sit aduluscentia liberior;. . . vincat aliquando cupiditas voluptasque rationem, dum modo illa in hoc genere præscriptio moderatioque teneatur . . ." (xviii). We will see these themes below in the mouth of the *Provinciales'* Jesuits, especially in chapter 4, "Revelation/Revolution."

Abbey of Port-Royal; "fellow travelers" such as Pascal; and a vast network of their friends, relations and readers. However, it is important to bear in mind that Augustine's prestige and influence were then such that he had hosts of admirers, whether real or merely professed, even among the opponents of the "movement." The Jesuits themselves could praise Augustine, however much they might rage against the Augustinians whom they stigmatized, and who allowed themselves to be stigmatized, as "Jansenists."[3]

In the event, the Jesuits, powerfully backed by the state, emerged victorious. The lot of the losers included prison, exile, disgrace, disbanding, even disinterment. But, as the pamphlet war of the *Provinciales* was to reveal, very many people besides "movement" Augustinians could be profoundly scandalized by what Pascal portrayed as the Jesuits' sly bid to gain universal influence through policies of innovation and accommodation— "All for the times and nothing for the truth." A landmark of French prose, the *Provinciales* so efficaciously derided and denounced the Jesuits, and especially moral laxities authorized by their casuists (IV–X), that they inflicted lasting wounds on the reputation of the Society. As for the Jansenists, if they still suffer from a stigma of heresy, they also benefit from the pathos evoked by brutal persecution, and from the romance attached to a nobly fought Lost Cause.

In addition to the six previously published studies, there are two new essays, one introductory and one concluding, "book-ends" if you will. Although they could be taken together as a Pascal-centered reflection on the philosophy of religion, they are presented here as a frame for the other essays and, in the case of the concluding one, as a lead-in to a question that I think every book of this kind should end with. And so? *Après?*

Much that is found in Pascal resonates immediately with a modern audience. But despite his incomparable gifts of expression, some of his views and matter are dark or alien to most modern readers. In the essays that follow, I have tried to be lucid without sacrificing worthwhile nuances. As Einstein said, things should be as clear as possible, but not clearer. At the least, I hope not to have visited upon the patient reader the plague of Egyptian darkness that can easily descend on topics such as those lying before us. Nor to have blotted the page with jargon and needless terms of art, "words that would make Quintillian stare and gasp." How successful this particular "essay" has or has not been the reader may decide.

[3] This ordinarily pejorative term not only shifts the focus from Augustine, but, by invoking a near-contemporary (Jansenius died in 1638), disparagingly hints at innovation and novelty. In addition, "Jansenism" labels its adherents as members of a sect and so, by insinuation, heretics (via the term's Greek root *hairesis*). The topic of innovation is taken up in chapter 4, "Revelation/Revolution."

# TEXTS AND CITATIONS

Pascal's *Pensées* is cited according to the Classiques Garnier edition of Philippe Sellier by *pensée* or fragment number, e.g., fr.S 43. Pascal's own quotations aside, text in italics was crossed out by him.

The readings of Sellier's edition are the best, and it best preserves the integrity of individual fragments as well as the ordering of them made definitive by Pascal's death. This order, that of the "Second Copy" of the notes and drafts found by Pascal's family after his death, is found in the Oxford World's Classics partial translation by A. H. Levi and is to be followed in Roger Ariew's forthcoming translation from Hackett. Ariew's translation is also to include all of the fragments from Sellier's edition that do not figure in the "Second Copy." Readers may consult Sellier's Introduction for details on the very complex questions of edition surrounding the *Pensées*.

References to the *Provinciales*, first published individually in a clandestine series of anonymous Letters, are given by Roman and Arabic numeral for letter and page of the Classiques Garnier edition edited by Louis Cognet and revised by Gérard Ferreyrolles.

Other Pascal references are, when preceded by "OC," to volume and page of Jean Mesnard's edition of his *Œuvres complètes* (four volumes to date), or, as indicated in a few cases, to the page of Louis Lafuma's one volume *Œuvres complètes* in the L'Intégrale series.

Greek and Roman, and other standard or "canonical" authors—for example, Aquinas, Montaigne, Nietzsche, and Bunyan—are referenced by book and/or numbered section or line when these are the same in all editions. (When, in a few instances, page references for translations of classical authors are needed, they are given by volume and page in Harvard's Loeb Classical Library edition.) All other references are given in full on their first appearance in the notes, and in a shortened form thereafter. There is a Select Bibliography at the end of the volume.

Fine translations by A. J. Krailsheimer of both *The Provincial Letters* and the *Pensées* have appeared in the Penguin Classics series, though the latter follows the less preferable "First Copy" order of L'Intégrale and the former is unfortunately out of print. The Classiques Garnier and the most recent Penguin edition of the *Pensées* contain a concordance that correlates the numbering orders of the First and Second Copies.

Background to, exposition of, and commentary on the *Pensées* and *Provinciales*, along with the rest of Pascal's thought, can be found in the *Cambridge Companion to Pascal*. The introductions to the Oxford and Penguin *Pensées* are helpful. For a detailed account of the *Pensées*, see Jean Mesnard's magisterial *Les Pensées de Pascal*. Leszek Kolakowski's fine *God Owes Us Nothing* and Gérard Ferreyrolles's concisely informative *Les Provinciales* provide valuable discussions of the *Letters* and their background. Walter Rex's *Introduction to the Provincial Letters* is also quite helpful for background while Richard Parish's *Pascal's Lettres Provinciales* is an illuminating analysis of their polemical art. In English, Krailsheimer's *Pascal* furnishes a concise overview of his life and work while Marvin O'Connell's *Blaise Pascal* is a good recent biography.

Schopenhauer managed to be, along with Nietzsche, the most readable of German philosophers despite such titles as *Parerga and Paralipomena*—surely a publisher's nightmare—and despite including a multitude of untranslated quotations in their original English, Spanish, Italian, French, and Latin (though for the benefit of the ignorant he translated into Latin the citations he gave in Greek). Lacking Schopenhauer's daring no less than his learning, I have thought it best to include translations of non-obvious foreign language material that appears in the text. Save for biblical texts they are mine unless otherwise noted, though I have occasionally consulted published versions. As the translations are of passages offered chiefly to ground or to illustrate links in a chain of reasoning, they are on the literal side and have no great pretention to literary merit.

As allowed by the essay format, and in ludicrous imitation of two of my idols, Schopenhauer and Montaigne, I have sprinkled the texts with a few quotations from literary sources. Sometimes they illustrate anticipations, parallels, or echoes of Pascalian themes, but more often than not they simply speak my mind better than I could possibly do. These are chiefly from the Latin classics, a specialty to us but intellectual pith and marrow to the early moderns.

# ACKNOWLEDGMENTS

Thanks for financial support for this project, including a sabbatical during which much of the final work was done, are due to St. John Fisher College. The earlier work on the original essays extended over many years, much of it done in relative isolation from major research libraries and departments of French literature. That isolation sometimes made the task at hand more laborious and uncertain than it would otherwise have been—laborious trifling, *magno iam conatu magnas nugas*, was a recurrent fear!—but the work was almost always enjoyable.

I am grateful to the publishers of the six previously published essays for permission to use them in this book.

Particular thanks must go to John A. Gallucci of Colgate University for a close and astute reading of a draft of this manuscript as well as for remarks on an early draft of "Révelation/Révolution." It is part of a larger indebtedness for stimulating, though all-too-infrequent, intellectual contact over many years. Thanks are due as well to my colleague Robert Brimlow, a philosopher of religion, who also offered insightful remarks on a draft of this book. Nor should I omit to mention colleagues and audiences gathered at Portland State University, where a much more concise "Proof in Pascal's *Pensées*" was given at the invitation of the University Honors Program, and at meetings of the North American Society for Seventeenth Century French Literature (NASSCFL), where other essays were presented. My wife, Joanna Natoli, kindly helped with the final edit and the proofreading. If not for her expertise in English literature, the misfortunate reader would have been compelled to wend his way through syntax even more labyrinthine than that before him. My friend and colleague Douglas Howard, steeped alike in Jacobean drama and the *dernier cri*, also lent a hand with the proofs as did Timothy Madigan, another colleague and friend.

Well does Pascal say that, though an author may speak of "my book," if one were to subtract from it all that came from others, little would be left. This is apt to be especially true of books on Pascal himself. In the last half-century in particular, he has been unusually fortunate in the quality of the scholars he has attracted, most notably, but not only, in France. Like all contemporary students of Pascal, I am generally and deeply indebted to them, and I count it a privilege to have known the ones I have been fortunate enough to meet. Special mention must be made of the groundbreaking work of Philippe Sellier and of Jean Mesnard, and of the *rayonnement* of their influence. It extends far beyond the many first-rate scholars they have mentored in France to those they have inspired in Japan, the United States, and elsewhere.

For any errors or misjudgments, though, I am indebted only to myself. I can only hope that I should not be saying, along with Scarron in his prefatory "Au lecteur scandalisé," that this book is its own Errata.

# PLACES OF FIRST PUBLICATION

"Proof in Pascal's *Pensées*: Reason as Rhetoric." In *Meaning, Structure and History in the* Pensées *of Pascal: A Colloquium Organized by the University Honors Program of Portland State University* (*April 5–6, 1989*), ed. David Wetsel, 19–32. Paris-Seattle-Tübingen: Biblio 17, 1990.

"Pascal: mystique/anti-mystique." *Cahiers du dix-septième: An Interdisciplinary Journal* 7, no. 1 (1992): 113–24.

"L'importance fondamentale de la justice dans l'apologétique de Pascal: le Dieu caché." In *Justice et Force. Actes du colloque «Droit et pensée politique autour de Pascal». Clermont-Ferrand, 20–23 septembre 1990*, ed. Gérard Ferreyrolles, 297–305. Paris: Éditions Klincksieck, 1996.

"Les *Provinciales*: ruse contre ruse, force contre force?" In *Le rayonnement de Port-Royal. Mélanges en l'honneur de Philippe Sellier*, ed. Dominique Descotes, Antony McKenna, and Laurent Thirouin, 289–99. Paris: Honoré Champion, 2001.

"S'aimer mieux dans un tronc d'arbre: The *Provinciales* as *Heauton timo-roumenos*." In *Philosophies of Classical France/Philosophies au siècle classique en France*, ed. Ziad Elmarsafy, 149–60. Berlin: Weidler, 2001.

"Révélation/Révolution: une réflexion sur la nouveauté dans les *Provinciales* de Pascal." In *Le savoir au XVIIe siècle. Actes du 34e congrès annuel de la North American Society for Seventeenth Century French Literature*, ed. John D. Lyons and Cara Welch, 243–53. Tübingen: Gunter Narr, 2003.

# CHRONOLOGY

The following has been compiled from the researches of others and is offered merely for the reader's convenience. For greater detail, the reader is referred to the chronology in Sellier's Classiques Garnier edition of the *Pensées*. For much greater detail, one should consult the very full chronologies by Jean Mesnard in OC I–IV.

1616? Marriage of Étienne Pascal (b.1588) and Antoinette Begon (b.1596).

1620. January 3. Baptism of Gilberte Pascal.

1623. June 19. Birth of Blaise Pascal at Clermont-Ferrand.

1625. October 5. Birth of Jacqueline Pascal. Mother Angélique Arnauld, abbess of Port-Royal, establishes a new house for her nuns, Port-Royal de Paris.

1626. Death of Pascal's mother.

1631. November. The Pascal family moves to Paris. In the nine or so years that follow, Blaise will be educated at home by his father. A prodigy, Blaise will be introduced by him to leading figures in mathematics, science and literature.

1638. Solitaries, laymen imbued with Augustinian piety, retire to the vacant abbey of "old" Port-Royal, now called Port-Royal des Champs.

1640. Spring. The Pascal family goes to Rouen where the father has been put in charge of tax collection.

Pascal's "Essai sur les coniques" ("Essay on Conics") appears in Paris.

Posthumous publication of the *Augustinus* of Cornelius Jansen (d.1638).

1641. June 13. Gilberte Pascal marries Florin Périer.

1645. Pascal perfects an arithmetical calculating machine, the product of three years of work, designed to aid in his father's work as a tax official.

1646. January to March. After falling on the ice and breaking his thigh, Étienne Pascal is tended by two pious Norman gentlemen, the Deschamps brothers, followers of the Augustinian teachings of Jansen's friend Jean Duvergier de Hauranne, abbot of Saint-Cyran (d.1643). Introduced by them to the deeply Augustinian piety of Saint-Cyran and the Cistercian abbey of Port-Royal, the entire family undergoes a conversion to its principles, beginning with Blaise (his "first conversion").

1647. Pascal, suffering severe headaches and in delicate health since the spring, and his sister Jacqueline move to Paris in the summer.

In September (23 and 24) he is visited by Descartes (several others are also present). The first day's discussion revolves around the arithmetical machine and the possibility of the vacuum. For the second day's discussion fewer are present, and Descartes offers observations on Pascal's illness.

Blaise and Jacqueline begin to frequent Port-Royal de Paris, where they attend Singlin's sermons.

In October, Pascal publishes his *Expériences nouvelles touchant le vide* (*New Experiments Regarding the Vacuum*).

1648. January 26. Pascal states his adherence to the Augustinian doctrine of grace in a letter to Gilberte.

September 19. At Pascal's request, his brother-in-law, Florin Périer, performs an experiment at Puy-de-Dôme which confirms that atmospheric pressure varies inversely with altitude. This leads to the publication of a further work on the vacuum, *Récit de la grande expérience* (*Account of the Great Experiment*).

Nuns from Port-Royal de Paris, led by Mother Angélique Arnauld, take up residence again at Port-Royal des Champs. Solitaries return to its environs.

1649. May. The Pascal family leaves Paris on account of the civil broils of the Fronde and takes up residence till November of the following year with Florin and Gilberte Périer at Clermont-Ferrand.

1651. September 4. Étienne Pascal dies in Paris.

1652. January 4. Jacqueline Pascal enters Port-Royal de Paris to become a nun despite her brother's strong misgivings.

1653. May 31. On the "question of right," Pope Innocent XI condemns five propositions alleged to be found (the soon-to-be-famous "question of fact") in Jansenius's *Augustinus*. For Pascal, a "wordly period" largely dedicated to the glories of the mind, and in particular to mathematics and science, begins to wane.

June 5. Jacqueline Pascal takes her vows at Port-Royal de Paris.

1654. Pascal finishes his *Traités de l'équilibre des liqueurs et de la pesanteur de la masse de l'air* (*Treatises on the Equilibrium of Liquids and on the Weight of the Air Mass*) which will be published posthumously in 1663.

He writes a *Traité du triangle arithmétique* (*Treatise on the Arithmetical Triangle*). It too will be published posthumously (1665).

His disdain for "the world" deepens. On the night of November 23, he undergoes a profound mystical and religious experience, his celebrated "nuit de feu," that will seal his "second conversion." He will carry with him a document memorializing the experience (the "Mémorial," fr.S 742) sewn and re-sewn into the lining of his clothing for the rest of his life.

1655. January 7–28. Pascal is on retreat at Port-Royal. The *Entretien avec M. de Sacy sur Epictète et Montaigne* (*Interview with M. de Sacy on Epictetus and Montaigne*) may date from this time.

He composes the *Abrégé de la vie de Jésus-Christ* (*Shortened Account of the Life of Christ*) and two versions of *De l'esprit géometrique* (*On the Geometrical Mind*). He begins work on the *Écrits sur la grace* (*Writings on Grace*), which will continue till early in the following year.

1656. About January 20. Pascal spends a few days with the Jansenist theologian Antoine Arnauld, who has been condemned (January 14) by the Sorbonne's Faculty of Theology on the "question of fact." He commits himself to the defense of Arnauld in the Letters that will be known as the *Provinciales*.

January 23. Title date of the first of Pascal's eighteen *Provinciales* (*Provincial Letters*). The first three are in support of Arnauld, who is now menaced with condemnation by the Faculty of Theology on the "question of right." They are too late to prevent his condemnation on this score as well (January 29), though it will be brilliantly derided in Letter III. Letters IV–X will be directed against the laxity of the Jesuits' casuists, and the remainder of them against the proceedings and practices of the Society itself.

March 24. "Miracle of the Holy Thorn." Marguérite Périer, Pascal's niece, is cured of a lachrymal fistula by the application by touch of what is alleged to be one of the "holy thorns" from Christ's crown. Pascal begins to think and write on miracles, a project that will expand to an "Apology" for the Christian religion, and survive in the fragments that his family and friends will call *Pensées*.

September–February 1657. Correspondence of Pascal with the Roannez, including the famous letter on the hidden God to Charlotte de Roannez (October 26).

1657. March 24. The Eighteenth and final *Provinciale* appears.

October 18. News of the condemnation of the *Provinciales* reaches Paris (it has been placed on the Church's Index of Forbidden Books).

1658. Spring. Pascal finishes *Sur la conversion du pécheur* (*On the Conversion of the Sinner*) and *Comparaison des chrétiens des premiers temps avec ceux d'aujourd'hui* (*Comparison of the Early Christians with Those of Today*).

June? He begins classifying notes he has taken for his Apology into twenty-seven bundles or dossiers (*liasses*) with titles. Perhaps as a result of this activity, he gives a conference at Port-Royal on the argument of his projected Apology (fr.S 182).

Late 1658–early 1659. Pascal writes and publishes treatises on the problem of the cycloid and other mathematical works.

1659. February to June. Pascal's health is drastically impaired. In November he will write *Prière pour demander à Dieu le bon usage des maladies* (*Prayer to Ask God How to Make Good Use of Illness*).

1660. He is seriously ailing for most of the year. He writes texts that Pierre Nicole will flesh out and publish in 1670 as *Trois discours sur la condition des grands* (*Three Discourses on the Condition of the Great*).

1661. February 1. An anti-Jansenist oath (the first "Formulaire") is imposed by the Assemblé du Clergé. If ordered by their Bishop, clergy and *maîtres d'écoles* must sign under pain of being accounted a heretic.

The nuns at Port-Royal, including Pascal's sister, Jacqueline, are powerfully pressured to sign. Jacqueline, full of remorse at signing, will die on October 4.

Pascal opposes signing, and will quarrel bitterly on this issue with Arnauld and Nicole. Disenchanted, he works more and more on his Apology.

Autumn. The Périer family moves to Paris.

1662. Pascal and the Duc de Roannez launch an omnibus service in Paris (the "carrosses à cinq sols").

June 29. The gravely ill Pascal goes to Gilberte's home so that she, who has been caring for him at his own lodgings, will not contract the small-pox of a child living there.

Early July. Pascal receives several visits from doctors. Noting that he has no fever, they declare that his illness is not mortal.

August 17. At about midnight Pascal, having suffered violent convulsions, receives the Eucharist he has long been requesting. His last words before losing consciousness for the final time are "Que Dieu ne m'abandonne jamais!" (May God never abandon me!)

August 19. He dies at one o'clock in the morning. He will be buried two days later in the church of Saint-Étienne-du-Mont in Paris.

Gilberte composes a short biography of her brother, *Vie de M. Pascal.*

1670. January 2. Publication of a selection of the "most finished" of Pascal's papers by a group of Pascal's family and friends. Some texts are retouched so as to avoid controversy. The editors call the collection *Pensées sur la religion et sur quelques autres sujets (Thoughts on Religion and on Some Other Subjects)*. This, the "Port-Royal edition" of the *Pensées*, appears with an important preface by Étienne Périer, Pascal's nephew.

1684. Publication of Gilberte's *Vie de M. Pascal.*

1687. Death of Gilberte Périer.

# PART ONE

## OPENING

# 1

## FIRE IN THE DARK

impiaque aeternam timuerunt saecula noctem.

And the unholy ages feared the everlasting dark.

Virgil, *Georgics,* 1.468

Though Blaise Pascal's years were few (1623–1662), they were replete with versatile accomplishment. For he was not only the inventor of a sophisticated computing machine, and the designer of a public transportation system for Paris, but a mathematician, physicist, philosopher, Christian apologist, theological controversialist, and rhetorician of striking genius. But although, like Leibniz after him,[1] he could pass for the very model of a modern-era polymath, his claims on the attention of posterity, like Leibniz's, far exceed those of mere breadth or of mere knowledge. He is a spiritual blood-brother to every one of us, believer or not, who has, like Jacob, wrestled with the angel. What has made him so is the testimony of his pen, above all in the fragmentary remains known to us as the *Pensées.* They, together with the exquisitely finished *Provinciales,* have secured him a place in the foremost rank of France's immortal writers and thinkers. As contributions to the modern world's intellectual and literary capital, his achievements are *un acquis.*

---

[1] Even so, comparison with Leibniz soon falters given that Pascal, apologist though he is, fails to attempt a theodicy of the type essayed in Leibniz's celebrated *Théodicée* (1710)—that is, one that would account for the moral and physical evil of the world in terms of principles acceptable to *le sens commun.* (See chapter 6, "The Fundamental Importance of Justice.") By implication Pascal is even a kind of anti-Leibniz inasmuch as the first ten of his *Provincial Letters* pillory the Jesuits' moral theology in much the way that Voltaire's *Candide* laughed Leibnizian theodicy out of the court of respectable opinion. (See chapter 3, "Preferring to Live in a Tree Trunk.")

But the foregoing grandiose platitudes should not be allowed to mislead, true as Gospel though they are. (And how true that is, readers who have experienced the haunting insight and penetrating expression that Pascal marshalled on behalf of the Faith are peculiarly well-equipped to say.) For, although Pascal was well aware of his abilities—and was, indeed, proud of them—unlike, say, Thucydides, he never set out to bequeath to posterity a "possession for all time." Nor, indeed, did he aim to confect "literature" at all. Yet, certainly with the *Pensées,* and arguably with the *Provinciales,* he not only succeeded, but succeeded eminently at doing both. However, his literary success is not only largely incidental insofar as it is a success, but also, from his point of view, insofar as it is "his." For like his master, St. Augustine, he was deeply imbued with a conviction that seemed both demanded by orthodoxy and confirmed by introspection—to wit, that the credit for "our" good is properly not ours at all but Another's. *Non nobis, Domine.*

## THE GUEST WHO TARRIETH BUT A DAY

ἐπάμεροι· τί δέ τις; τί δ’ οὔ τις; σκιᾶς ὄναρ ἄνθρωπος.

Creatures of a day! What is someone? What is no one? Man
is the dream of a shadow.

Pindar, *Pythians,* 8.95–96

But, unlike many another author of a literary or philosophical monument more enduring than bronze, the proverbial *monumentum aere perennius,* Pascal is no mere quarry for literary Burkes and Hares, "resurrection men" of academe. Like Montaigne, arguably the chief of his adversaries of election, he has been and remains a living presence to readers across a wide spectrum of *le public honnête*—that is to say, to a multitude of that quite respectable element, in the world and of it, whose moral address lies somewhere between Babylon and Jerusalem.[2] He has proved to have a remarkable ability to engage, not only the otherworldly, but a sizable number of the hard-headed ranks of the free-thinking and easy-living, the *libertins* from his day to ours. In great measure, this is due to his refusal to flinch in his stark, forceful, portrayals of our human condition—nay, our plight. With these jolting and sobering depictions, he strives to awaken his readers from the doze of their banal illusions, to bring them face to face with themselves,

[2] The universality of Pascal's appeal is evidenced by its allure to even his real or seeming antipodes. For one such case see my *Nietzsche and Pascal on Christianity* (Berne: Peter Lang, 1985).

and thus to discover themselves. They will then stand revealed as enigmas adrift on universal flux (fr.S 748); as wayfaring strangers, passing on after only a day; and as the lost, engulfed by infinities past and future, large and small, viewed *en abyme*.

> Quand je considère la petite durée de ma vie absorbée dans l'éternité précédente et suivante, *memoria hospitis unius diei praetereuntis*, le petit espace que je remplis et même que je vois, abîmé dans l'infinie immensité des espaces que j'ignore et qui m'ignorent, je m'effraie et m'étonne . . . . (fr.S 102; cf. 230)

> When I consider the brief span of my life absorbed in the eternities that precede it and come after, *[as] the remembrance of a guest that tarrieth but a day* [Wisdom 5:15], and the little space that I fill and even that that I see, engulfed in the infinite immensity of spaces that know me not nor I them, I am terrified and astounded . . . .

"Twilight and evening bell, and after that the dark!" That, at the end of a mere day, we must find ourselves "Crossing the Bar," mere Philosophy can tell us of ourselves. But, just as grace perfects nature, so, for Pascal, Philosophy's Delphic injunctions to "Know thyself" and "Have a care for thyself" can only be *completely* fulfilled by a power above Philosophy, one that alone can reveal our origin and goal. And so, at the last, Pascal would explain his readers to themselves by bringing them to glimpses, though they be but in a glass and darkly, of a hidden God's elusive revelations in the world's *chiaroscuro*. But before we can see the half-light, we must see the dark.

> . . . en regardant tout l'univers muet et l'homme sans lumière abandonné à lui même et comme égaré dans ce recoin de l'univers sans savoir qui l'y a mis, ce qu'il est venu faire, ce qu'il deviendra en mourant, incapable de toute connaissance, j'entre en effroi comme un homme qu'on aurait porté endormi dans une île déserte et effroyable [. . . .] [J]e demande [aux autres] s'ils sont mieux instruits que moi. Ils me disent que non. Et sur cela ces misérables égarés, ayant regardé autour d'eux et ayant vu quelques objets plaisants, s'y sont donnés et s'y sont attachés (fr 229; cf. 195–8).[3]

> . . . on seeing the whole universe to be silent and man, without light, abandoned to himself and as if lost in this corner of the

---

[3] Cf. "Quid autem mirum est, si in his circuitibus errantes nec aditum nec exitum inveniunt? Quia genus humanum atque ista nostra mortalitas nec quo initio coepta sit sciunt, nec quo fine claudatur . . . ." Augustine, *De civitate dei* XII 15.

universe, not knowing who has put him there, what he has
come to do, what will happen to him on dying, incapable of
any knowledge, I become terrified like a man who has been
transported while asleep to an out of the way[4] and terrifying
island [. . . .] I ask [other people] if they are better informed
than I am. They tell me no. Then these wretched, lost people, having looked about them and seen some pleasant
objects, gave themselves over to them and attached themselves to them.

For Pascal can hope to appeal only to unbelievers who feel, or who
can be brought to feel, something of the world's mystery, and so be
brought to quest for its unriddling. To the unbeliever like Turgenev's
Bazarov—"I only look up to heaven when I want to sneeze"—he will
remain a closed book. Rather, his appeal will be to readers who have sat
nights at mead with the anonymous counselor to King Edwin in Bede.
A pagan, but one who is weighing coming to the New Faith, in a debate
thereon before the king he famously likened the life of man to a sparrow,
which, winging in under the hall's open eaves from the stormy dark
outside, is briefly lit by the glow of the sheltering hall's central fire, and
speeding out goes straightaway into the dark again.[5]

> Talis mihi videtur, rex, vita hominum praesens in terris, ad
> comparationem eius quod nobis incertum est temporis, quale
> cum te residente ad coenam cum ducibus ac ministris tuis
> tempore brumali, accenso quidem foco in medio et calido
> effecto coenaculo, furentibus autem foris per omnia
> turbinibus hiemalium pluviarum vel nivium, adveniensque
> unus passerum domum citissime pervolaverit qui cum per
> unum ostium ingrediens, mox per aliud exierit. Ipso quidem
> tempore quo intus est, hiemis tempestate non tangitur, sed
> tamen parvissimo spatio serenitatis ad momentum excurso,
> mox de hieme in hiemem regrediens, tuis oculis elabitur. Ita
> haec vita hominum ad modicum apparet; quid autem
> sequatur, quidve praecesserit, prorsus ignoramus. Unde si

[4] A. H. Levi renders "île déserte" as the more obvious "deserted island," but this, if
construed strictly, belies what follows. Clearly, if the island were uninhabited save
for oneself, there would be no others to ask for information. A. J. Krailsheimer's
"desert island" can suggest climate, which is not at issue.
[5] That the sparrow's passage into fleeting security and visibility is at night follows
from its occurrence during the evening meal (*coenam*) at or about the time of the
winter solstice (*tempore brumali*). The translation above is J. E. King's version
(based on Thomas Stapleton's 1565 translation) in Bede, *Historical Works*
(Cambridge, Mass. and London: Harvard University Press, 1930), vol. 1, 283, 285,
with a few changes.

haec nova doctrina certius aliquid attulit, merito esse sequenda videtur (*Hist. eccles.* II 13).

Such seemeth to me, o king, the present life of men here on earth for the comparison of our uncertain time to live, as if, at the time of winter's longest dark, a sparrow should come to the house and very swiftly flit through; which entereth at one opening and straightaway passeth out through another, while you sit at supper with your captains and servants; the parlour being then made warm with the fire kindled in the midst thereof, but all places abroad being troubled with raging tempests of winter rain and snow. Right for the time it be within the house, it feeleth no smart of the winter storm, but after a very short space of fair weather that lasteth but for a moment, it soon passeth again from winter to winter and escapeth your sight. So the life of man here appeareth for a little season, but what followeth or what hath gone before, that surely we know not. Wherefore if this new teaching hath brought us any better surety, methinks it is worthy to be followed.

A sparrow, not an eagle. We are figured, not in the mastery of a bird of prey, but in the vulnerability of a bird for prey. A sparrow, not an owl, whose superb ability to see into the dark makes it so fitting an image of the wisdom we do not have.

Then again, because he may be expected to be less docile initially, Pascal's reader might be better thought of as one who, worldling though he is, echoes at times the indignant plaint of Fitzgerald's Omar Khayyám (xxx):

> What, without asking, hither hurried Whence?
> And, without asking, Whither hurried hence!

And who echoes "Old Khayyám's" response, an emphatic even if distressed *carpe diem*! Pluck the Day! Pluck the Grape!

> Another and another Cup to drown
> The Memory of this Impertinence!

Let there be an end to futile searching.

> But leave the Wise to wrangle, and with me
> The Quarrel of the Universe let be:
> And, in some corner of the Hubbub coucht,
> Make Game of that which makes as much of Thee. (xlv)

Rather, recline in the perfumed bosom of "objets plaisants." Pluck *divertissements*.

> Here with a Loaf of Bread beneath the Bough,
> A Flask of Wine, a Book of Verse
> —and Thou
>
> Beside me singing in the Wilderness—
> And Wilderness is Paradise enow. (xi)

The prodigiously difficult and delicate task of Pascalian rhetoric will be to rouse such a one from his cups, pry him loose from his verse and his mistress, jolt him out of his indifference, and, finally, guide him through the "wrangles of the wise." It will be to bring man without light, "l'homme sans lumière" (fr.S 229), to see the dark as a calamity since the truth it veils may be of the utmost moment (fr.S 680–82), and thus to seek with groans (fr.S 24) until emerging into a light that both reveals and blinds. At which point, the apologist can only hope that the God the dark envelops will, of his grace, kindle faith in the heart.

But when all is said, just Whom does this light enshroud?

## "WHO DO YOU SAY THAT I AM?"

"And you," he said to them, "who do you say that I am?"

Matt. 16:15 [repeated in Mark 8:29 and Luke 9:20]

Strictly speaking, in his *Pensées* Pascal disparages the rhetorical rather than the logical power of the traditional proofs of God's existence from nature (fr.S 222). But, in any event, since they do not conclude to Christ, they are of little use to an apologist. For to infer the existence of a Primordial Truth as a ground for eternal verities of mathematics is not to make great strides towards one's salvation (fr.S 690). When it comes time to speak of God, and especially to speak of Him to unbelievers, for Pascal the question of *who* God is is always, even if unvoiced, the foreground concern. It frames or over-shadows the question of his mere existence even when the latter question infrequently emerges. To follow Pascal's thinking carefully, whether we have before us apologetic texts, such as the fragment containing his cele-brated wager, or polemical and/or expository ones, such as the *Provincial Letters* and the *Writings on Grace*, we would do well to keep this point present to mind. A few remarks on the argument called the wager may serve by way of illustration.

### 1. A MODEST WAGER

Led by Laurent Thirouin, recent scholarship has made it clear that this famous argument (fr.S 680), which aims, not to establish the existence of

God, but the eminent reasonableness of *believing* that God exists, was intended by Pascal to figure in an extensive and carefully wrought preamble or overture to his projected Apology for the Christian faith.[6] The argument's principal task would be to persuade an unbelieving reader to stake his all on a *belief* in divinity and eternal life. But, to learn in the here and now whether his "wager" is a good one, the unbeliever must proceed to a search for the truth of the matter, "le dessous du jeu." This will lead him to the scrutiny, and, hopefully, to the acceptance of, "proofs" of the Christian faith to be offered later.[7] The wager is only a step, not a destination.

But it is important to see, not only Pascal's intentions for the placing of the wager within his overall apologetic argumentation, but the logical weight that the argument was best suited, and apparently intended, to bear. All things considered, I think, though it is decidedly a minority view, and though the evidence is not absolutely conclusive either way, that the wager is best understood as being made on behalf of belief in *a* god, one not yet identified as the Christian God.[8]

One must, Pascal argues, either believe in a god who concedes infinite, eternal felicity to those who believe in him and who live accordingly, or refrain from such a belief. (Given the law of the excluded middle, there can be no other option.) Though we do not *know* whether or not such a being exists, it is in the highest degree advisable to *believe* that he does. For, as the chance of his existing is 50/50 (or at least not infinitely small), the magnitude of a possible infinite reward offsets the hazard of any finite stake (in this case, a lifetime of god-oriented belief and conduct). One must have renounced reason not to take a bet when one is as likely to win as not, and when the payoff would be infinite but your stake only one (eternal and hence infinite bliss to be won, one lifetime to be staked).

However, once the reader is brought to this self-interested realization, the question of who this god is, and thence of what he wishes from us by way of conduct, becomes the foreground concern. In short, the entire

---

[6] Pascal's intentions regarding the placement of the wager emerge in Laurent Thirouin's very rich discussion in *Le modèle du jeu dans la Pensée de Pascal* (Paris: Vrin, 1991), 170–90. Cf. esp 188–89. For a clear statement of key reasons underlying the placement see Philippe Sellier, "L'Ouverture de l'Apologie," *Port-Royal et la littérature*, vol. 1. *Pascal* (Paris: Honoré Chamion, 1999), 59–61.

[7] The projected sequence of themes in the entirety of Pascal's "Ouverture" is meticulously delineated from the available evidence in Sellier, "L'Ouverture de l'Apologie." Cf. also David Wetsel's introduction to his *Pascal and Disbelief* (Washington, D.C.: Catholic University Press, 1994), esp. 12–13. Sellier's, however, is the consensus view that the wager is for the Christian God.

[8] A version of the argument that follows above appeared in my "The Role of the Wager in Pascal's Apologetics," *The New Scholasticism* 57: 1 (1983):98–106. The reader is referred to it for additional details.

remainder of the Apology takes aim at the question, "Who do you say that I am?"

In support of this interpretation we may note, for example, Pascal's use of indefinite articles. In "framing" text preceding the articulation of the wager proper, we find "Ainsi on peut bien connaître qu'il y a un Dieu sans savoir ce qu'il est" (Thus one can well know that there is a God without knowing what he is). The thought here is most suggestive in light of the argument to follow. And what we may fairly take as the first words of the wager argument proper are, "S'il y a un Dieu . . ." (If there is a God).

Understanding the wager in this way—as opposed to an argument concluding directly to belief in the Christian God, and so as an Apology in itself—has, moreover, two distinct logical advantages.

First, it eludes the very obvious objection that besets a wager explicitly for the Christian God, viz., why wager on Him and not on some other deity dispensing infinite reward? Why not wager on Allah and houris? Or, as facetiously intimated in Smollett's *Humphrey Clinker*, on Jupiter and Elysium?

Second, understood as above, the wager bridges what would otherwise be a logical gap in Pascal's argumentation. It is a gap that would otherwise occur at the transition from the knowledge of man to the knowledge of God. In the dossier (*liasse*) of fragments titled *Transition*, the reader, having been incited to search for the truth, and having been shown the futility of Philosophy, is made to say: "Je vois plusieurs religions contraires, et partant toutes fausses excepté une" (I see several religions contrary to one another and hence all false, except for one, fr.S 229). The "except for one" presupposes prior belief in the existence of *a* god (at least one), whose revelation and cult the non-false religion would reveal. Pascal can hardly take "except for one" as axiomatic for an unbeliever—quite the opposite!—but he could assume it here if he understood it to rest on the reader's prior acceptance of the wager.

But even if this view of a rather more modest wager is suggested by the text, is more logically defensible, and is clearly serviceable, is it consistent with the specifically Christian elements of the text of the argument? For there are elements that, when coupled with our background knowledge of Pascal's faith and apologetic purposes, may make it seem self-evident that the wager leads directly to the Christian God. (A similar contamination by imported assumptions would see the wager as predicated on the avoidance of eternal punishment, even though the text is wholly silent on this score.)

Apparently decisive against the limited view of the wager being advanced here are the first words of the paragraph following the argument's opening ("S'il y a un Dieu"). "Qui blâmera donc les chrétiens de ne pouvoir rendre raison de leur créance, eux qui professent une religion dont ils ne peuvent rendre raison?" (Who then will blame Christians for not being able to provide a rational basis for their belief, they who profess a religion for which they cannot provide a rational basis?)

But these words are not necessarily a gloss on, and restriction of, the preceding "Dieu," and so they are from nullifying the term's indefinite article. Quite to the contrary. For these words may be naturally taken as logically following from the indefinite article in its context. "S'il y a un Dieu," Pascal says, "il est infiniment incompréhensible, puisque, n'ayant ni parties ni bornes, il n'a nul rapport a nous. Nous sommes donc incapables de connaître ni ce qu'il est, ni s'il est" (If there is a god, he is infinitely imcomprehensible, since, having neither parts nor limits, he bears no relation to us. We are thus incapable of knowing either what he is or whether he exists).

That is, since we cannot rationally prove the existence of a god, i.e., of any god, then *a fortiori* the Christians cannot vindicate their religion by proving their God. Indeed, by professing to be unable to give reasons, they conform to the demonstrable truth that a god would be beyond the reach of our reasons. Christians' professed inability to give reasons is thus, if anything, a mark in their favor!

Another apparently decisive objection to our interpretation of the wager occurs just after the argument has been articulated and accepted. An imaginary interlocutor, having been forced by the wager's logic to give his assent to it, is bid by Pascal to act *as if* he believed in the *Christian* God, "en prenant de l'eau bénite, en faisant dire des messes, etc." (by taking holy water, having Masses said, etc.).

But this counsel comes only *after* the interlocutor has asked "N'y a-t-il point moyen de voir le dessous du jeu?" (Is there no way at all of seeing how the bet turns out?). And, of course, for Pascal, to discover in this life how the wager will turn out will necessitate coming to Christianity. And so his anwer is, "Oui. L'Écriture, et le reste etc." (Yes. Scripture, and the rest, etc.). It will be only after one has intellectually assented to the wager that masses and holy water are invoked as a regimen to instill, through repetitive behavior, conviction of what will turn out to be the truth—namely, Christianity. The regimen will help one to diminish one's passions and so be receptive to its yet to be encountered "proofs," Scripture and the rest.[9] What is specifically

---

[9] Thus, of course, these proofs cannot be included in the "augmentation des preuves de Dieu" that the imaginary interlocutor is bid to forego a few lines down. This phrase can only be taken as referring to the traditional philosophical arguments for God's existence. Even if they were successful, such arguments only conclude to a first mover, first cause, necessary being, etc.—descriptions that are compatible with the Christian God, but that cannot be taken, without much more ado, as uniquely designating him.

In fr.S 681, a key part of Pascal's projected *Ouverture*, the apologist gives his own, possibly unique "preuve de Dieu." The astounding indifference of some of mankind to a question so momentous as God's existence is so utterly incomprehensible, it can only have a supernatural cause!

Christian here comes only *after* the wager has been made, and points, not to the wager, but to its outcome. The specifically Christian elements follow on the wager, not from it.

In fact, that the interlocutor is not a Christian yet is also indicated by several expressions just a few lines further on. In the most notable, Pascal asks him "Vous voulez aller à la foi . . .?" (Do you want to arrive at the Faith . . .?) He is not there yet!

## 2. STANDING IN THE WINGS, SAINT AUGUSTINE

FEU
Dieu d'Abraham, Dieu d'Isaac, Dieu de Jacob
non des philosophes et savants

FIRE
God of Abraham, God of Isaac, God of Jacob
not of philosophers and scholars

Pascal, Mémorial (fr.S 742)[10]

These famous lines from the Memorial are only the most striking reminder that, for Pascal, God is not the mere conclusion of a philosophical argument. But neither is it the Christian God in a generic or unqualified sense to whom Pascal would shepherd his reader. Or from whom, in the *Provinciales*, he would keep him from straying. It is indeed of the God of Abraham, Isaac, and Jacob, that Pascal speaks, the "Hidden God" who emerges into an ambiguous, concealing/revealing half-light in the Incarnation, the Eucharist, and Scripture. *But it is this God as represented by prevailing orthodoxy, who on close consideration will be understood, in what of his will pertains to morals and to salvation, in light of the sense of St. Augustine.*

Of course, this is a qualification that extends far beyond Pascal. One of the great achievements of French literary scholarship in the last half-century is to have revealed what Philippe Sellier aptly called the "submerged continent" (continent englouti) of Augustine's colossal influence on the *grand siècle*. Stretching far beyond wholly obvious instances such as Port-Royal, its *ancien élève* Racine, and its sometime collaborator and fellow traveler, Pascal, Augustinianism saturates or imbues a host of others, including, among

---

[10] Though now included in the *Pensées*, the paper and parchment copies of what we call the Memorial were found sewn into Pascal's clothing after his death. For the text of each see OC, III 50–51. The document evokes the experience of his celebrated "nuit de feu" (November 23, 1654). For a discussion see chapter 7, "Mystic/Anti-Mystic: Speech and Silence in Pascal's Mémorial."

the most notable, La Rochefoucauld, Mme. de Sévigné and Mme. de Lafayette.[11] Today one can say, without risk of hyperbole or whiff of paradox, that the seventeenth century in France can well be called the age of Augustine.

Our own age, however, is very far indeed from being the age of Augustine,[12] notwithstanding that the *Confessions* remain widely read, in fact a perennial best seller. Nor is it any longer the age of Augustine even in the Church. The process of separation from Augustine, begun in seventeenth-century disputes over grace,[13] has continued to our day, though usually at a glacial pace, as the Church has gradually distanced itself from the somber conception of divine justice that Augustine's views on grace implied and reflected.

But before we go any further, there are at least three closely related considerations that, though they are hardly unknown, it is profitable for a modern reader to keep present to mind.

The first—and it would be hard to overstress—is the absolute centrality of the doctrines of the Fall and Original Sin to the faith of earlier times. They are quite simply the linchpin of the whole Christian account of things. For if we are not fallen, and so enter the world without Original Sin, what need is there of a Redeemer? From what would we be redeemed? The Fall also accounts for God's being hidden from mankind; we are unworthy of his presence. This, in its turn, makes a Revelation necessary if we are to encounter Him even mediately. But to be sure respecting a Revelation, we need it to be authoritatively identified and interpreted, whence the need for a Church.

Second, prior to nineteenth-century advances in geology, biology, and literary-textual criticism, the historicity of the Garden of Eden story is taken as a matter of course. It is simply the most ancient part of ancient history. And so, when in the opening books of *Paradise Lost* Pascal's great

---

[11] For an excellent illustration of the breadth and depth of Augustine's influence see the two-volume collection of Philippe Sellier's studies, *Port-Royal et la littérature*. See also the essays collected in Dominique Descotes, Laurent Thirouin, and Antony McKenna, eds., *Le rayonnement de Port-Royal. Mélanges en l'honneur de Philippe Sellier* (Paris: Honoré Champion, 2002).

[12] After reading this sentence, a philosopher of religion of my acquaintance confessed to having been disparaged by professional colleagues as a "neo-Augustinian."

[13] The steps whereby, to all but the most submissive eyes, the Church condemned Augustine's views on grace (though not under his name) are briefly set forth by Leszek Kolakowski in *God Owes Us Nothing* (Chicago: University of Chicago Press, 1995), 3–9. Cf. also Sellier, *Port-Royal et la littérature*, vol. 2. *Le siècle de saint Augustin, La Rochefoucauld, Mme de Lafayette, Sacy, Racine* (Paris: Honoré Champion, 2000), 19–20, 52.

contemporary Milton narrates the temptation, the Fall, and the ensuing divine resolve to send a Redeemer, his account is offered—and received— not as an unalloyed poetic fiction, but as something, even in its details, very like the truth. Neither Milton nor Pascal is really very far from the outlook of Gregory of Tours in the sixth century. Wishing to put his *History of the Franks* (*Historia Francorum*) in a full perspective, Gregory matter of factly begins it with the Creation and the Fall, and confidently proceeds to tally the score of years from Adam to David, thence to Jesus, and thence to the Frankish kingdom.

Third, accepting the possibility of corporate guilt is made far easier, though not less paradoxical, if one does believe in the historicity of the Fall as an event. For, regardless of how the matter should seem to our common (all-too?) human conceptions of right, what is *in fact* decreed by the highest justice is something whose justice is *possible* because it is *actual. Ab esse ad posse.* For that matter, despite the insistence of our less clan-oriented, more individualistic age on *personal* responsibility, the notion of *corporate* guilt (or entitlement), though for very many in the West all but inconceivable, has by no means vanished from among us. (Cf. "white guilt," reparations for slavery, post-World War German "war guilt," Marxists on capitalists and proletariat, etc.) Indeed, the responsibility of the tribe for the actions of individuals is still axiomatic in many other parts of world.

What has just been said about corporate guilt in general applies as well to one specific kind, hereditary guilt, which is presupposed by the story of the Fall. As late as the mid-nineteenth century, when the Fall was still history, southern slave owners could readily persuade themselves that their chattels were expiating the sin of their ancestor Ham, Noah's son. Though paradoxical, even impossible in the light of our most commonly shared convictions about justice, hereditary guilt is nonetheless something that many among our contemporaries are well able to believe too, as more than a few Christians, and not only Christians, will still bear witness. (A close analogue to hereditary guilt is found in still prevalent notions of hereditary uncleanness or unworthiness—consider, for example, the status of the untouchables in India.) Perhaps it is even natural to wonder if we are not somehow implicated in the crimes of our ancestors, especially if present horrors seem too great to be retribution for merely personal guilt. Virgil needed no Christian theology to protest, not dogmatically but neither as a mere literary flourish, that in the bloodletting of the civil wars Rome had now sufficiently expiated the guilt of her Trojan ancestor Laomedon.[14]

---

[14] "satis iam pridem sanguine nostro/ Laomedonteae luimus periuria Troiae" (*Georgics*, I 501–2).

In Pascal's texts there is a gulf, or even an abyss, that separates his understanding of grace, and, by implication, of divine justice, from both *le sens commun* of his age and the *de iure* and *de facto* orthodoxies of our own. To appreciate what a "hard sell" he has, one need only examine his account of Augustine's views in *Writings on Grace*. (The "hard sell" he has when it comes to morals will emerge in chapter 3, "Preferring to Live in a Tree Trunk.")

In fact, the mystery of a divine justice that can appear utterly unjust to fallen mankind—a conception underlying, not only Augustine's theology of grace, but the whole orthodox doctrine of salvation in Pascal's day—was, not surprisingly, a "stone of stumbling" even to the believer of his time. This emerges starkly in fr.S 164 where the apologist, confronting the doctrine of the damnation of unbaptized infants—and this for a sin committed four thousand years before they were born!—candidly avows that nothing is a greater shock to our reason or to the conceptions of our "misérable justice." Or, in other words, nothing is harder to believe than orthodoxy and Augustine.

Augustine held that prior to their Original Sin, our first parents were, as Milton would later put it, "sufficient to stand but free to fall."[15] That is, their natural powers, as yet uncorrupted, were sufficient for them freely to coöperate (or not) with a divine grace that would enable them to do and to persevere in good.[16]

But for Augustine, the situation after the Fall is vastly different from Milton's effectively Molinist description. The entire human race has inherited the guilt of Adam and Eve's sin, and so, in strict justice, merits damnation. We have also suffered, again as a consequence of their sin, a radical corruption of our wills and our understanding. As a result, it is wholly impossible for us to choose and to persevere in the good by virtue of our unaided efforts. They alone cannot bring us to salvation.[17]

---

[15] Augustine's views on grace emerge clearly and concisely in *De correptione et gratia* (*On Admonition and Grace*). Sellier gives a clear account of its crucial points that is quite helpful. See Sellier, "Qu'est-ce que le Jansénisme," in his *Port-Royal et la littérature*, vol. 2, especially 57–64.

[16] The Molinist view of a "sufficient grace" that God makes available to all believers is in essence today's orthodoxy respecting the situation *after* the Fall of Adam and Eve. Pascal's views on some of the machinations behind its incipient success amusingly emerge in the droll satire of the first four *provinciales*.

[17] To believe the contrary is of course to fall into the error of Augustine's contemporary and *bête noire* Pelagius. Though his view may seem more indulgent and optimistic as regards our salvation, for Augustine this is far from being the case. For not only does it contradict our experience of ourselves, but its corollary—that since, through our unaided efforts, moral perfection is possible for us, *therefore it is obligatory*—would, if true, only compound the guilt of our sins.

Indeed, so corrupt is our post-lapsarian nature that no assistance less overwhelming than an "efficacious grace" can make us salvageable. A gift of God freely bestowed on those (few) whom He elects to save, bestowed without any prevision of independent merit, it is a grace so powerful that it irresistibly determines the will to coöperate with it and so to elect and to persevere in the good. As the *Provincial Letters* make clear (V 78–79), the necessity for a so potent a grace is grounded, not only in the apalling extent of our radical corruption, but in God's exigence. How good must we be to be good enough? To enable us to be good in the exalted sense in which, on an Augustinian understanding, God would have the saved be good, nothing less than efficacious grace will serve, grace that is *irresistibly* effective in orienting human will to what is good.

Thus, for Augustine, it is of God's pure mercy, by his determining will, and to the glory of both that a person is saved. But as it is by our determining will that a human soul is lost, its fate thus redounds to the glory of God's justice. From a certain point of view—one widely held in premodern and early modern philosophy and theology—an account of this sort is not only attractive, but indispensable. For God cannot be too greatly praised, and by magnifying Him while abasing and incriminating man, we glorify Him all the more by maximizing the distance between us. Contrariwise, the more God's judgments might be in keeping with those of a human race corrupt in will and understanding, the greater the risk will seem of imputing to Him a kind of imperfection by association.

In sum, then, efficacious grace is necessary for salvation, and it alone is truly sufficient grace. It may be withdrawn from one at any moment—as it was from Peter when he denied Christ. But they, and only they, who will be finally maintained in it—and we cannot in this life discern who they are—will inevitably[18] be saved.

But the God of Pascal's day differs from today's even when seen through the lens of believers who were opposed to the spirit of their age's Augustinian revival. Here, of course, the most obvious example is furnished

---

[18] This grace operates through a necessity that is internal rather than external (as opposed to what the Jansenists saw as the necessity operative in Calvinistic election). It does not, as it were, seize a sinner and forcibly remove him from the mire of sin— nor is it a "sweet chariot, comin' for to carry me home"—rather, it is a grace that inevitably attracts and secures the coöperation of the will. On this view, the freedom of the human will, though it excludes external constraint, is compatible with (inner) necessity.

This, by the way, is an understanding of freedom implicit in the orthodox view that, though the blessed and damned both retain their freedom of will, it is impossible for the latter to repent, or for the former to sin. See, for example, Aquinas, *De Veritate* Qu. XXIV art. VIII, X. Pascal contrasts the essentials of the Augustinian view of grace with those of Calvin and Molina in *Écrits sur la grace*, OC, III 781–99.

by the Jesuits, arch-foes of Port-Royal and of Pascal. In the pillory of *Provincial Letters* I–X, he derides them for legitimizing moral laxity and dispensing cheap grace. But even the Jesuits' God, though easily carica-tured as content with "Easy Virtue" (the title of one of their books), and as readily fobbed off with absurd legalisms and ruses, starkly affronts modern sensibilities in the matter of his justice. For the Jesuits were just as ortho-dox, and no more "obligeants et accommodants" than the Augustinians, when it came to glossing texts such as Acts 4:12, where salvation can be through the name of Jesus alone, and the famous John 3:5, wherein this implies being born again of Spirit and water, i.e., baptism.

The gulf between traditional soteriology and our modern sensibilities can be nicely illustrated by the oft-remarked story of the reaction of Gregory the Great (d. 604) to the sight of handsome young Britons—pagans—on sale at the slave market in Rome. Whereas a modern could be expected to sorrow at their plight—Oh, the shame that such glorious youths are sold like cattle!—or, indeed, at the institution of slavery itself, Gregory sorrows instead that folk so comely of face and form are all going to Hell! " 'Heu, pro dolor!' inquit, 'quod tam lucidi vultus homines tene-brarum auctor possidet' " ("Alas! Ah, Grief!" he said. "That the Author of Darkness possesses folk whose faces are so full of light!"). And so, when later he becomes Pope, he will famously send the missionary Augustine to Britain to convert these Angles into angels.[19]

A correlate to the severity of this venerable orthodoxy lies in another Augustinian notion, one underlying, for example, La Rochefoucauld's *Maximes*,[20] that the "virtues" of unbelievers, grounded wholly in human nature, and hence in corruption, are but veiled vices. Hence, the Augustinian indictment of the whole life of the unbeliever as a sin. "Omnis infidelium vita peccatum est."[21] Such a view of the utter and unutterable sin-fulness of natural man helps us to appreciate *its* correlate—jaw-dropping astonishment and awe at the salvific power of Christ. As St. Jerome had

---

[19] Bede, *Historia Ecclesiastica* (II 1) in *Historical Works*, vol. 1, 201 (Loeb). The story also nicely illustrates the revolution in sensibility that, beginning in the eigh-teenth century, separates the modern Western world from earlier times. For us a paradigm of injustice, slavery hardly emerged as a moral issue at all to pre-moderns. Much the same is true of torture. We are a long way from the mind-set of the ancient Sicilians in Plutarch's *Life* of Timoleon (xxxiv) who, on the day of their lib-eration from a tyrant, immediately called off school so that the children could be present at his death by torture. Beccarria's *Of Crimes and Punishments* (1764) both reflected and reinforced a new humaneness with respect to the pain of others.

[20] For three revealing essays on La Rochefoucauld's Augustinianism see Sellier's *Port-Royal et la littérature*, vol. 2, 139–89.

[21] Cited ibid., 59 n. 20; cf. 142–43. This striking and famous formulation is by Prosper of Aquitaine.

said, "Ante Christum, Abraham apud inferos; post Christum, latro in paradiso" (Before Christ, Abraham was in the infernal realm; after Christ, the
thief is in Paradise).[22]

Though the seventeenth century is commonly accounted the beginning
of the modern era, almost all of us moderns are more modern than it, and
so, whether pious or not, little likely to concede many things that Pascal's
age readily could and did. No doubt this stems largely from background
assumptions that seem self-evident to us in light of the axiomatic value we
accord our democratic heritage. Our idea of justice is that it is the same for
all, both rulers and ruled. It must embody "fair play," a "level playing field,"
an equal chance for all—*not* the will or *bon plaisir* of a monarch, nor the
arbitrary life and death power of a *paterfamilias* over his children (after all,
they are his property!). And so, on the subject of salvation and damnation,
we find ourselves markedly less willing to acquiesce in the justice of shock-
ingly severe edicts by an inscrutable Higher Power than were the early
moderns, who tended to figure justice in terms of paterfamilial or kingly
power and prerogative. Or even, following Scripture (Rom. 9:14–21), in
terms of the power of a potter over his clay.

In addition, our recognition of the self-correcting character of so successful and prestigious an enterprise as science dovetails nicely with our
habituation to the give and take of criticism characteristic of democracy. All
of these conceptions foster and reinforce our conviction that regnant
powers and orthodoxies can be in error, and that we will progress in our
ideas by challenging them and, if not overthrowing, at least refining them.
Hence, our era is fond of innovation. And hence, it is far from reflexively
submissive to claims advanced on authority, whether of church, book, or
king, or to any claims advanced as definitive, even if as part of an "immutable
deposit of faith."[23]

In short, it takes a robust "suspension of sensitivity"—that is, a kind of
Pyrrhonism of susceptibilities—for us to appreciate the choices facing a
seventeenth-century unbeliever pondering conversion, or to feel some of
the allures that helped recruit and retain both Jesuits and Jansenists. But,
without such a suspension, we can hardly enter imaginatively into a world-
view wherein, as a matter of course, under the highest justice even those
unbelievers are damned who have never heard of the Gospel, including
unbaptized infants. Indeed, Augustine insists that the latter are not spared
the fire: in the world to come, it is either bliss or torment, *regnum* or
*supplicium*.[24] Whence it follows, as a sort of *non plus ultra*—but one from

---

[22] Letter LX (Ad Heliodorum), 3.

[23] For more on this theme see chapter 4, "Revelation/Revolution."

[24] For a concise account of the Augustinian view of the damnation of unbaptized
infants along with relevant citations, notably from *De natura et origine animi* and

which a logical age did not shrink—that were it not for the sacrament of baptism, it would be a grave sin to have children at all! Parents would simply be glorifying the devil by supplying combustibles for Hell. As Malebranche says,

> Il est vrai que depuis le péché ils [maris et femmes] n'engen-drent que pour le démon, et par une action toute brutale; et que sans JÉSUS-CHRIST notre médiateur, ce serait même un crime épouvantable que de communiquer à une femme cette misérable fécondité, d'engendrer un ennemi de Dieu, de damner une âme pour jamais, de travailler à la gloire de Satan, et à l'établissement de la Babylone infernale.[25]

> It is true that since Original Sin married people engender off-spring only for the devil, and by a wholly brutal act; and that without JESUS CHRIST our mediator it would even be a frightful crime to visit this wretched fecundity upon a woman, to spawn an enemy of God, to damn a soul forever, to work for the glory of Satan and the establishment of the infernal Babylon.

Or, perhaps, the *non plus ultra* would rather lie in the following inference drawn by Leszek Kolakowski. Its irony is maybe the least hostile response that seventeenth-century orthodoxy could fairly hope for from a modern reader.

> [A]ccording to common belief, the elect will feel enormous delight at the sight of the torments of the damned and so we should suppose that if the parents of the unlucky babies happen to be themselves baptized and saved (and babies frequently died just after birth), they will jubilate on seeing their offspring devoured by everlasting flames (this is an extrapolation: I have not seen this point specifically made by any Jansenist author).[26]

However, we should also bear in mind that logical inference from the orthodox view that outside the Church there is no salvation, *extra ecclesiam nulla salus*, also led to a sense of the appalling gravity and urgency

from Jansen's *Augustinus* (1640), see Kolakowski, *God Owes Us Nothing*, 82–86, 128 and relevant notes.
[25] Nicholas Malebranche, *Traité de morale*, in *Œuvres complètes*, vol. 2 (Paris: Gallilmard [Pléiade], 1992), 610.
[26] Kolakowski, *God Owes Us Nothing*, 83–84. The "common belief" has theological support in passages from Aquinas (*Summa theologiae*, III, Supplementum Q.94 art. 1) and Tertullian (*De spectaculis*, xxx) that received famously sardonic comment from Nietzsche in *On the Genealogy of Morals*, I 15.

of the apologist's task, and of missionary work in general. From it sprang both the zeal of Pascal and that of the small band of Jesuit missionaries to the Indians of New France in the wilds by Lakes Huron and Ontario. These truly heroic contemporaries of Pascal underwent the severest hardships, typically ending only with death through slow torture, so that, by bringing the grace of baptism, they might snatch a few "brands from the fire"—that is to say, souls of the Hurons, Algonquins, and Iroquois from the very jaws of the devil. It is a heroism one would hardly expect from the sly, easy, accommodating Jesuits of the *Provincial Letters*. On occasion, though, it was a heroism that could stoop to ruses not unworthy of the latter—as when, by what amounted to sleight of hand, a Jesuit would surreptitiously baptize a dying child before the very eyes of parents who had expressly forbidden it.[27]

Of course, to accept the absolute necessity of baptism, whatever its warrant in Scripture and in the Fathers of the Church, was not always easy, even for the orthodox.[28] In a Letter to Jerome, Augustine himself confesses to be uncertain as to what reason might conceivably underlie what, since it is incontestably the faith of the Church and the plain sense of Scripture, must incontestably be a just decree. Moreover, he professes himself to be anguished at being compelled to distress the faithful with the doctrine's horrific implications for unbaptized children and catechumens.[29] In the *Divine Comedy*, the justice of God on this matter is depicted as, though no longer a stone of stumbling for the character Dante, still an impenetrable mystery. In *Paradiso* XIX, he asks the celestial Eagle how it can be just to

[27] Fr. LeMercier's account of such *industries* (devices) [tr. from LeMercier's *Relations des Hurons* (1637) 165] appears in chapter 8 of the twenty-fifth edition (1885) of Francis Parkman's classic *The Jesuits in North America,* in *France and England in North America*, vol. 1 (New York: Library of America, 1983), 466–68; cf. also 481. Parkman too sees in this conduct an image of the Jesuits of the *Provinciales*.
[28] Cardinal Newman's 1855 novel *Callista* seems by its obliqueness to show an incipient soft-pedaling of (or "bad conscience" about?) this severity. It is even put into the mouth of St. Cyprian, the very champion of *extra ecclesiam nulla salus.* Callista, though close to conversion, flatly declares to the priest Caecilius [St. Cyprian] that "Nothing will ever make me believe that all my people [sc. pagan Greeks] have gone and will go to an eternal Tartarus." Faced with this, Caecilius immediately dodges, though not without an elliptical intimation that such indeed will be their fate. "Had we not better confine ourselves to something more specific, more tangible? . . . I suppose if one individual may have that terrible lot, another may—both may, many may. Suppose I understand you to say that *you* will never go to an eternal Tartarus." John Henry Cardinal Newman, *Callista: A Tale of the Third Century* (London: Longman, repr. 1901), 216–17 (ch. 19). But in the final analysis, even though it is no longer, as in the age Newman depicts, *Christianos ad leones*, it is still *paganos ad ignes.*
[29] Letter 166, ch. 16–27.

damn a virtuous man who, living by the waters of the Indus, has through no fault of his own failed even to hear of the Gospel. In response, he is roundly insulted and told to mind his own business, for he cannot presume to fathom all the depths of the divine mind. The impression of severity is mitigated in the next canto: the unexpected salvation of the pagans Trajan and Ripheus shows that God may will better for us than we had a right to hope. Still, as the Eagle says, "Certo ha colui che meco s'assottiglia, se la Scrittura sovra voi non fosse, da dubitar sarebbe a maraviglia" (XIX 82-4) (Had he not the Scriptures over him, he who splits hairs with me would certainly have marvelous matter for doubt).

But for Pascal, as we saw above, the matter is even worse than mere matter for doubt: for in this decree of the divine justice we confront, not only impenetrable mystery, but an affront to our reason. Hence, as the essay "The Fundamental Importance of Justice" tries to show above, it is indispensable for Pascal's apologetic enterprise to tackle mystery and paradox head-on by making a case to the *libertin* reader that they do indeed call for submission on the part of our reason, *soumission de la raison*. No easy task, since, in any era, the essence of being a *libertin* (cf. *libertinus*, freedman) lies in thinking and/or living "freely," without master or other constraint. That is, it consists precisely in being *insoumis* to authorities![30] But, if Pascal cannot make such a case, the unbeliever whom he would bring to the God of orthodoxy and Augustine—for orthodoxy then was only beginning to part company with Augustine—will be mightily inclined, indeed may feel obliged, to halt the discussion by inverting the saint with "Mendacium, non mysterium" (It is no mystery, but a lie). And he is like to come to his end, full of days, and no doubt of iniquities, ruefully saying with "old Khayyám" (xxvii),

> Myself when young did eagerly frequent
> Doctor and Saint, and heard great Argument
> About it and about: but evermore
> Came out by the same Door as in I went.

If, however, Pascal can convincingly make a case for *soumission de la raison*, then, like Dante in the *Paradiso*, the *libertin* may feel entitled, even impelled, to acquiesce in mysteries, severities included. But unless reason takes its last step by acknowledging its own incapacities, faith cannot take its first.

It is a dramatic step that can be viewed, in the spirit of a comment of Nietzsche on Pascal, as tragedy: "[His] faith . . . resembles in a gruesome

---

[30] The development of these and other senses of *libertin*—including criminal and *philosophe*(!)—and of their enmeshings up to and through the eighteenth century are fascinatingly captured in Patrick Wald Lasowski's preface to *Romanciers libertins du XVIIIe siècle* (Paris: Gallimard [Pléiade], 2002).

manner a continual suicide of reason—a tough, long-lived wormlike reason that cannot be killed all at once and with a single stroke."[31]

Or, as implicit in a remark of Molière's Chrysale in *Les femmes savantes*
(597–98), as farce:

> Raisonner est l'emploi de toute ma maison
> Et le raisonnement en bannit la raison.
>
> My whole household's set to reasoning
> Which has banished reason from the house.

Yet, in the final analysis, would not the absence of mysteries be a
greater puzzlement than their presence? Pascal might be entitled to expect
that even an unbeliever would be ready to concede that, if there is a God,
then in principle his nature would demand them. For how could infinite,
transcendent deity be fully captured by categories of thought accessible to
our finite and immanent selves—an insight whose spirit is nicely signposted
in the Augustinian tradition by the *Confessions'* exaltation of God as "most
omnipotent" (omnipotentissimus).

Or, as Pascal puts the general point, "La dernière démarche de la raison est de reconnaître qu'il y a une infinité de choses qui la surpassent
[. . . .] Que si les choses naturelles la surpassent, que dira-t-on des surna-
turelles?" (Reason's last step is to recognize that there is an infinity of things
which surpass it. [. . . .] If natural things surpass it, what shall we say of
supernatural ones?, fr.S 220; cf. 680).

But, to concede that mystery might be legitimate is to concede that a
church might be authentic, for church and revelation *as such* are inextricably tied to mystery. It is no accident that, as has often been remarked, in
controversies over grace, Trinity, the nature and person of Christ, etc.,
Christian orthodoxy has, over the course of its establishment, repeatedly
shown a marked preference for the more mysterious over the more readily intelligible and explicable. It is little likely to be otherwise. Revelation,
along with a church to establish and to explain it, is hardly necessary to
point the way to the intelligible and the explicable. Mere Philosophy might
essay as much! A church is *essentially* a guide to mysteries, while a believer
is *essentially* an initiate of the same. A church, in short, is a mystagogue,
not a pedagogue.

But all is not bafflement and severity; and after dark, the light. Nothing
would affront and distress Pascal and his fellow Augustinians more than the
imputation that their religion was a sad one. Indeed, one of the pillars of

---

[31] Nietzsche, *Beyond Good and Evil* (46) in Kauffman, *Basic Writings of Nietzsche*,
250.

Pascal's apologetic strategy is to reveal Christianity as so lovable that good people will wish that it might be true.

> Ordre.
> Les hommes ont mépris pour la religion, ils en ont haine et peur qu'elle ne soit vraie. Pour guérir cela il faut commencer par montrer que la religion n'est point contraire à la raison. [. . . .] La rendre ensuite aimable, faire souhaiter aux bons qu'elle fût vraie . . . (fr.S 46; cf. 203).

> Order.
> People despise religion, they hate it and are afraid it might be true. To remedy this one must begin by showing that religion is not contrary to reason. [. . . .] Then make it lovable, make good people wish that it were true.

Fear is cited here as an *obstacle* to belief, and in any event Pascal is adamant that he means to instill religion, not terror. Unlike Augustine himself, who authorizes force in the famous (or infamous) Letter 93, and unlike the Jesuits of New France, who found lurid pictures of Hell the most effective tool for conversion,[32] Pascal has no use for trying to impart religion "par la force et par les menaces" (fr.S 203).

He would surely remind us that if, as is hardly surprising, we should find mystery in God, we can also find the profound intimacy with Him so exquisitely revealed and instanced by the *Confessions*. And if, as revealed in *On Admonition and Grace*, our salvation be matter for fear and trembling, it is no less true that, as in the *Confessions*, God seeks for the stray, calling out from afar to the one whom He Himself has prompted to seek Him.

---

[32] The Jesuit missionaries not only wrote back to France asking for more pictures of Hell, but gave explicit instructions on how it should be depicted for maximum effect. When, in 1977, Lorne and Lawrence Blair journeyed to inner Borneo and found members of a "lost" people, nomadic and semi-nomadic Punan Dyaks, they discovered that native Christian missionary scouts had arrived shortly before, bringing paints and brushes that they used to decorate the walls of the Punan longhouses with pictures of Hell. In both cases fear, though deeply troubling, seems to have proved less potent than love, in particular love of kin. Assured by the missionaries that their non-Christian ancestors were all in Hell, the Huron and the Punan both were so hard of heart that they preferred to go to Hell with them. For the Punan see Lorne and Lawrence Blair, *Ring of Fire* (Rochester, Vt: Park Street Press, 1991), 247, 250, 255, along with their accompanying PBS video, *Ring of Fire: Dream Wanderers of Borneo* (Mystic Fire Video). For the Jesuit mission to the Hurons see Parkman, *The Jesuits in North America*, 461–2, 493, 513 (this time the Algonquins). In fact, the Indians had almost a greater fear of Heaven than of Hell. Since, as you Jesuits tell us, there is no hunting or fishing in Heaven, if we go there we will starve!

In the *Provinciales*, Pascal censured the Jesuit missionaries to the Indies and China for suppressing Christ's fate on the Cross so as to make Christian teaching more palatable to potential converts (V 76). Thus, it is not at all surprising that, in the *Pensées*, he does not try to conceal hard-to-swallow truth, shutting it up like some crazy aunt in the attic. But though he is ardent on behalf of *la grâce efficace* and the mysteries of divine justice, it is the spirit, not of *On Admonition and Grace*, but of the *Confessions* that saturates the *Pensées*.[33] For if the mystery of the divine justice that falls on the reprobate is somber to our darkened eyes, not so is the free gift of grace and heaven to the elect, unentitled and undeserving though they are. "Or la justice envers les réprouvés est moins énorme et doit moins choquer que la miséricorde envers les élus" (But his justice towards the reprobate is less out of our measure,[34] and should be less shocking, than his mercy towards the elect, fr.S 680). The ineffable divine mercy is just cause for ineffable joy.

Not only the joy of the world to come, union with Him by whom and for whom we were made, and which alone can fully satisfy the longing human heart. But joy even in this world, where the turning of the heart to God, whether on the part of unbeliever or the lukewarm believer, will transform it into a heart reborn, *un cœur nouveau*.[35] Even here and now, our life will be transfigured by our love for the Love which is Love Itself, and by the love for us of Him who has a care even for the sparrow that falls.

[33] See Sellier, "Des *Confessions* aux *Pensées*," in his *Port-Royal et la littérature*, vol. 1, 195–222. See his "Pascal et Saint Augustin: théologie et anthropologie," ibid., 249–62, for the comparatively slight presence in the *Pensées* of the anti-Pelagian writings. He notes that the Augustinian emphases are reversed in the (largely controversial) writings of Antoine Arnauld and Pierre Nicole (249).

[34] The term *énorme* implies, not just size, but the exceeding of rule or measure. Cf. our "monstrous."

[35] *Le Cœur nouveau* is the title of a little work by Saint-Cyran. "L'ouverture du cœur à l'amour de Dieu suscite une joie pure et stable. De là une célébration de la joie évangélique du chrétien diamétralement oposée aux idées toutes faites sur le 'jansénisme'. Dans la conversion 'on ne quitte les plaisirs que pour d'autres plus grands' (Pascal). Saint-Cyran répétait que nul ne serait heureux dans le ciel s'il ne l'avait été sur la terre. La vie éternelle commence avec la transformation du cœur: 'Nul n'est heureux comme un vrai chrétien' (Pascal)." Sellier, "Port-Royal: littérature et théologie," in his *Port-Royal et la littérature*, vol. 2, 13.

# PART TWO

## STRAIT IS THE GATE/FAITH OF OUR FATHERS

The *Provinciales*

# 2

# THE *PROVINCIALES*: RUSE AGAINST RUSE, FORCE AGAINST FORCE?

'Άριστος τρόπος τοῦ ἀμύνεσθαι τὸ μή ἐξομοιοῦσθαι.

The best revenge lies in not doing likewise.

Marcus Aurelius, *Meditations* (VI 6)

For good or ill, the noses of readers who comprise the lay, *honnête* public to which the *Provinciales* are addressed do not have the final cause of providing a platform for casuists' high-magnification spectacles. And so, it is not surprising that, as their author intended, a reading of the *Provinciales* often leaves them profoundly scandalized. This is especially true of Letters I–X which are, as it were, Pascal's *Candide*. In them we see the Jesuits' methods and, especially, their moral theology pilloried and ridiculed with consummate address and dramatic art. The applause of the very public that the lax, debonnaire morality authorized by the Jesuits aimed to please testifies to the overwhelming triumph of the campaign of the *Provinciales*.

However, Pascal's rhetorical methods and tone provoked murmurs of criticism even at Port-Royal among fellow Augustinians—to say nothing of the cries of rage and bafflement they wrung from the Jesuits and their backers in the civil authority. One of the many reproaches aimed at the *Provinciales* since Pascal's day is especially ironical and piquant: it is that, in his polemic for Port-Royal and Augustinianism, Pascal sometimes proceeds in a manner that is all-too Jesuitical (a term of opprobrium thanks in no small part to the the *Provinciales* themselves). "[R]use contre ruse, force contre force," as Sainte-Beuve said, though not without admiration.[1] Indeed, Pascal himself seems to admit to a certain resemblance to his foe. "[V]ous blâmez en moi comme horribles les moindres impostures que vous

---

[1] Charles Sainte-Beuve, *Port-Royal*, vol. 2 (Paris: Gallimard [Pléiade], 1953), 66.

excusez en vous, parce que vous me regardez comme un particulier et vous comme IMAGO" (You call the smallest deceits in me horrible, but you excuse them in yourselves because you regard me as a mere individual and yourselves as IMAGO, fr.S 450).[2] But did the Jesuitical spirit, "l'esprit de la Société"[3] that he so artfully delineated and so vigorously opposed, really insinuate itself into his own methods in the *Provinciales?*

According to the Jansenist friend, "l'esprit de la Société" aims to satisfy everyone (V 75). Hence, we can fairly say that it must be in close accord with "l'esprit du peuple" in the term's widest sense. From this, it follows that the great diversity in moral teachings of individual Jesuits, which at first glance seems to refute the hypothesis that there is but one spirit animating the whole Society, on the contrary confirms it. For without this smorgasbord of moral opinions, where there is an option for every taste, the Society's goal of governing "toutes les consciences" could not be realized. And from the fact that few persons can long tolerate moral strictures that are "évangéliques et sévères"—so great is the corruption of Fallen Man!—it follows that the

[2] "Dans *Imago primi saeculi*, la Compagnie de Jésus procédait a un bilan satisfait de ses cent ans d'existence . . ." [Sellier's note].

[3] On the noxious character of "l'esprit de la Société," Sainte-Beuve is even more vehement and damning than Pascal. "Au reste, pour le reconnaître vrai, cet esprit dénoncé et décrit par Pascal, cet esprit caressant, câlin, énervant, qui tente toujours et chatouille à l'endroit de l'intérêt, cet esprit diabolique et calomniateur, et qui en même temps ne sait pas haïr d'une haine honnête et vigoureuse; qui est toujours prêt à vous flatter si vous revenez, comme ce bon Père de la cinquième Provinciale (*il me fit d'abord mille caresses, car il m'aime toujours*); qui vous offre toutes les facilités et toutes les dispenses, mais seulement si vous lui donnez des gages et si vous êtes à lui; esprit adultère de l'Évangile; tout à soi et aux siens; qui est comme un petit souffle demi-parfumé, demi-empesté, mortel à l'âme chrétienne aussi bien qu'à l'âme naturelle, empoisonneur de Plutarque comme de Saint-Paul, et qui, sous air de douceur, et en l'adulant, convoîte éternellement le royaume de la terre;—pour le reconnaître, cet esprit, et le proclamer vrai chez Pascal, nous n'avons pas besoin de l'aller étudier bien loin dans le passé: tous ceux qui l'ont vu [. . .] à travers toutes les politesses de détail, toutes les exceptions et les réserves légitimes, lui sauront dire, en le démêlant dans son essence et en le détestant jusqu'au bout dans sa moindre haleine: *Toi, toujours toi!*" Sainte-Beuve, *Port-Royal*, vol. 2, 148–49, notes omitted.

By positing one, all-embracing "esprit de la Société," Pascal gives himself the rhetorical advantage, which in the event proved insuperable, of making the whole Society answerable for the extravagant opinions of any and all individual Jesuits. Contrariwise, as we shall see (pp. 36–39), by remaining anonymous and by disassociating himself from any party ("je suis seul") he makes it very difficult indeed for the Jesuits to carry the attack to him. But is Pascal's characterization correct, or are there in fact well nigh as many "esprits" as there are Jesuits? Cf. Dominique Descotes, "La Responsabilité collective dans les *Provinciales*" in Roger Duchêne, *L'Imposture littéraire dans les* Provinciales *de Pascal*, 2nd ed. *Suivie des actes du colloque tenu à Marseilles le 10 mars 1984* (Aix-en-Provence: Université de Provence, 1985), 350–62.

ordinary moral teaching of the Society, veritable *pot-bouille* in the sense of Zola,[4] will be characterized by permissiveness and laxity, *relâchement*.

Of course, if indeed the Jesuits aimed above all to please universally, the ferocity of anti-Jesuit sentiment through at least the nineteenth century powerfully belies their reputation for cleverness and address. In some cases, it amounts to an obsession or mania, as in Eugène Sue's *Le Juif errant* (1844–45), an immensely popular thousand-page tale of reptilian Jesuit skullduggery at whose climax an Indian *thug* forsakes the murder cult of Kali for the more terrible Society of Jesus!

In making an appeal to public opinion through satire and comedy, Pascal too engages "l'esprit du people." Thanks to their education and their interests—both far more strongly oriented toward religious subjects than the public's today—Pascal's readers are not without a certain theological sophistication, though they are far from having the competence of professional theologians.[5] Indeed, at the outset, the *Provinciales'* fictive author declares that his readers have already been duped by his adversaries (I 3).

But does his desire to please a wide public, to instruct it while diverting it with raillery, lead to the seduction of those whom Pascal wished to disabuse? Did a desire to vanquish the Jesuit enemy who seemed to corrupt, not only morals, but the rules of morals, at times seduce Pascal himself,[6] despite his evident sincerity and profound respect for truth, into rhetorical strategies that are the image of those he imputes to the Jesuits? The endeavor to please the tastes of creatures corrupted by the Fall may well lead one astray, especially if it includes a desire to establish a Reign of Truth in the here and now—itself the veil of another desire, to triumph on one's own account,[7] and the father of the desire to "gouverner toutes les consciences." For, as Balzac says, "Rien n'est si jésuite qu'un désir" (Nothing is so Jesuitical as a desire, *Illusions perdues*).

---

[4] This is "[L]a cuisine de tous les jours, cuisine terriblement louche et menteuse sous son apparente bonhomie [. . . .] la marmite où mijotent . . . tous les relâchements de la morale." Paul Alexis, cited by Henri Mittérand, ed., in Émile Zola, *Les Rougon-Macquart*, vol. 3 (Paris: Gallimard [Pléiade], 1964), 1638 n.1.

[5] See Jean Mesnard in the Round Table discussion in Duchêne, *L'Imposture littéraire*, 385–87, and Richard Parish, *Pascal's* Lettres Provinciales: *A Study in Polemic* (Oxford: Clarendon Press, 1989), 47–51.

[6] According to Michel LeGuern, he was led astray by his own inexperience and by his colleagues. See "Les *Provinciales* ou les excès d'un polémiste abusé," in Duchêne, *L'Imposture littéraire*, 309–14.

[7] "Mais quoi! on agit comme si on avait mission pour faire triompher la vérité, au lieu que nous n'avons mission que pour combattre pour elle. Le désir de vaincre est si naturel que, quand il se couvre du désir de faire triompher la vérité, on prend souvent l'un pour l'autre et on croit rechercher la gloire de Dieu en cherchant en effet la sienne." "Fragment d'une lettre de Pascal à M. et Mme. Périer," towards the spring of 1657 (OC, III 1206).

The struggle depicted in the *Provinciales*—one between modernizers and reactionaries, moral laxists and moral rigorists, those who would magnify the Lord while abasing man and those whose apparent aim is the reverse—is, as even this partial description suggests, a contest that is little likely to cease. The *Provinciales* is thus the kind of text that will always have its partisans and its quarrels. Our topic demands that we revisit some of the them in their green old age, re-engaging disputes that would seem to put to the test Sainte-Beuve's dictum (I 153) that "on ne peut tout dire des *Provinciales*" (one can't say all there is to say about the *Provinciales*).

## THE CONDEMNATION OF ARNAULD/THE CONDEMNATION OF THE CASUISTS: FORCE AGAINST FORCE?

εἶτ᾽ ἐξάνοιγε μηχανὰς τὰς Σισύφου·
ὡς σκῆψιν ἀγὼν οὗτος οὐκ εἰσδέξεται.

Come now, disclose your Sisyphean ruses:
This case will acknowledge no mitigating circumstances![8]

Aristophanes, *Acharnians*, 391–2

In the third Letter the fictive narrator, "je," seeks to understand the Sorbonne's condemnation of the Augustinian theologian and Port-Royal stalwart Antoine Arnauld for a proposition whose words and sense are clearly present in Saint Augustine and Saint John Chrysostom. As the proposition is found in these Fathers of the Church it must be orthodox; is it not then pointless for the Jesuits and their allies in the Sorbonne to denounce it in terms "de *poison*, de *peste*, *d'horreur*, de *témérité*, *d'impiété*, de *blasphème*, *d'abomination*, *d'exécration*, *d'anathème*, *d'hérésie* . . .?"(44). The narrator boldy affirms that their censure is perforce in vain, but a Doctor of the Sorbonne disabuses him.

Si vous connaissiez l'esprit du peuple, me dit mon docteur, vous parleriez d'une autre sorte. Leur censure, toute censurable qu'elle est, aura presque tout son effet pour un temps; et quoiqu'à force d'en montrer l'invalidité il soit certain qu'on la fera entendre, il est aussi véritable que d'abord la plupart des esprits en seront aussi fortement frappés que de la plus juste du monde. Pourvu qu'on crie dans les rues: *Voici la censure de M. Arnauld, voici la condamnation des Jansénistes,*

[8] This translation is by Jeffrey Henderson in the Loeb *Aristophanes*, vol. 1 (Cambridge, Mass. and London: Harvard University Press, 1998), 105. As he indicates in a note, Sisyphus was proverbial for his cunning.

les Jésuites auront leur compte. Combien y en aura-t-il peu
qui la lisent? combien peu de ceux qui la liront qui l'entendent? combien peu qui aperçoivent qu'elle ne satisfait point
aux objections? Qui croyez-vous qui prenne les choses
à cœur, et qui entreprenne de les examiner à fond? (46–7)

If you knew the spirit of the people, my doctor said to me, you
would speak otherwise. Their censure, though deserving of
censure itself, will be almost wholly effective for a time; and
although by force of demonstration its invalidity will be shown,
it is also true that at first the majority of minds will be as
strongly struck by it as by the most just censure in the world.
Provided that one cries out in the streets: *Here is the censure of
M. Arnauld, here is the condemnation of the Jansenists*, the
Jesuits will have gained their object. How few of the people
will read the censure? How few of those who read it will
understand it? How few will perceive that it does not satisfy
objections? Who do you think takes these matters to heart, or
undertakes to examine them in depth?

Despite the many very real excesses that Pascal attacks in the
*Provinciales*, do not the ridicule and indignation provoked by his handling
of the casuists often owe their being to the same causes, and in particular
to "l'esprit du peuple"? Of the public at large, how many are there who, to
judge between Pascal and his opponents, will read tomes of casuistry? How
few of those who will read them will understand, or will undertake to
examine their matter in depth?

The following passages from Filiutius and Sanchez, read to the narrator by the ever-obliging Jesuit *bon père*, could well serve as touchstones for
readers of a casuistical bent. (Pascal enlivens the latter with an expression
from Diana, a Theatine.) It is for this reason that they appear here rather
than from hope of adding anything new.

> *Celui qui s'est fatigué à quelque chose, comme à poursuivre
> une fille, est-il obligé de jeûner? Nullement. Mais s'il s'est
> fatigué exprès pour être par là dispensé du jeûne, y sera-t-il
> tenu? Encore qu'il ait eu ce dessein formé, il n'y sera point
> obligé.* Eh bien! l'eussiez vous cru? me dit-il. En vérité, mon
> père, lui dis-je, je ne le crois pas bien encore (V 82–3).

> *En quelles occasions un religieux peut-il quitter son habit
> sans encourir l'excommunication?* Il en rapporte plusieurs, et
> entre autres celles-ci: *S'il le quitte pour une cause honteuse,
> comme pour aller filouter, ou pour aller* incognito *en des lieux
> de débauche, le devant bientôt reprendre.* (VI 98)

> *Is a man who has tired himself out at something, such as chas-
> ing after a girl, obliged to fast? Not at all. But if he has delib-
> erately worn himself out so as to be dispensed from fasting,*

*will he be obliged to fast? Even if he had this expressly in mind,
he will not be obliged to fast.* Well! Would you have believed
it? To tell the truth, Father, I don't quite believe it yet.

*On what occasions can a monk not wear his robe without
incurring excommunication?* He [Sanchez] gives several
examples, among them these: *If he puts it off for a shameful
reason, such as going out to engage in sneak-thievery, or in
order to go* incognito *to places of debauchery, provided he
soon puts it back on.*

Here we have one of the more droll variations on the *Provinciales'*
great theme of Jesuitical laxity—why excuse evil when evil excuses us? *Qui
s'accuse, s'excuse!* The first impression of the wide public Pascal is addressing will almost certainly be that these authors, conformably to "l'esprit de
la Société," do indeed "tendent les bras à tout le monde" (offer an embrace
to everyone, V 75–6). Nor is it surprising that some specialist readers are of
the same opinion.[9] For in these passages Filiutius and Sanchez, inasmuch
as they explicitly censure nothing mentioned, can easily appear to extend
indifferently the innocence they concede to some of the actions mentioned
to all of them. They then seem as guilty themselves as the transgressors
they would seem to excuse.

But let us suppose readers—and how few there will be—who will
understand these passages in the dialectical and juridical spirit of casuistry.
Now some distinctions begin to take shape. It is licit or excusable (which
does not imply approbation) if one does not fast on account of bodily
fatigue. But the causes of the fatigue itself, including even reasons for
which it may be sought deliberately, are not in question as such. Likewise,
the frequenting of places of debauchery is not in question as such.
However, it is clear, as *le bon père* goes on to explain, that this behavior
would give rise to all the more scandal to the Church if monks frequented
them in their ecclesiastical garments. Is it a sign of *relâchement* to say that
here one may suspend a rule, and hence cancel a punishment for violating
it, when preserving the rule and inflicting the punishment would not only
weigh on the guilty but injure an innocent party—namely, the Church itself?
(And this when both the rule and the punishment are ecclesiastical.) What
consequences would ensue if the contrary principle—that the guilty must
receive their deserts regardless of harm incident to innocent parties—were
established as absolute! To readers of a fairly dialectical cast of mind, the

[9] One of the most recent is Kolakowski. "No unprejudiced reader can fail to be won
over to the side of the author when he peruses the *Provincial Letters* or to be
amused by quotations from various Jesuit writers who seem to have a ready-made
excuse for all kinds of human depravities and crimes." *God Owes Us Nothing*, 61.
He explicitly cites the monk without his robe.

judgments in the passages cited above may seem to be good or bad ones, or advisable or inadvisable, without at all seeming outrageous or ludicrous.

Now let us suppose readers who have examined these questions more in depth by virtue of having read the works of the casuists themselves. And although the narrator invites this (VIII 151–2)—in the event, not without result—at the end of the day, how few of the Letters' many readers will undertake this investigation![10]

The citation from Sanchez/Diana is exact save for the addition of "incognito." The text of Filiutius has given rise to much discussion.[11]

> Dices secundo, an qui malo fine laboraret ut ad aliquem occidendum vel ad insequendam amicam, vel quid simile, teneretur ad jejunium. Respondeo talem peccaturum quidem ex malo fine, at sequuta defatigatione excusaretur a jejunio; . . . nisi fieret in fraudem, secundum aliquos; sed melius alii, culpam quidem esse in apponenda causa fractionis jejunii, at, ea posita, excusari a jejunio.[12]

> You will ask if the one who has labored for an evil end, such as for killing someone or chasing after a woman-friend, shall be obliged to fast. I reply that such a one will indeed sin on account of the evil end pursued, but that, exhaustion having followed from it, he would be excused from fasting; . . . unless, some say, it is done in fraud [i.e., as a means of gaining exemption]; but others say, with better reason, that the wrong lies in procuring a reason to break the fast, but that, once it is present, one is excused from fasting.

In the dull, heavy style of his profession, Filiutius underscores that the one who has pursued a wrong end has sinned, an underscore absent from Pascal's citation. And he declares explicitly that, in the opinion of the case he finds preferable, to procure oneself a reason for breaking the fast is indeed a sin—a declaration not to be found in Pascal's citation either.[13] If it

---

[10] On the general, much-explored question of Pascal's citations in the *Provinciales*—a subject of great nuance, and still instructive—Roger Duchêne's discussion is extremely useful. See *L'Imposture littéraire*, 160–84. Cf. also Louis Cognet, introduction to the *Provinciales* (XXXVIII–XLII), and Sainte-Beuve, *Port-Royal*, vol. 2, 134–36.

[11] Fairly typical opposed reactions are those of Sainte-Beuve, *Port-Royal*, vol. 2, 134–36, and Ernst Havet (cited ibid. 1084 n.1). See also Erec Koch, *Pascal and Rhetoric: Figural and Persuasive Language in the Scientific Treatises, the Provinciales and the Pensées* (Charlottesville: Rockwood Press, 1997), 98–99.

[12] Cited by Sainte-Beuve, *Port-Royal*, vol. 2, 134–5.

[13] Does the responsibility for this omission lie with Escobar, from whose compilation Pascal takes the text of his citation? According to his sister, Marguerite Périer, Pascal verified the quotations he took from Escobar in the casuists' original texts (fr. 1002 [L'Intégrale]).

is subtle and legalistic, is it *relâché* to place the sin only in these places? The original text of Filiutius would hardly scandalize professional theologians, nor, were it brought before it, the public at large. The more the reader becomes informed, the more the indignation and ridicule evoked by Pascal wane and the force of his censure fades.

Few things in the *Provinciales* are more shocking, and rightly so, than the authorizing of the famous "pieux guet-apens" (pious ambush, VII 121), a name that, despite the smile it provokes, could serve as cover for some genuinely frightful cases. But even so, over the ages confessors and their penitents have lived under many a criminal regime, where, warped and perverted under a Hitler or a Stalin, the "justice system" is frankly murderous. If one proceeds from the principle that it is permissible, *if it is the sole means*, to preserve an *innocent life* by the death of a *guilty party*—guilty because aiming to take the innocent life (in VII 121, by judicial murder)— is it utterly outrageous to consider such a lethal *defense, perforce* preemptive, and carried out *perforce* by a private individual, to be debatable, perhaps even defensible? Pascal himself discusses the principles essential to such cases in Letter XIV, though without reference to life under a criminal regime. The rhetoric of the *Provinciales*, like that of *Candide*, risks leading the reader astray precisely in the measure that it portrays debatable issues as manifestly outrageous and hence beyond the pale of discussion, thus meriting ridicule rather than refutation.

Roger Duchêne's assessment is essentially my own. "On a condamné Arnaud sur des phrases qu'on a detournées de leur sens; on a condamné les casuistes sur des phrases qu'on a detournées de leur sens. . . ." (Arnauld was condemned on the basis of statements diverted from their meanings; the casuists were condemned on the basis of statements diverted from their meanings, 324).

When it comes to demonstration, decrying something in a comedy is quite on a par with crying it out in the street. Even without his rare formal inexactitudes of citation, Pascal's rhetorical techniques in Letters IV–X are similar to those he imputes to the Jesuits in the condemnation of Arnauld. Both are based on a strategy of *deflecting attention* from details and distinctions, from "fine print," notwithstanding that these are of the essence in the cases, so that each party can speak conformably, and hence with effect, to "l'esprit du people." *Esprit abusé ?* For in each case, appearance is decisive—whether the ridiculous impressions made by casuistry divorced from its context and methods, and by Pascal's puppet Jesuit who falls unwitting into all manner of traps, [14] or whether the impressions produced by the gravity and authority of those who denounce Arnauld, and by the violence

[14] For the "jésuite-marionette" see Sainte-Beuve, *Port-Royal*, vol. 2, 132 and Sellier in a discussion in Duchêne, *L'Imposture littéraire*, 348.

of their language. To say nothing of the impressions made by a kind of rhetorical osmosis through which, in the *Provinciales,* a whole case is colored by the presence of a bizarre or nefarious condition.

In Pascalian terms, it is the triumph of the imagination, of a power sometimes true but deceitful more often than not (fr.S 78).

If, in the Sorbonne, it was force that condemned Arnauld, in the *Provinciales* it is *vis comica* that triumphs over the monks who, brought in to make a "packed court" in the Sorbonne, were more numerous than the reasons of Arnauld's enemies.[15]

It needs to be strongly emphasized that, as Philippe Sellier points out, "Pascal n'est pas contre la casuistique . . . . On ne peut pas être contre la casuistique: elle est liée à la vie même" (Pascal is not against casuistry . . . . One cannot be against casuistry: it is bound up with life itself).[16]

Nonetheless, Pascal does give it short shrift, for he sometimes speaks as if denying the reality of conditions whose existence the casuist is presupposing. "*Que si le pénitent déclare qu'il veut remettre à l'autre monde à faire pénitence, et souffrir en purgatoire toutes les peines qui lui sont dues, alors le confesseur doit lui imposer une pénitence bien légère*" (*If the penitent declares that he wishes to put off the doing of a penance to the other world, and suffer in purgatory all the punishments that are owing him, then the confessor must impose a very light penance on him*), says the *bon père,* translating Escobar. To which the narrator replies: "[J]ugez-vous qu'un homme soit digne de recevoir l'absolution *quand il ne veut rien faire de pénible pour expier ses offenses?*" (Do you consider that a man is worthy to receive absolution *when he doesn't wish to do anything unpleasant to expiate his offenses?*, X 175, emphasis added). But this response presupposes rather than demonstrates the Jesuits' bad faith, the *Mentiris impudentissime!* It presupposes that casuistry involves a kind of complicity, a wink of an eye between a politic confessor and an impenitent penitent. "[V]ous avez suivi *votre méthode ordinaire,* qui est d'accorder aux hommes ce qu'ils désirent, et donner à Dieu *des paroles et des apparences*" (You have followed your usual method, which is to give men what they desire, and to give God *words and appearances,* XII 224, emphasis added; cf. VII 117).

This remark may be of some assistance in understanding the undoubted sincerity of Pascal's scrupulosity in the matter of citations, his "soin très particulier . . . de ne pas altérer ou détourner le moins du monde *le sens d'un passage*" (very particular care . . . not to alter or to twist in the least the *sense of a passage,* XI 204, emphasis added).

---

[15] See Sainte-Beuve, *Port-Royal,* vol. 2, 66, and Descotes and Sellier in a discussion in Duchêne, *L'Imposture littéraire,* 347–48.
[16] In a discussion in Duchêne, *L'Imposture littéraire,* 323.

The spirit of a Pascal, inclined to the aphorism, to cutting to the quick of a matter, has perhaps a natural tendency to become impatient with the moral *chiaroscuro*—sometimes bizarre, for it is bound up with life itself— that the casuist and the confessor must concern themselves with. To say, with the narrator, "Je ne me contente pas du probable . . . je cherche le sûr" (I am not satisfied with the probable . . . I am looking for the sure, V 84), is almost to renounce casuistry at a stroke. An ardent and powerful exponent of the mystery of the divine justice, it is only with difficulty that Pascal can enter into the Scholastic spirit that animates his adversaries—a spirit that is cold, legalistic, supple in its dialectic, and confident of its abililty to speak for God (cf. IX 157).

## "JE SUIS SEUL": RUSE AGAINST RUSE?

> When I mention religion, I mean the Christian religion; and not only the Christian religion, but the Protestant religion; and not only the Protestant religion, but the Church of England. [To say that this] will uphold, much less dictate, an untruth, is to assert an absurdity too shocking to be conceived.
>
> Fielding, *Tom Jones* (III 3)

Perhaps the most crushing criticism Pascal makes of the Jesuits is that among them truth counts for little, that they are willing to authorize the use of the most extravagant equivocations (IX 164), to say nothing of flat out lies and calumny (XV). "*Mentiris impudentissime!*"

But the forceful, clear claims by the author of the *Provinciales* in the Seventeenth Letter that "en propres termes *que je ne suis point de Port-Royal*," "*je suis seul*" (329), "sans liason," "sans relations," "sans attachment," "sans engagement" (331), and, in the Twelfth, "étant seul comme je suis . . . sans aucun appui humain" (216) (properly speaking I am not of Port-Royal/I am alone/without ties/connections/unengaged; alone as I am . . . with no human support), are, on their face, decidedly equivocal. For in the *Provinciales* Pascal is, at his own instigation, the defender of Arnauld, of Port-Royal and of the Augustinian movement it represents.[17] He conferred with Arnauld at Paris for several days around 20 January 1656, engaging himself ("sans engagement"?) in the campaign of the *Provinciales*, the first Letter of which bears the date of the twenty-third.[18] Moreover, he had the vigorous collaboration of Arnauld and his fellow Port-Royalist Pierre Nicole for documentation and review, and of Nicole for much in

---

[17] See Nicole, cited in Gérard Ferreyrolles, *Blaise Pascal: les* Provinciales (Paris: PUF, 1984), 36–7.
[18] See Mesnard in OC, III 447–48; 467–71.

letters XIII and XIV. Indeed, the *Provinciales* are, as Gérard Ferreyrolles says in his study of them, a work "dans une certaine mesure, collective" (38).

It is not difficult to understand the initial impression of Sainte-Beuve. "S'il se croit donc en droit de soutenir qu'il n'est pas de Port-Royal à la lettre, s'il ajoute d'un ton d'assurance qu'il est *sans attachement, sans liaison, sans relation[s]*, cela ne se peut entendre, on l'avouera, qu'en un sens quelque peu jésuitique" (If then he believes himself entitled to maintain that he is not literally of Port-Royal, if he adds in a tone of assurance that he is without attachment, without ties, without connections, one must confess that all this can only be understood in a somewhat Jesuitical sense).[19]

In fact, except for the first of them, these affirmations are easier to explain than to justify. As Philippe Sellier points out to us, the rhetoric of Pascal—a geometer the vigor of whose style derives from the prophets— shows little liking for qualifiers.[20] Moreover, Pascal's considerable respect for force in all domains is reflected in his penchant for hyperbole. It is clear that one must, as does Philippe Sellier, regard the remainder of the affirmations as hyperboles. No one can be *sensu strictissimo* "seul" ou "sans liaison" (save in a Leibnizian possible world containing only oneself), etc.

But insofar as the sense which would make these claims true is not evident to readers who do not know the identity and the circumstances of "je," are the claims not equivocal as well as hyperbolic?

The manifest goal of these claims is to keep the author of the *Provinciales*, whose anonymity insulates him personally from counter-attack by the Jesuits and the civil autorities, from bringing down the further vengeance of either upon Port-Royal. "Vous pouvez bien toucher le Port-Royal, mais non pas moi" (You can readily get at Port-Royal, but not at me, 330). "[P]ersonne ne répond de mes Lettres que moi" (No one is responsible for my Letters but I, 333). Thus, for the claims to succeed, they must be taken to deny, not some relation between Port-Royal and a fictive, authorial "je," a literary character—and not merely to deny residence at or formal attachment to Port-Royal on the part of a flesh and blood authorial "je"—but to deny *concerted action* between Port-Royal and the latter "je," between it and the actual person who is writing the *Provinciales*. To pretend, then, that the preceding claims of independence and isolation are true with respect to an authorial "je" who is a literary character, a creature of the text to whom the text attributes itself, would involve a colossal equivocation.

Let us turn from this pretension to the case in which, at least from Letter XI on, "je" is taken to designate Pascal himself.

[19] Sainte-Beuve, *Port-Royal*, vol. 2, 96, but cf. the revised assessment in the note on 107.
[20] Sellier, "Vers l'invention d'une rhétorique," in his *Port-Royal et la littérature*, vol. 1, 182.

Obviously one should take the expression "Je ne suis point de Port-Royal," preceded as it is by "en propres termes," in a qualifed sense. In fact, the preceding Letter has revealed it (301). And so Philippe Sellier and Dominique Descotes are right to insist that this affirmation means "Je ne suis pas de ces Solitaires qui . . ." (I do not belong to those Solitaries who), or "Je ne suis pas de ces Messieurs de Port-Royal qui y sont à demeure" (I am not one of those Gentlemen of Port-Royal who reside there), and that hence the expression is not equivocal.[21] It is the reader's responsibility for any misunderstanding if he attaches his own meaning to terms the author clearly and explicitly qualifies. However, it is fair to say that the vindication of this expression presupposes a respect for, and a fidelity to, a letter-limited interpretation of texts that the Letters do not always display in their drolleries on the adversaries' moral theology.

Like the one just noted, the other controversial expressions are only true, as their hyperbolic character proclaims, with restrictions. But *their* restrictions, with the exception of those for "sans attachement" (331), which is effectively glossed as "ni à quelque communauté, ni à quelque particulier que ce soit" (neither to any community nor to any individual whatever, 330), are not made explicit. For example, by *"je suis seul"* Pascal denies formal connection to Port-Royal, but without restricting the expression in this sense. It is very true that Pascal is only one person, *un seul*; that he is, unlike his adversaries, without the support of the civil authorities ("sans appui humain" *from them)*; and without formal link ("sans liason" *formelle)* to Port-Royal. (He does scrupulously admit at an earlier point [XVI 301] that he knows some of its Solitaries and honors the virtue of them all.) However, the restrictions necessary to make the expressions true are not evident to readers who are, perforce, ignorant of the circumstances of the *Provinciales'* anonymous author, and especially of the extent of his collaboration on them with Antoine Arnauld and Pierre Nicole. "[É]tant seul *comme je suis* . . . contre un si grand corps" (Being alone *as I am* [and in what way is that?] . . . against so great a body [emphasis added]). To be true this must be restricted to mean "I am an individual, and formally unaffililated, though I do not act alone."

These reflections take us back to the heart of the matter. The affirmations in question cannot attain their goal of forestalling the Jesuits and the police from action against Port-Royal and its associates and allies *unless one understands them as denying that the author is acting in concert with Port-Royal*. But this sense, though it is false with respect to Pascal, is one easily derived from the claims as they stand. They are thus, unequivocally, snares for the enemy. "Personne ne répond de mes Lettres que moi." Quite true in a sense. However . . .

---

[21] Sellier and Descotes in a discussion in Duchêne, *L'Imposture littéraire*, 364; but cf. Duchêne's remarks, ibid., 373.

One may say without being facetious that, despite a very real independence from Port-Royal on Pascal's part, for him to be entitled to claim
that here he trades in no *équivoques* he would need the benefit of some
fairly accomodating casuistry on the "interprétation de quelque terme"
(VI 96). It is a situation far from anomalous in the *duellum/bellum* called
polemics.

"At times Pascal is Jesuitical"—a reproach that is more than specious, but
how serious?

If the methods adopted by Pascal invite the seduction of the reader, at
the same time they invite him not to go astray. The comic masks of irony
and raillery serve as the announcements of a visage hidden underneath,
just as manifest hyperbole proclaims the need for some restrictions and
reservations in its interpretation. Indeed, Letters I–X cry out for them.
Though these *premières Provinciales* are less developed dialectically, they
have not only the irony of a Platonic dialogue but also its form, a form that
itself readily fulfills the maieutic function of a Socrates. For a dialogue
invites the reader to enter into it imaginatively, to make himself another of
the characters therein, to bring to the discussion objections and restrictions,
to demand clarifications, digressions, or even another main line for the
argument—all to be contributions on his part, and to be made according to
such lights as he has. The responsibility rests with him if he remains content with a first, superficial reading of a dramatic and ironic discourse—
especially a polemical one. Just as there is an ethic for the author of a
polemic, and especially a comic polemic (XI), so there is an ethic for the
reader that the author is in his rights to presuppose. It redounds to the
honor of a certain number of their first readers that the *Provinciales*
boosted the sales of Escobar.

But under the deceased Plato's pillow, we are told, lay comedies of
Aristophanes. Produced, like them, in a religious context, and likewise to
serve a conservative view, the *Provinciales* too unleash a raillery designed
to instruct and to improve the community. And like the raillery of
Aristophanes, that of the *Provinciales* is aimed at individual targets rather
than at types, though obviously the Letters are couched in a polished style
much closer to that of New Comedy. In the *Clouds*, whose influence was
so grave for Socrates in his trial before a public of 501 jurors, he is ridiculed
and maligned by Aristophanes from the common man's perspective, that of
*le sens commun* as embodied in public opinion. Therein Socrates is pilloried, not only for the general absurdity of various sophistic innovations, but
for subverting the traditional religion and *mores*. Indeed, by transmuting
the Better into the Worse, by making the Weaker Reason the Stronger, the
Socrates of Aristophanes, like Pascal's Jesuits, corrupts not only public
morals but the public's moral rules. The first ten *Provinciales* dress a stage

on which the nefarious and subversive Thinkery (φροντιστήριον) of *le bon père* and his Jesuit colleagues is exposed to catch the catcalls of the crowd.

But if Aristophanes wrongly defamed Socrates, and perhaps even the sophistic movement, is the censure of the *Provinciales* fundamentally just? The reply must be in the affirmative if, like Pascal and his Doctor of the Sorbonne, one is optimistic enough about the power of truth to believe that imposing on the public can only yield a vain and ephemeral triumph (III 46–7). (The Athenians quickly repented having put Socrates to death and went after his accusers.) The success of the *Provinciales* stems most of all from the fact that Pascal was able to evoke in the hearts and minds of his readers his own reaction to the reading of Escobar. "Disclose your Sisyphean ruses: this case admits of no mitigating circumstances!"

Thus, Pascal has the greatest confidence that the reading of his adversaries by his public will only confirm the success of the Letters (fr.S 801). Nor would the echoes of the *Provinciales'* controversies over more than three hundred years force Pascal to revise his conviction as to their final triumph. "Jesuitical" remains a reproach, and even today, though *le public honnête* has arguably acquiesced in "defining deviancy down" in its moral and theological ruminations—which are by and large far less informed than those of Pascal's public—this acquiescence, though widespread, has met with strong resistance. Although it would not use these terms, the lay, *honnête* public is still largely unconvinced that *pot-bouille* is nectar, or that *pot-bouille* would require a God to bring it to mankind—though, alas for Pascal and his party, it is decidedly unconvinced that nectar needs to be consumed while living in the trunk of a tree, or while retiring to the pensive solitude of a crypt or cemetery on holidays (IX 159). Paradoxically, it is the defender of the Jesuit cause who will need to paint human nature in darker colors than his Augustinian opponents if he wishes to explain this long resistance to truth on the part of fallen man.

In the final reckoning, to defend Port-Royal by trusting to the power of Truth acting over time—in effect, by trusting in the power and mercy of Providence—could pass for the most saintly, and yet the most clever, ruse of all. It insinuated itself even into the rhetorical practices of those non-polemicists who were not "sans liason" and "sans attachement" but were, on the contrary, very literally of Port-Royal—to wit, the Solitaries and religious who defended it only with their prayers. "[L]a vérité subsiste éternellement, et triomphe enfin de ses ennemis, parce qu'elle est éternelle et puissante comme Dieu même" (Truth subsists eternally and in the end triumphs over its enemies, for it is eternal and powerful like God himself, XII fin).

# 3

## PREFERRING TO LIVE IN A TREE-TRUNK: THE *PROVINCIALES* AS *HEAUTON TIMOROUMENOS*

[C]'est encore une des contradictions qui défigurent nôtre espèce. Veu le penchant que nous avons à satisfaire la nature, nous devrions courir aprés ceux qui nous prêcheroient que tout est permis: cependant nous les détesterions. Puis qu'une morale relâchée nous paroit abominable, nous devrions nous attacher à la morale la plus rigide: cependant nous la fuyons. C'est donc que nous voulons un juste milieu, qui nous permette quelque chose, et qui ne nous permette pas tout? Mais si on y prend garde, on trouvera que ce milieu même ne nous accommode pas . . . .

[I]t is yet another one of the contradictions that disfigure our species. In view of the inclination we have to satisfy our nature, we ought to run after those who would preach that all is permitted; however, we would detest them. Then again, inasmuch as a lax morality appears abominable to us, we should embrace the strictest morals; however, we flee from them. Is it then that we wish a golden mean that permits us some things, but does not permit us everything? But if one looks closely, one will find that this very mean does not suit us . . . .

Pierre Bayle, *Pensées diverses sur la comète*, CLXXXIX

In the *Provinciales* IV–X, Pascal shows remarkable rhetorical address in maneuvering his "jésuite-marionette," the sublimely fatuous "bon père," into enthusiastic accounts of the Jesuits' genius for accommodating Christian morality to the lifestyles of people of all sorts and conditions—in effect, into accounts of evident moral enormities declared permissible. These, quite unbeknownst to their expounder, will leave far the greater part of the Letters' public agog, amused, aghast, and finally indignant. We are thus treated to the deliciously droll spectacle of the Jesuits, in reputation consummately clever, and by self-proclamation "tous conduits par la sagesse divine" (all guided by the divine wisdom, V 72),[1] unwittingly indicting, convicting, and executing themselves in the court of public opinion.

The success of the *Provinciales* against the Jesuits as moral laxists has been as striking as *Candide*'s against Leibniz. Only in the "best of all possible worlds," where "Tout est bien," does "Jesuitical" imply no reproach. But may there not be another success, surely unintended, against the Augustinian severities dear to Pascal and Port-Royal? For if, under the spur of the *Provinciales*, public opinion both seconded and anticipated the Church in censuring the laxity of Jesuit (and other) casuists, neither—again like the Church—did it react by embracing the rigors of Pascal and Port-Royal's Augustinianism.[2]

Both of these outcomes can be traced to a common cause: the necessity each party faces, when addressing even a well-informed public of *honnêtes gens* rather than one of professional theologians,[3] of pleading against common conceptions before the tribunal of *le sens commun*—a tribunal that paradox can quickly transform into a pillory. It is a judge that, if scandalized by the apparent moral enormities licensed by Jesuit casuists—dueling, killing from ambush, and dispensation from loving God are perhaps the most shocking—is nonetheless little likely to be attracted by Augustinian severity. In varying degrees, this severity is discernible by implication throughout Letters IV to X, wherein the Jesuits are pilloried for

---

[1] The buffoonery of unwitting self-subversion on the part of *le bon père* and the authors he quotes not only gives comic bite to the *Provinciales*, but deftly insinuates a serious point: can "authorities" who are *si peu habiles* be trusted on matters where salvation, our all, is at stake?

[2] On the issue of laxism, see Ferreyrolles, *Blaise Pascal*, 10–14. On the censures (of 110 propositions, 17 of which figure in the *Provinciales*), see LXIX–LXX of the introduction to Cognet et Ferreyrolles's edition of the *Provinciales* and their notes to Letters IV–X.

As regards the reception accorded rigorism, Racine relates what may be taken as a foreshadowing. When Mother Angélique Arnauld reintroduced the rigors of the rule of Saint Benedict at Port-Royal, "Plusieurs maisons non seulement admirèrent cette réforme, mais résolurent même de l'embrasser." However, "[La réforme] fut extrêmmement désapprouvée par un fort grand nombre de moines et d'abbés même, qui regardaient la bonne chère, l'oisiveté, la mollesse, et, en un mot, le libertinage, comme d'anciennes coutumes de l'ordre [de Cîteaux] où il n'était pas permis de toucher. Toutes ces sortes de gens déclamèrent avec beaucoup d'emportement contre les religieuses de Port-Royal, les traitant de folles, d'embéguinées, de novatrices, de schismatiques même, et ils parlaient de les faire excommunier." *Abrégé de l'histoire de Port-Royal*, in *Œuvres complètes* (Paris: L'Intégrale, 1962), 316.

[3] For an encapsulating discussion of the "grand public" of "honnêtes gens" to which the *Provinciales* are addressed, see Mesnard in the Round Table in Duchêne, *L'Imposture littéraire*, 385–87.

legitimizing very apparent moral laxity. But in Letter IX the author, in his zeal for what his party accounts the true Christian moral ideal, thrusts its severity naked before the reader. By these revelations he, too, unwittingly enacts a self-undoing before the bar of *le sens commun*.[4]

*Le sens commun* can be understood as a part as well as a product of *le bon sens*, the ability to distinguish between the true and false, itself *commun* in the heavy irony of Descartes's opening words of the *Discours de la méthode* ("la chose du monde la mieux partagée" [the best shared-out thing in the world]). Understood as the product of *le bon sens*, *le sens commun* refers to a web of widespread because apparently correct beliefs and assumptions—what Aristotle called *endoxa*. Understood as a part of *le bon sens*, *le sens commun* refers both to the faculty that endorses *endoxa* as true, and to the role that these assumptions play in the making of moral and other judgments by forming a background whose truth is taken as "given," a background with whose truth new judgments are thus required to agree.

Pascal is decidedly of two minds—at first glance, even inconsistent—on the reliability of *le sens commun* as a judge. In the *Pensées*, unbelievers too indifferent to investigate Christianity's pretensions to know what awaits us all in the world to come can be confounded "par les premières vues du sens commun et par les sentiments de la nature" (by the first inspection on the part of *le sens commun* and by the instincts of [our cognitive] nature, fr.S 682). But, in a world where, if we speak but according to our natural lights, the search for truth ends in impasse, and hence in Pyrrhonist suspension of

[4] Likewise, there is a certain amount of unwitting self-undoing on the part of the author before the bar of Port-Royal, and of its friends even of today. "Il y a une réponse aux *Provinciales* dans les *Mémoires* de Lancelot. Celui-ci raconte la vie de Saint-Cyran, avec un chapitre intitulé 'De la raillerie'. C'est une réfutation en forme de la onzième Provinciale. Saint-Cyran avait beaucoup réfléchi sur ce qu'il appelle 'l'onction' [. . . .] [Il] disait: 'Quand vous discutez avec un adversaire, vous pouvez frappez, mais il faut qu'à tout moment votre adversaire sente que vous êtes un frère pour lui.' Or, franchement, il y a beaucoup de textes dans les *Provinciales* où l'on ne sent pas que le jésuite est un frère pour Pascal! Celui-ci a inventé le personnage du jésuite-marionette, qui a fait une grande carrière dans la littérature française [. . .] avec Saint-Evremond et Voltaire. Ça ne sonne pas chrétien, et je comprends bien l'hostilité de la mère Angélique, de Singlin, de Lancelot à la pratique des premières *Provinciales*." Sellier in a discussion in Duchêne, *L'Imposture littéraire*, 348.

Robin Howells plausibly sees self-subversion in the Letters in that, though contrary of course to Pascal's intention, through ridicule of its "authorized representatives" and its "theological discourses" they "subject the Church to comic debasement and lay judgment." "Polemical Stupidity in the *Lettres provinciales*," in *Pascal/New Trends in Port-Royal Studies*, eds. David Wetsel and Frédéric Canovas (Tübingen: Gunter Narr, 2002), 236–37.

judgment ("le pyrrhonisme est le vrai," fr.S 570), *le sens commun* can be a blind guide. And "vae caecis ducentibus! vae caecis sequentibus!" (Woe to blind guides! Woe to blind followers! XI 203 [quotation from Augustine]). For it can be corrupted by errors inculcated at a young age, which acquire a sort of *ius primi occupantis* (cf. fr.S 78), and it has been corrupted by the Fall (frs.S 94, 498). Indeed, its opposition renders the perpetuity of Christian truth—"Le Messie a toujours été cru" (The Messiah has always been believed in, fr.S 314)—all the more amazing, if not miraculous. "La seule science qui est contre le sens commun et la nature des hommes, est la seule qui ait toujours subsisté parmi les hommes" (The only knowledge that is against our common human understanding [cf. God's justice as it emerges in fr.S 164] and our human nature is the only knowledge that has always existed among humankind, fr.S 680, end).

There is a like two-mindedness in the *Écrits sur la grâce*. Although it counts against the doctrine of Calvin that, humanly speaking, it is intolerable ("insupportable aux hommes"), the fact that the doctrine of Molina "flatte le sens commun que l'autre blesse" (flatters the common human understanding that the other [Calvin's] affronts, OC, III 786) can be discounted. In the *Provinciales* IV–X, these ideas are combined. Pascal's Jesuits, anxious lest the rigors of the Gospel be "insupportable aux hommes," and thus striving to accommodate Christian morals to us rather than to conform us to them, will flatter *le sens commun* so grossly and maladroitly as to render themselves "insupportable[s]" to the very object of their flattery.

Given the limitations of *le sens commun*, and hence of public opinion, why make an appeal to it by writing a work such as the *Provinciales*? Small wonder that the Jesuits subsequently denounced the Letters for airing disputes before an incompetent tribunal, just as, in 1644, Antoine Arnauld complained that the theologal Habert had appealed to public opinion against the Jansenists.[5] In the *Pensées*, Pascal himself voices this reservation on the subject of discerning between probative and nonprobative miracles.

> Ce n'est point ici le pays de la vérité. Elle erre inconnu parmi les hommes. Dieu l'a couverte d'un voile qui la laisse méconnaître à ceux qui n'entendent pas sa voix. Le lieu est ouvert au blasphème, et même sur des vérités au moins bien apparentes. Si l'on publie les vérités de l'Évangile, on en publie de contraires, et on obscurcit les questions en sorte que le peuple ne peut discerner (fr.S 425).

[5] In the préface of *l'Apologie de M. Jansenius*; cited in Sellier, *Port-Royal et la littérature*, vol. 1, 172 n. 9.

> This is not the land of truth. It wanders unknown among mankind. God has covered it with a veil which makes it unrecognizable to those who do not understand his voice. The way is open to blasphemy, and even about truths that are, to say the least, very apparent. If the truths of the Gospel are published, so are contrary "truths," and the questions are obscured so that the people cannot discern aright.

Of course, every moralist must take common moral belief at least as a point of departure. But the more particular answer to the question "Why appeal to public opinion?" is rooted in Pascal's censure that "l'esprit de la Société n'est pas celui de la sévérité chrétienne" (The spirit of the Society [the Jesuits] is not that of Christian severity, V 74). Aiming to govern all consciences, "toutes les consciences," the Society wishes to accommodate and hence to satisfy everyone. But since "les maximes évangéliques et sévères [. . . .] ne s'accordent pas aux desseins de la plupart des gens" (evangelical and rigorous maxims [. . . .] do not fit in with the designs of the majority of people, V 75), the Jesuits' morality for day-to-day consumption—*le pot-bouille,* so to speak[6]—is one of laxity, *relâchement,* that abases and infects not only moral conduct, but, worse, moral rules. In short, the Society poses a public danger, and so it is public opinion that must be warned (cf. fr.1002 in L'Intégrale).

## THE JESUITS IN THE PILLORY

And who better to warn that the Jesuits have poisoned the fonts of morality than a Jesuit? And so Pascal has *le bon père,* as proud of his colleagues' finesse as he is naïve, explain to the fictive narrator of the *Provinciales* I–X how the Society's casuists have been able to accommodate all sorts of persons by legalistic subtleties that would legitimize what, to the less besotted, must seem paradigm cases of wickedness. Among the most shocking examples are dueling, and assassination from (pious) ambush—the famous *pieux guet-apens* (VII 121)—to say nothing of the abolition of love for God as needful for salvation. The Jesuit father is even piqued when his interlocutor seems merely astounded at the cleverness that can reconcile dueling with the Gospel (VII 115). *Proh pudor! O tempora, o mores!*

Of course, to casuists, confessors, philosophers and theologians, the precise circumstances and conditions, no matter how unusual or bizarre,

---

[6] As noted above, this is "[L]a cuisine de tous les jours, cuisine terriblement louche et menteuse sous son apparente bonhomie [. . . .] la marmite où mijotent [. . .] tous les relâchements de la morale." Paul Alexis, cited by Henri Mittérand, ed., in Émile Zola, *Les Rougon-Macquart,* vol. 3 (Pléiade), 1638 n. 1.

that may attend a moral case are of very great importance. Indeed, as a practical matter, confessors, to whom works of casuistry are primarily addressed, must expect to be confronted with, and to judge of, even the most unusual and bizarre ones. But to the wide, lay public of *honnêtes gens*, such "fine print," when visible, and when not amusing on account of its fantasticality, will be easily obscured by the blazingly evident moral enormity of things such as duels, ambushes, and lack of love for God considered simply and without qualification.[7] The polemical genius of the *Provinciales* lies precisely in allowing this enormity, itself beyond discussion, to permeate and to color the entire discussion of a case by a sort of rhetorical osmosis. And so, Letters IV–X do not give a trial to the Jesuits, or a hearing to the moral cases they have pronounced upon. For, as we read in Letter XI (200), to do so would require taking them seriously, and so accord them some respect.

> Et comment aurait-on pu traiter autrement la plupart de ces matières, puisque ce serait *les autoriser que de les traiter sérieusement*, selon Tertullien?
> Quoi! Faut-il employer la force de l'Écriture et de la tradition pour montrer que c'est tuer son ennemi en trahison que de lui donner des coups d'épee par derrière, et dans une embûche; et que c'est acheter un bénéfice que de donner de l'argent comme un motif pour se le faire résigner?

> And how else could one have treated the greater part of these matters, since, as Tertullilan says, *to treat them seriously would be to invest them with some authority?*
> What! Must we avail ourselves of the force of Scripture and of Tradition to show that it is killing an enemy treacherously if one stabs him with sword-thrusts from the rear, and from ambush; and that it is really buying an ecclesiastical office if one gives [the incumbent] money as a motive for resigning from it in one's favor?

Rather, in lieu of finely weighing conditions and distinctions, and so in effect doing casuistry themselves, Letters IV–X laugh the Jesuits out of court—a proceeding implicitly condemned elsewhere by Pascal himself ("Jésus-Christ n'a jamais condamné sans ouïr" [Jesus Christ never condemned without

[7] "[D]eux pensées [sur la théologie morale] s'entrechoquent, dont aucune n'évolue, ne se soumet à l'autre. Au lecteur de choisir! Ce qui va condamner la conception des jésuites, c'est la rigueur de la radiographie effectuée (qui fait apparaître les principes et les grandes lignes) et le rassemblement rapide des concessions. L'ensemble apparaît alors, à l'évidence, comme en contradiction avec les exigences illimitées du *Sermon sur la Montagne*." Sellier, "Les premières *Provinciales*," in his *Port-Royal et la littérature*, vol. 1, 150.

hearing, fr.S 460]). Nor can the Jesuits hope to vindicate an opinion[8] save by doggedly insisting upon the importance of crucial distinctions in a case's "fine print"—that is to say, by stupefying or infuriating a lay public with the niceties of casuistry, thus repeating their original "offense," and so condemning themselves anew.

And yet, after all, is Pascal fair in seeing the Jesuits' distinctions and conditions as mere fig leaves to cloak their moral *pudenda*? "[V]ous avez suivi votre méthode ordinaire, qui est d'accorder aux hommes ce qu'ils désirent, et *donner à Dieu des paroles et des apparences*" (You have followed your usual method, which is to grant men what they desire and *give God words and appearances*, XII 224, emphasis added).

For example, might one be permitted to fight a duel if it were the only means of guarding an innocent from destruction? Does Scott depict a murderer in Ivanhoe, who accepted a duel to preserve the life of the innocent Rebecca? And was it not to preserve truth, surely an innocent, that Pascal entered into a polemic with the Jesuits—that is to say, into a duel (*polemos=bellum=duellum*)? One could make an accommodation for the *Provinciales* as not a duel *sensu strictissimo*, but this would be to speak *en casuiste non strictissimus*.

And what of the "pious ambush"? Under a brutal regime—where, like so many in our century, the Jansenists found themselves—the machinery of justice can be corrupt, even frankly murderous. If, under such a regime, a case arises wherein a Resistance can preserve the innocent against faithless and corrupt, even murderous civil authorities only by ambush, is it morally permissible? In defense of truth, Pascal in the *Provinciales* clandestinely attacks a foe he deems corrupt and faithless ("Mentiris impudentissime!" [XV 294–95]), in fact murderous in the license it grants in questions of homicide (VII). It is, moreover, a foe that is powerfully backed by the official machinery of State. Does he not, as a clandestine author, strike from ambush, and with a force well-nigh sufficient for a sort of rhetorical lethality? Are the *Provinciales* not then a kind of *pieux guet-apens*? If so, their author stands in some small need of being accommodated by the kinds of principles, distinctions, and allowances that festoon the Jesuits in the pillory in which he has placed them. It is ironic that the *Provinciales*, themselves the voice of a moral and theological Resistance, treat as beyond all discussion, as patent moral enormities, expedients to which a Resistance might arguably not only be driven but entitled.

---

[8] For perceptive remarks on the Jesuits' rhetorical options, and on their long failure to appreciate the rhetorical dilemma in which Pascal placed them, see Descotes, "La Responsabilité collective dans les *Provinciales*," and LeGuern, "Les *Provinciales* ou les excès d'un polémiste abuse."

Finally, is it really, as the narrator indignantly exclaims, "le mystère d'iniquité accompli" (the mystery of iniquity accomplished, X 191), to suppose that the love of God is not absolutely necessary for salvation in all cases? To suppose that attrition (repentance from fear of punishment) may possibly suffice in lieu of contrition (repentance from love of God)? Consider, *ex hypothesi*, a man who imagines that he has committed the unpardonable sin, and so is irrevocably cut off from divine grace—a state of mind movingly described by Pascal's great contemporary John Bunyan in *Grace Abounding to the Chief of Sinners.*[9]

> And now I was sorry that God had made me a man . . . . The beasts, birds, fishes, etc., I blessed their condition, for . . . they were not to go to hell after death; I could therefore a [have] rejoiced had my condition been as any of theirs. (87,88)

He goes on to lament that he had not been made a dog or a toad, and so without a soul that was sure to be lost (104).

Is it beyond all possibility that a virtuous man, living and dying in this arguably pathological state, all that might have been love of God stultified by terror and despair, might yet be saved? Even if it is mistaken to affirm it, is it monstrous, let alone the *non plus ultra* of enormities, "the mystery of iniquity accomplished"? After all, the famous Pascalian contention that the human self is hateful, "Le moi est haïssable" (fr.S 494), implies that God should be dispensed from any obligation to love mankind; and it warrants Jonathan Edwards's no less famous view that God abhors us. Would the severity of *these* conclusions affront the *Provinciales'* public so much less than the doctrine of attrition?

---

[9] Sellier rightly explains Port-Royal's revulsion to the possibility of salvation without love of God by insisting on its conception of the radical turning of the heart towards God required for true conversion (*Port-Royal et la littérature* II, 13–16; cf. Jan Miel, *Pascal and Theology* (Baltimore and London: Johns Hopkins University Press, 1969), 127–36. The case of Bunyan as revealed in the text above is arguably conformable to "une situation d'école, à moins qu'il ne s'agisse de compulsions psycho-pathologiques purement profanes" (15) of the kind that Sellier taxes some casuists with having imagined. This underscore of the element of the bizarre is a fair one. Yet, life is so various that even the strangest cases can and do occur, whence the need of casuists and confessors to allow for them.

A long note by Cognet to the tenth *provinciale* (182–83 n. 2) provides very helpful background and precisions to the vitally important attrition/contrition distinction. Albert R. Jonsen and Stephen Toulmin's *The Abuse of Casuistry: A History of Moral Reasoning* (Berkeley and London: University of California Press, 1988) furnishes a useful overview of casuistry and its critics, of whom Pascal is arguably the most influential.

Pascal has little reason to fear such cavils from the wide public of *honnêtes gens*. When, by the consummate address of his ventriloquism, his opponents not only take, but glory in taking, the exceptional, the bizarre, and the deplorable as serious, even decisive elements in moral judgment— a proceeding their profession as casuists demands—then, by their own devisings, they appear, rightly or wrongly, to be either ludicrous or monstrous, and out of their own mouths they stand condemned.

## PREFERRING TO LIVE IN A TREE-TRUNK: FROM POST TO PILLORY

Again, what of "les sévérités chrétiennes" to which Pascal would have his audience resort once it has recoiled from the laxities of the Jesuits? Will its *sens commun* not recoil from them as well once they are recognized in the lines of the *Provinciales*?

To a worldly reader who is attentive, even if oblivious to a professional moralist's subtleties, at least two potentially disquieting themes emerge, one in foreground, the other in background. The former is that the saintly ideal, by implication the ideal for all Christians, is one of heroic asceticism and utter detachment from the world. And, lest *le public honnête* should comfort itself with the reflection that heroic virtue is, fortunately, not required of us all, there is the latter: mere saintliness is not enough.

What will the *public honnête* of the *Provinciales* think when confronted with this caricature of a certain type of *dévot* from the Jesuit Le Moyne's *Peintures morales (Moral Portraits)*—one utterly unlike the "saints polis et dévots civilisés" (cultivated saints and the civilized among the devout) commended to the public in his *Dévotion aisée (Easy Devotion)*— and one who goes far beyond the love of silence and withdrawal, "le silence et la retraite," evinced by *dévots* "qui n'ont que du flegme dans les veines et de la terre sur le visage" (who have only phlegm in their veins and dirt on their faces)?

> Il est sans yeux pour les béautés de l'art et de la nature. Il croirait s'être chargé d'un fardeau incommode, s'il avait pris quelque matière de plaisir pour soi. Les jours de fête, il se retire parmi les morts. Il s'aime mieux dans un tronc d'arbre ou dans une grotte que dans un palais ou sur un trône. (IX 159)

> He is blind to the beauties of art and of nature. He would consider himself to be bearing an awkward burden if he had taken any pleasure for himself in anything. On festival days he withdraws to a cemetery. He prefers to be in a tree-trunk or a grotto rather than in a palace or on a throne.

To complete the picture, Le Moyne adds that this *dévot* is as insensible to insults and affronts as a statue, is oblivious to honor and glory, and is blind before the beauty of women.

Or rather, what will *le public honnête* think when it sees the narrator, "je," profoundly shocked by Le Moyne's mockery, retort that this depiction seems "faite à dessein de tourner les saints en ridicule" (made with the set purpose of ridiculing the saints), that it is, in reality, "l'image d'un homme tout à fait détaché des sentiments auxquels l'Évangile oblige de renoncer" (the picture of a man completely detached from the sentiments the Gospel obliges us to renounce, IX 160)?

It would be sanguine indeed to hope that such a public will fail to conclude that the narrator, in fleeing the laxist morals of the Jesuits, has rather embraced what *le bon père* calls "les mœurs ridicules et brutales d'un fou mélancolique" (the ridiculous and brutish *mores* of a melancholic madman, 159). For if, in this public's view, *pot-bouille* is not nectar, neither is dust and ashes.

It would be more than sanguine to hope that *le public honnête*, if it conceded that this portrait is in truth of the saintly ideal, would also concede that the heroic virtue of embodying this ideal is required of *it*. Not surprisingly, the world is loath to believe that it must be dead to the world. And, even if it were to concede both of these paradoxical severities, would it be disposed to grant the clear implication by the narrator in Letter IV's discussion of intention that, for salvation, such saintliness is not enough?

In the *Provinciales*, intention plays not merely contrary but contradictory roles in the moral notions (and strategies?) of the opposing parties. Pascal's Jesuits, aiming to make sin difficult and virtue easy, require a specific intention to do ill for an act to be sinful. Hence, a valet who holds a ladder while his master climbs though his mistress's window can, if he is subtle, avoid sin. Since the act of holding a ladder is itself morally indifferent, he need only direct his intention away from aiding in the consummation of an illicit amour to an innocuous end—for example, to the mere earning of his wage (VI 109). Here, the intention is the determining factor in judging whether an act is blameworthy. But when it comes to making an act morally creditable, intention is scarcely required. Thus, the Jesuit de Barry writes that to say the Ave Maria daily in honor of the Heart of Mary assures one of winning her heart. Provided we also give her our own? "Cela n'est pas nécéssaire," replies de Barry through *le bon père*, "quand on est trop attaché au monde" (It is not necessary when one is too attached to the world). The narrator drily observes that "il n'y aura personne de damné après cela" (No one will be damned after this), but the Jesuits take a darker view of human nature. What of the hard of heart who would like to be saved, but only "sans quelque application de mémoire" (without some effort of the memory)? For them, writes de Barry, it will suffice "d'avoir jour et nuit un chapelet au bras en forme de bracelet, ou de porter sur soi un rosaire, ou bien une image de la Vierge" (to wear day and night a chaplet in the form of a bracelet, or to bear with one a rosary, or, for that matter, a picture of the Virgin, IX 154–55).

Pascal, who would have it that sin is easy but virtue hard, likewise gives a varying value to the importance of intention as opposed to that of an act's intrinsic good or evil, but in the inverse sense. Thus, in the discussion just preceding, the *Provinciale's* fictive narrator, who is by now of Pascal's party, is clearly unconvinced that a good action is meritorious in the absence of a good intention. This signals that here it is the (lack of) intention that overrides the intrinsic goodness of an act in determining whether the act is meritorious. But Pascal also holds, following Saint Augustine, that one sins all unknowingly, and without any intention of doing ill, provided that, in God's eyes even if not in ours, the act itself is wrong. Here, the intrinsic ill of the act overrides (an innocent) intention to make the act blameworthy. As a result, as the Jansenist friend points out, even the saintly can be hated by God.

> Mais que dira-t-on de ceux qui se porte avec ardeur à des choses effectivement mauvaises, parce qu'ils les croient effectivement bonnes . . . ce qui n'empêche pas, selon les Pères, qu'ils n'aient péché dans ces occasions?
> Et sans cela, comment les justes auraient-ils des péchés cachés? Comment serait-il véritable que Dieu seul en connaît et la grandeur et le nombre; que personne ne sait s'il est digne d'amour ou de haine, et que les plus saints doivent toujours demeurer dans la crainte et dans le tremblement, quoiqu'ils ne se sentent coupables en aucune chose . . . ? (IV 65–66)

> But what shall we say of those who ardently pursue things that are in fact bad because they believe them to be in fact good . . . which, according to the Fathers of the Church, does not prevent them from sinning on these occasions?
> And were this not so, how could the just have secret sins? How would it be true that God alone knows their magnitude and their number, that no one knows if he is deserving of love or hatred, and that the holiest must always remain in fear and trembling though they are unaware of any guilt . . . ?

Of course, from the Augustinian perspective, nothing really suffices for salvation save God's free and irresistible gift of efficacious grace, made to some but not to others without any prevision of merit. This is a doctrine that, on Pascal's view in the *Écrits sur la grâce*, unlike Calvinism and Molinism neither wounds nor flatters *le sens commun* but, its disciples "marchant avec plus de lenteur et de considération" (proceeding more slowly and with greater thoughtfulness), strikes a middle path (OC, III 787). But even if this be so, Augustine's views on grace rest on what Pascal himself concedes to be a repellent severity. For their truth is the consequence of the guilt that we all, even to a babe new born, have inherited from our first ancestors for a sin committed four thousand years before we were born—a mystery so great "qu'il n'y a rien qui choque plus notre raison" (that there is nothing that shocks our reason more, fr.S 164).

As they stand, the severities implicit in the *Provinciales* IV–X, if they are to be persuasive to a *public honnête*, must be vindicated by the *Pensées'* brief for skepticism, and thence for *soumission de la raison*. There, in the ultimate act of self-undoing, reason hales itself before its own judgment seat, weighs itself in its own balance, and finds itself to be wanting (fr.S 164). At the end of the day, "le pyrrhonisme est le vrai," and so we must be prepared to submit ourselves to paradox even if "il n'y a rien qui choque plus notre raison."[10] It is a submission that will become easier once we realize that it is *fallen* reason that is outraged!

It is in the *Pensées*, then, that Pascal's most fundamental criticism of the Jesuits' moral doctrines is given voice. Not only is the *morale* they advance *raisonnable* rather than *sainte*, but it is corrupt by virtue of being *raisonnable*.

> Les casuistes soumettent la décision à la raison corrompue et le choix des décisions à la volonté corrompue, afin que tout ce qu'il y a de corrompu dans la nature de l'homme eût part à sa conduite. (fr.S 498)
>
> The casuists submit the decision to our corrupt reason and the choice of decisions to our corrupt will in order that all that is corrupt in the nature of man may have its part in directing him.

Yet, as a polemicist addressing a wide, lay public—one more reasonable than saintly—Pascal himself can hardly do otherwise than to make his primary appeal to his audience's sense of reasonableness, its *bon sens* and *sens commun*. Moreover, as a satirist he will also make an appeal to its sense of humor—from an Augustinian point of view, a sense perhaps no less corrupt and no more reliable than those others.

In fine, in the rhetorical framework of the *Provinciales* the Augustinian severities of easy sin and hard virtue, be they ever so true, will have the potential to affront *l'honnêté* and *le sens commun* just as do the Jesuit

---

[10] For more on the importance in Pascal of accepting mystery and paradox, see chapter 6, "The Fundamental Importance of Justice."

laxities of hard sin and easy virtue. And when they are called upon to judge, paradox calls forth dismissal and a smile. If, as many have, we take the first *Provinciales* (I–X) to enact a comedy, then perhaps, following Menander and Terence,[11] it should be called the "Self-Punisher" (possibly "Self-Executioner")—*Heauton timoroumenos.*

[11] This title is also found ending in "-umenos," and sometimes as one word.

    Needless to say, Port-Royal, following Saint Augustine, voiced grave moral reservations about the theater. Cf. Thirouin, *L'Aveuglement salutaire: le réquisitoire contre le théâtre dans la France classique* (Paris: Honoré Champion, 1997), and Pierre Nicole, *Traité de la comédie et autres pièces d'un process du théâtre* (Paris: Honoré Champion, 1998). Nonetheless, Pascal, in his famous *entretien* with Sacy, speaks approvingly of Epictetus's likening of human life to a comedy and of his insistence on our responsibility to play well the role assigned us by the master. See Nicholas Fontane, *Mémoires ou histoire des solitaires de Port-Royal* (Paris: Honoré Champion, 2001), 600. For his part, Sacy seems to have found at least three plays of Terence to be safe since he presented and translated them "en y changeant fort peu de choses" for the use of the *petites écoles* of Port-Royal, notwithstanding that, as the then estranged Racine implicitly reproached him, "Cicéron n'est pas moins nécéssaire que lui [pour apprendre la langue latine]; il est assurément moins dangéreux . . . ." Racine, "Lettre aux deux apologistes de l'auteur des 'Hérésies imaginaires,'" in *Œuvres complètes*, 314.

# 4

## REVELATION/REVOLUTION: A REFLECTION ON NEWNESS IN THE *PROVINCIALES*

Il semble que les premiers mots des *Métamorphoses* d'Ovide,
*in nova fert animus*, soient la devise du genre humain. . . .

It seems that the first words of Ovid's *Metamorphoses*, "The
mind is carried to new things," are the motto of mankind . . . .

Voltaire, Dictionnaire philosophique, "Nouveauté"

Quelle chimère est-ce donc que l'homme, quelle nouveauté,
quel monstre, quel chaos . . . .

What a chimera man is, what a novelty, what a monster, what
a chaos . . . .

Pascal, Pensées (fr.S 164)

Although it is customary to date the modern era from the seventeenth century, the scant esteem in which it holds what is new[1]—at the time, a way of thinking so old as to be immemorial—clearly distinguishes that century from a more modern modernity, one on which the Enlightenment succeeded in imposing a veritable cult of innovation—a new idol before which postmodernity, a more modern modernity still, also bends in worship. For

---

[1] Even Bacon, who, perhaps owing to his appreciation of science, was more open to innovation than most of his contemporaries, decidedly qualified such endorsement as he bestowed on it in "On Innovations" (1625). For if innovations, including political ones, should be called for (religion is pointedly unmentioned), it is in large part because "a froward retention of custom is as turbulent a thing as an innovation." Francis Bacon, "On Innovations," in *Major Works* (Oxford: Oxford University Press, 2002), 388.

innovation, having dethroned the *mores maiorum* under the auspices of the Goddess of Reason, proceeded to accomplish yet another revolution— *novae res novae*—by installing itself in the high seat of that now outmoded deity.

At the time of the *Provinciales*, innovators, *les novateurs*,[2] are, after the model of Catilina in Sallust, neither more nor less than revolutionaries. According to the topos of malefic novelty of which Catilina is a paradigm in the rhetorical tradition,[3] these enemies of the public peace are so many *furieux* who would risk setting all ablaze as a prelude to a new order, *res novae*, itself a prelude to *novae tabellae*, the abolition of the colossal debts they have amassed under the goad of their unbridled vices, debts which they could never hope to liquidate otherwise.

And so, on their first arising, *les novateurs* in religion are held to be, in the manner of a Luther, nothing less than heretics, revolutionaries insurgent against Revelation, *furieux* whose hubris risks sending all and sundry to eternal fire. Do they not know that the Faith, having always existed—for "Le Messie a toujours été cru" (The Messiah has always been believed in, fr.S 314)—is the antithesis of an innovation? They are so rash as to have it that the *fundatissima fides* of so many popes, councils, peoples, and centuries can and should change. But this is not only heresy, but a contradiction in terms, since orthodoxy, by virtue of its orthodox definition, is the faith of all, always and everywhere (Vincent of Lerin's famous *quod ubique, quod semper, quod ab omnibus creditum est*). To the verdict of so great a weight of authority, *les novateurs* have the megalomania to oppose their

[2] This term, which appears largely in the domains of theology and politics, is always pejorative. See s.v. "novateur" in *Le grand Robert de la langue française* (Paris: Dictionnaires Robert, 1963).

[3] For example, in Fénelon, "Mémoire concernant la cour de Rome" (1688), *les novateurs* are "des esprits emportés secouant le joug" and "La Hollande . . . embrassa la nouveauté en se révoltant." *Œuvres*, vol. 1 (Paris: Gallimard [Pléiade], 1983), 519. Cicero treats great debts as sufficient reason to conspire for *res novae*, whence the following facetious aside: "Itaque nunc me scito tantum habere aeris alieni [after the purchase of a magnificent residence on the Palatine] ut cupiam coniurare, si quisquam recipiat" (*Epistulae ad familiares*, V 6). These *nexus idearum* long remained unbroken. Thomas Jefferson, whose passion for innovation pushed him to the point of denying that the laws and contracts made by one generation ought to bind generations that followed, made his friend John Adams wonder if his Jacobinism was not rooted in his colossal debts to English creditors. See David McCullough, *John Adams* (New York: Simon and Shuster, 2001), 442, 450. Jefferson's great adversary Alexander Hamilton, the conservative chief of the Federalists, American *optimates*, is very quick to see in political innovation the hostile van of *res novae*. See "Draft of a Defense of the Neutrality Proclamation," in *Writings* (New York: Library of America, 2001), 795. Indeed, assuming the name and style of Cicero, he denounces political innovators as so many new Catilinas. "Tully III," ibid., 830–32.

own mere endorsement—and this as the last word! It is in this sense that
Thomas More, whose polemical diversity in some ways anticipates the
Pascalian doctrine of the three orders,[4] attacks Luther on behalf of Henry
VIII, all the while parading Lutheran pronouncements fit to make the hair
of a Pascal stand on end.

> Hic sto. Hic maneo. Hic glorior. Hic triumpho. Hic insulto
> papistis, Thomistis, Henricistis, sophistis, et omnibus portis
> inferi. Neque curo, si contra me stent mille Augustini, et mille
> Cypriani.[5]

> Here I stand! Here I stay! Here I boast! Here I exult! Here I
> insult the papists, Thomists, Henricists, the "wise" and all the
> gates of Hell! Nor do I care if a thousand Augustines and a
> thousand Cyprians should stand against me.

To top it all, railing against a famous Augustinian affirmation of the
absolutely fundamental authority of the Church—"Ego vero Evangelio non
crederem, nisi me catholicae ecclesiae commoveret auctoritas" (Truly,
I would not believe in the Scriptures did not the authority of the Catholic
Church persuade me to do so, *Contra ep. Man.* I 5)—Luther exclaims:
"[Q]uis est Augustinus? Quis nos coget illi credere? Qua auctoritate eius ver-
bum est articulus fidei?" (Who is Augustine? Who forces us to believe him?
By what authority is his word an article of faith?).[6]

In the *Provinciales* Pascal, like More and so many other theological
polemicists, assails the adversary with the perennially effective accusation
of innovation. Why are the Jesuits so accommodating—that is to say, at
once *novateurs* and laxists[7]—in both morals and doctrine? According to the
Jansenist friend, who is unveiling the Jesuits' true nature and grand strategy
("l'esprit de la Société") to the fictive author of the *Provinciales*,

> Ils ont assez bonne opinion d'eux-mêmes pour croire qu'il est
> utile et comme nécessaire au bien de la religion que leur crédit
> s'étende partout, et qu'ils gouvernent toutes les consciences.
> Et parce que les maximes évangéliques et sévères sont propres
> pour gouverner quelques sortes de personnes, ils s'en servent

---

[4] See Louis Martz, *Thomas More: The Search for the Inner Man* (Yale, 1990), 31–51.
[5] Thomas More, *Responsio ad Lutherum* in *The Complete Works of Thomas More*,
vol. 5, pt. 1 (Yale, 1969), 573 (II 18).
[6] Ibid. 600 (II 21).
[7] As is apparent in chapters 2 and 3, I find the laxism imputed to some casuistical
judgments in the *Provinciales*, including some of the most famous, to be more
debatable than the incomparable art and profound sincerity of Pascal would lead
the reader to think.

dans ces occasions où elles leurs sont favorables. Mais commes ces mêmes maximes ne s'accordent pas au dessein de la plupart des gens, il les laissent à l'égard de ceux-là, afin d'avoir de quoi satisfaire tout le monde (V 75).

They have a high enough opinion of themselves to believe that it is useful and, as it were, necessary for the good of religion that their good standing should extend everywhere, and that they should rule all consciences. And because severe and evangelical maxims are fit for ruling some kinds of people, they use them when circumstances are favorable. But since these same maxims do not at all fit in with the plans of most people, they abandon them in their case so as to have something to satisfy everyone.

*Esprit de la Société, esprit de Port-Royal*—the spirit that would make truth pleasing to mankind, and the spirit that would make mankind pleasing to Truth. A protean, shape-shifting spirit and a spirit *semper isdem*. To come to grips with, and to get a hold on the times—a high necessity for a Church that would be catholic (universal)—the spirit of the Society is willing to undergo and to accomodate continual metamorphosis and renewal. Contrariwise, the other spirit's unchanging will to conform to Supreme Being rather than to Supreme Becoming, and its lurking fear that God may be a poor casuist indeed, require the upper case letter that its Truth displays like the stigmata. Two spirits no less powerful than universal, their striving and struggle—sometimes raucous sometimes silent, at some times sublime and at others *peu estimables*—constitute rather than characterize the Church.[8]

Conformably to "l'esprit de sa Société," the Jesuit *bon père* of the *Provinciales* assures their fictive author that "Les Pères [de l'Église] étaient bons pour la morale de leur temps; mais ils sont trop éloignés pour celle du nôtre. Ce ne sont plus eux qui la règlent, ce sont les nouveaux casuistes" (The Fathers of the Church were good for the moral teaching of their times; but they are too far removed from ours. It is no longer they who hold sway on morals, but the new casuists, V 90). Authorized by the postpatristic doctrine of "probable opinion," by a kind of moral alchemy the new casuists transmute what was yesterday sin into innocence today (VI 101–3). They are able to coin still more moral judgments that are *tout nouveaux, peu beaux* by having recourse to the "direction of the intention," a stratagem that "les Anciens n'ont point connu" (the Ancients knew nothing of, VII 117).

---

[8] "The present author's sympathies and antipathies are divided when he reflects on the conflict between Jesuit modernizers and Jansenist reactionaries. 'So miserable is human destiny that the lights which deliver man from one evil throw him into another [Pierre Bayle].'" Kolakowski, *God Owes Us Nothing*, x.

The fictive author, a faux naïf, feigns astonishment that "un seul casu-iste peut à son gré faire de nouvelles règles de morale et disposer, selon sa fantaisie, de tout ce qui regarde la conduite des mœurs" (one mere casuist can, at his pleasure, make new moral rules and, at his whim, settle all that pertains to moral conduct, VI 101). That these innovations subvert, or rather, invert the Christian ideal is crisply pointed out for us by *l'ami janséniste*.

> [C]omme si la foi, et la tradition qui la maintient, n'était pas toujours une et invariable dans tous les temps et dans tous les lieux; comme si c'était à la règle à se fléchir pour convenir au sujet qui doit lui être conforme; et comme si les âmes n'avaient, pour se purifier de leurs taches, qu'à corrompre la loi du Seigneur; au lieu *que la loi du Seigneur, qui est sans tache et toute sainte, est celle qui doit convertir les âmes* [Psaume XVIII 8] et les conformer à ses salutaires instructions! (V 78)

> As if the Faith, and the Tradition that upholds it, were not always one and the same in all times and places; as if the rule should bend in order to agree with those who, on the con-trary, must conform to *it*; and as if souls, to be purified of their stains, needed only to corrupt the law of the Lord; whereas instead *the law of the Lord, which is without stain and utterly holy, is that which must convert souls* and conform them to its salutary precepts!

But although the Jesuits' novelties are clearly subversive, they are no less patently ridiculous. What new authorities do the Jesuits presume to oppose to the Fathers, to the popes, to the councils, to tradition? What great Doctors dare deny that, as per More's hyperbole, "all men alone" should be believed? The list of thirty-two authorities with which Pascal would feign to have the *bon père* impress the fictive author has acquired a certain comic celebrity. "Villalobos, Coninck, Llamas, Achokier, Dealkozer, Dellacrux, Veracruz, Ugolino . . ." "O mon père! lui dis-je tout effrayé, tous ces gens-là étaient-ils chrétiens?" (O Father! I said to him all afright. Were all of these people Christians? V 92–3).

Inasmuch as the argument *tu quoque* ("you too do what you condemn") is no less fashionable in polemics than are other types of inconsistency, it is almost needless to add that the Jesuit adversaries of Pascal and Port-Royal also avail themselves of the accusation of innovation—for example, in the dispute raging over the Augustinian and Molinist accounts of grace. This time it is a Doctor of the Sorbonne who would enlighten us.

> [A]dmirez les machines du Molinisme qui font dans l'Église de si prodigieux renversements . . . que la doctrine si ancienne

de saint Augustin est une nouveauté insupportable ["The New Gospel of Port-Royal," according to the Jesuit Rapin]; et que les inventions nouvelles qu'on fabrique tous les jours à notre vue passent pour l'ancienne foi de l'Église. (III 51)

Wonder then at the devices of the Molinists, which effect such prodigious reversals in the Church . . . that Saint Augustine's teaching, though so ancient, becomes an intolerable novelty; and that the new inventions fabricated every day in our plain sight pass for the ancient Faith of the Church.

Later, Racine will report that the enemies of Port-Royal have described the nuns cloistered there as "de folles, d'embéguinées, de novatrices" (mad-women, besotted, innovators), whereas, for his part, "je puis vous protester devant Dieu que je ne connais ni ne fréquente aucun homme qui soit suspect de la moindre nouveauté" (Before God I can protest to you that I neither know nor frequent anyone suspected of the least novelty).[9]

To sum up, though at the risk of unduly prolonging this bacchanal of quotations: "mira, nova, falsa" (amazing, new, false [Bossuet]).[10]

Of course, none of this undermines the fact that, as Philippe Sellier points out, for Port-Royal true conversion consists in newness.

La conversion véritable consiste en un retournement du cœur. De là le titre, emprunté à Ézéchiel (XVIII, 31), d'un opuscule de Saint-Cyran, *Le Cœur nouveau*, et l'insistance sur la nouveauté chrétienne, défi aux vieillesses de la vie et aux routines des tièdes, l'urgence du renouvellement intérieur.[11]

True conversion consists in a returning of the heart. Hence the title, borrowed from Ezechiel (XVIII, 31), of a little work of Saint-Cyran, *The New Heart*. Hence the insistence on Christian newness, on bidding defiance to the old in life and to the routines of the lukewarm, and on the urgency of inner renewal.

But the newness demanded by such a conversion is of a special kind. It is a *return*—to Scripture, to the Fathers of the Church, to the fervor of the early Christians. In short, in religion, the new that is good is the past once more.

---

[9] Racine, *Abrégé de l'histoire de Port-Royal* in *Œuvres completes*, 316; Racine, Lettre à Mme. de Maintenon [4 mars 1698], ibid., 526.

[10] Bossuet, *Nouvelles ecclésiastiques*, le 15 avril 1684, cited by J. Le Brun, ed., in Fénelon, *Œuvres*, vol. 2, 1489. (Malebranche's view of grace is at issue here.)

[11] Sellier, "Port-Royal: littérature et théologie," 13.

Of course, in domains wherein authority is not the rule of truth, Pascal is far from being opposed to innovations.[12] As is well known, the *Provinciales* themselves abound in them. They are a theological and moral polemic, but comic and dramatic. Destined not just for theologians but for a lay, *honnête* public, women emphatically included, they are in the vulgar tongue. And they are, despite Port-Royal's reservations as to a want of charity therein—perhaps the sole point of accord between Port-Royal and the unhappy Escobar!—far less violent than the common run of the genre. Indeed, a modern defender of Thomas More, Louis Martz,[13] the editor-in-chief of the Yale edition of his *Complete Works*, would excuse More's intemperance and insults towards Luther—who, for his part, is even less delicate in his own expressions—by invoking the traditions, if not the requirements, of the theological polemic! Whoever reads what follows, one of More's countless displays of "sanctified bitterness," may well feel entitled to ask himself if Port-Royal's reservations on the charitableness of the *Provinciales*, even if strictly speaking just, do not testify to a somewhat Proustian delicacy of sentiment.

> Martyne Luther hym selfe, beynge specyally borne agayne & new created of the spyryte, whom god in many places of holy scypture hath commaunded to kepe his vowe made of chastyte when he then so far contrarye there unto toke out of relygyon a spouse of Cryste, wedded her hym selfe in reproche of wedloke, called her his wyfe, and made her his harlot, and in doble despyte of maryage and relygyon both, lyeth wyth her openly and lyeth wyth her nyghtly, in shamefull inceste and abominable bycherye: dothe he the whyle after Tyndalys hyghe wordes serche the depe secretys, and neuer leue serchynge tyll he come to the botome, the pyth, the quycke, the lyfe, the spyryte, the mary, and the very cause of that commaundement why, and so iudgeth all thynges?[14]

> Antiqui patres odisse te [Luther] non poterant: qui tot ætatibus ante defuncti sunt, quam quisquam suspicari posset, quod te merdam talem cacodemon aliquis, aliquando foret excavaturus in terram.[15]

---

[12] But, rather paradoxically, if he finds a scientific innovation to be good, in part it is because of its antiquity—indeed, its eternity! "[Q]uelque force enfin qu'ait [l']antiquité, la vérité doit toujours avoir l'avantage, quoique nouvellement découverte, puisqu'elle est toujours plus ancienne que toutes les opinions qu'on en a eues . . . ." "Fragment de préface pour un *Traité du vide*," OC, II 784–85.

[13] Martz, *Thomas More*, 19–22.

[14] Thomas More, *The Confutation of Tyndale's Answer*, in *Complete Works*, vol. 8, pt. 1, 48–49.

[15] Thomas More, *Responsio ad Lutherum*, in *Complete Works*, vol. 5, pt. I, 570 (II 18).

The ancient Fathers of the Church, having passed away so
long ago, were unable to hate you, Luther; no one would
have been able to suspect that someday some evil spirit
would void shit such as you upon the earth.

Pascal pointedly ignores this tradition of the theological polemic, a
genre he consciously renews in the *Provinciales*. But whoever would like
to see a specimen of what he could have reproached the Jesuits with in a
tone like More's need only read the passages of Sanchez that Voltaire, who
also scorned the casuists "que l'éloquent Pascal a trop épargnés" (that the
eloquent Pascal spared too much), did not hesitate to cite in a note to his
"Relation de la maladie, de la confession, de la mort et de l'apparition du
jésuite Berthier" (Account of the Illness, Confession, Death and Apparition
of the Jesuit Berthier).[16] To peruse them in the realization that Pascal was
aware of such things but declined to bring them forward (cf. IX 166) is to
realize that, even though he strikes the Jesuit adversary with a hard and
a high hand, he falls well short of the proverbial *odium theologicum*, a
bared hatred that bares all.

More than a few critics have echoed Sainte-Beuve's very just remark
that the rhetoric of the *Provinciales* displays all of the vigor of the great
speeches of Demosthenes. But Demosthenes does not hesitate to vituper-
ate his rival Aeschines, and his father, and to hurl the grossest of insults at
his mother. He picturesquely describes her as a whore who plied her trade
in a shed or outhouse (κλεισίον), and who was popularly known as
Ἔμπουσα (a shape-changing hobgoblin), thus implying both her hideous-
ness and the variety of her means of pleasing.[17] Pascal, however, says nothing against the mother of Escobar.

The *Provinciales* also renew the theological polemic by virtue of their
mélange of genres. The first ten Letters, in which we see the beginnings of
the journalistic interview, can be viewed as an epistolary novel that
recounts the author's conversion from indifference to what seemed a mere

[16] Voltaire, "Relation de la maladie, de la confession, de la mort et de l'apparition
du Jésuite Berthier," in *Mélanges* (Paris: Gallimard [Pléiade], 1961), 340. "Ce frère
Sanchez examine 'Utrum femina quae nondum seminavit, possit, virili membro
extracto, se tactibus ad seminandum provocare' ([*De Matrimonio*] Lib. IX, disp.
XVII, no. 8.) 'Semen ubi femina effudit, an teneatur alter effundere, sive inter
uxores, sive inter fornicantes? Utrum liceat intra vas praeposterum, aut in os fem-
inae, membrum intromittere, animo consummandi intra vas legitimum, etc.' (Lib. IX,
disp. XVII, depuis le no. 1, 2, 3, 4.). Ce même Sanchez pousse l'abomination
jusqu'à examiner sérieusement 'An virgo Maria semen emiserit in copulatione cum
Spiritu Sancto?' (Lib. II, disp. XXI, no. 11). Et il tient pour l'affirmative!" Ibid.
1396–7 n. 1.
[17] Demonsthenes, *De Corona*, 129–30.

quarrel among theologians to incandescent indignation against corruptions authorized by the Jesuits. Another novelty lies in the fact that these Letters are a mix of theological polemic and comedy.[18] As noted above, in theme (though hardly in idiom!) they are reminiscent of Aristophanes' *Clouds*. In their pages, we catch sight of the ludicrous extravagances hatched in the "Thinkery" of the new sophists, the Jesuits, like their ancient counterparts arch-corrupters of both religion and morals.

However, the "No" to novelty in religion which permeates the *Provinciales*[19] has drawbacks that are no less serious than obvious for the Augustinians in their struggle with the Jesuit innovators. In particular, this denial commits them to a grand strategy of dubious consistency. For in effect, they would correct the Church by the rule of conformity to the thought of Saint Augustine, himself an innovator in his day. It is as if, having once bestowed approval on his teaching, the Church were bound to it once and for all; as if his innovations were to be the last; and so, henceforth, as if he and not it should be the rule of Faith.

At bottom, then, it is as if the Augustinians would be more Catholic than the Church—to say nothing of more Augustinian than Saint Augustine. For, far from having the least pretension to be the rule and arbiter of Faith, the *kanon*, a second Messiah as it were, Augustine explicitly insists, as we saw above, that the foundation of the Christian faith is naught but the Church itself, its authority serving as the warrant even for Scripture—whence the fury of Luther and other Reformers, apparent victims of something like a magician's misdirection. (For, though seeking above all to anchor faith directly in God, *not* in Church or tradition, all the while they are implicitly *lending faith to the Church's endorsement and establishment of traditions* regarding the inspired status of Scripture, its canon, the divinity of Jesus, the Trinity, etc. Though at the devotional level the Church points to God as the fundamental object of our faith, on the epistemological level, as Augustine's words imply, it is the Church itself that is its object.) And, in a recently discovered sermon (1990), Augustine underscores the point that, with the exception of the Scriptural authors, a Christian can only write on matters of faith as an explorer, as one making progress and learning something new every day. He even

---

[18] One comic device, mockery, is defended by Pascal in Letter Eleven largely on biblical grounds. Perhaps one might defend comedy in a larger sense on scriptural grounds as well. For God even produces and directs a little comedy, one not without "sanctified bitterness," when He commands his prophet Hosea to marry a whore so as to symbolize his relationship to a Jewish nation that gives itself to other gods as well as to Him (Hosea 1:2–8).

[19] "Étrange théologie de nos jours!" (XI 191)—for example, the "rédemption toute nouvelle" of Fr. Bauny (IV 57).

declares that he would be angrier at a reader who would take his own writings as canonical ("canonicum") than at one who would criticize him wrongly.[20]

In other words, it is not only Luther, but the saint himself, who would have us ask "Who is Saint Augustine?" Nor, very arguably, has the Church itself failed to ask this—and answer it. Leszek Kolakowski and Philippe Sellier are perhaps only the most recent commentators to affirm, as did Port-Royal, Pierre Bayle and others, that in condemning Jansenius and his followers on grace the Church effectively condemned the teaching of Saint Augustine as well.[21]

In a word, it is the Church that canonized Augustine; it is not Augustine who will canonize the Church.

But if Augustine, who was in a position to see key elements of future Catholic belief take shape, not only before his very eyes, but in his very hands, had an intimation that a faith we might call Parmenidean, a unity eternally one and changeless, was impossible for fallen beings in a Heraclitean world where flux alone is eternal, and where the Christian sees but "through a glass and darkly," the same is not true of Pascal. For him, "je cherche le sûr" (I seek the certain, V 84) could well serve as a device. But, alas, flux is uncertain, and only the stable, the unchanging is sure. "Les fleuves de Babylone coulent, et tombent, et entraînent. O sainte Sion, où tout est stable, et où rien ne tombe!" (The rivers of Babylon flow, and fall, and carry away. O holy Sion, where all is stable and nothing falls!)[22]

Where the Faith is concerned, Pascal and his fellow Augustinians are decidedly of the Parmenidean persuasion. But this persuasion requires a heroic commitment to paradox; it must maintain that "change" is but an

---

[20] Cited in Peter Brown, *Augustine of Hippo*, rev. ed. (Berkeley and London: University of California Press, 2000), 451. This passage (from sermon 162C) is found in full in Edmund Hill, trans., *Sermons: Newly Discovered Sermons of Saint Augustine* (New York: New City Press, 1997), 176–77. Cf. Aquinas, *Summa Theologiae*, II–II, qu. 10 art. 12.

[21] See Kolakowski, *God Owes Us Nothing* 3–9; and Sellier, *Port-Royal et la littérature*, vol. 2, 19–20. The latter cites a decree of the Holy Office in 1690 which condemns the proposition that "as soon as one has found a doctrine clearly founded on Saint Augustine, one can hold it and teach it with out regard to any pontifical bull whatever." As Sellier says, "Cette dernière déclaration, capitale, affirmait enfin clairement, après plusieurs décennies de louvoiements peu estimables, que l'Église pouvait prendre ses distances à l'égard de certaines thèses augustiniennes." Ibid., 52.

[22] Fr.S 748; cf fr.S 460. "[L]a hantise de 'l'écoulement' obsède à ce point la vision pascalienne du monde que ces deux courts poèmes en prose, loin d'apparaître comme erratiques, isolés, dans les *Pensées*, nous livrent l'une des clés de leur lecture." Sellier, "'Sur les fleuves de Babylone': la fluidité du monde et la recherche de la permanence," in his *Port-Royal et la littérature*, vol. 1, 239.

appearance, an illusion that reason can dissipate. Thus, the Church's draw-back from long-accepted truth in Saint Augustine and his followers may be shown to be illusory by deploying the famous distinction between questions of right and questions of fact, *le droit et le fait. Of course*, one may say, the Church cannot err in the condemnation of a given doctrine. But it can indeed err in attributing a doctrine to a certain text or author, as in the famous condemnation of the Five Propositions the Church claimed to be found in Jansenius's *Augustinus*. Likewise, in an earlier day, the Church rightly condemned a position that it wrongly claimed to be present in a decree of Pope Honorius (XVII 346–47).

Unfortunately, this line of argument might be taken to augur well for others than Jansenius and Honorius. Such a use of *le droit* and *le fait*, a distinction in itself irreproachable, has the potential to eradicate the totality of heretics more efficiently than the stake—but by getting them off the hook, and so putting them beyond the reach of the stake, that *ultima ratio theologorum* (Nietzsche). An Arius would be able to affirm that he certainly approved of the condemnation of doctrines that the Church—always, alas! subject to error in questions of fact—imputed to him in a sense that was not quite his own.

Or, perhaps, if the Church should seem to depart from established truth, it may do so by mistake or inadvertence rather than by intention, and thus not really depart from truth after all. For in the eyes of the Jansenists—"selon l'usage où nous les verrons de toujours savoir les intentions des Papes mieux qu'eux-mêmes" (according to the habit we shall see of their always knowing the intentions of popes better than the popes themselves [Sainte-Beuve])[23]—it is an unhappy fact that "Le pape est très aisé à être surpris à cause de ses affaires et de la créance qu'il a aux jésuites" (The Pope is easily taken unawares on account of the press of his affairs and of the trust he has in the Jesuits), and "Toutes les fois que les jésuites surprendront le pape, on rendra toute la chrétienté parjure" (Every time the Jesuits take the pope unawares, all Christendom is made to commit perjury, fr.S 744).

"Toute la chrétienté"! For even though it be true, as Port-Royal affirmed,[24] that by right only an ecumenical council can speak definitively for the whole Church, in fact, as Pascal confesses in this passage, it is Rome that does so. If, for Port-Royal, the claim that "Rome has spoken, the case is closed" is very bad ecclesiology—for them, it curtails Christian liberty; indeed it is tyrannical—nonetheless, it correctly describes the Church *comme elle va*, so to speak. Adding insult to injury is the fact that this

---

[23] Sainte-Beuve, *Port-Royal,* vol. 2, 40.
[24] See Sellier, *"Port-Royal: littérature et théologie,"* 27–30.

expression derives from a sermon of Saint Augustine himself (131) referring to papal condemnation of Pelagian error. "Causa finita!"

"Parjure"! This word says it all. The Church, having promised the faithful that it speaks for God, and so truly, must—like God himself (fr.S 428)—stand fast in its word.

At the end of the day, given that the Church has continually proclaimed the Good News of a New Testament, and promulgated new decrees and anathemas of new councils, synods, popes, etc., there seems little likelihood of its saying nothing new henceforth—and this despite a tradition which is one of its most constant (if indeed it is not consubstantial with it), a rhetorical tradition that proclaims the Church ever unchanging, *semper eadem.*[25]

Whence, for example, Gladstone's merely apparent inconsistency in his public controversy with Cardinal Newman over the "Vatican Decrees." All the while advancing as one of his four principal theses that "Rome has substituted for the proud boast of *semper eadem*, a policy of violence and change in faith," Gladstone does not hesitate to censure the anathema of Pius IX against the opinion that "Romanus Pontifex potest ac debet cum progressu, cum liberalismo et cum recenti civilitate sese reconciliare et componere" (The Roman Pontiff can or ought to reconcile himself to and be in harmony with progress, liberalism, and modern civilization).[26]

The tradition of a rhetoric of immutability effectively prevents the Church from metamorphosing with the innovative fluidity of the Dunkers, one of whose founders, Michael Welfare, explained to Benjamin Franklin that they had no inalterable dogmas at all since their faith changed from day to day, according as the Lord afforded them more light. (It is a view that, if advanced as a *reductio ad absurdum*, would well encapsulate a Port-Royalist verdict on the whole notion of *aggiornamento*.) Thus, the

---

[25] *Semper eadem, sed semper eunda*. It would be superfluous to point out that at the time of the *Provinciales* the personal infallibility of the pope and the Assumption of the Virgin Mary were not yet *de fide*, though they have since been added to the deposit of the Faith. On the other hand, as noted in chapter 1, in Canada a small band of Jesuit missionaries was performing prodigies of heroism because *extra ecclesiam nulla salus*, an article of Faith as well founded in the Fathers of the Church and tradition as it is repugnant to the ecumenical spirit of the contemporary Church. As a sign of this repugnance, consider the fate of one of the principle's more vocal modern exponents, the Jesuit Leonard Feeney, condemned in the celebrated "Boston Heresy Case." (It is noteworthy that his excommunication [1953] was technically founded, not on his espousal of the principle, but on disobedience to superiors.)

[26] Alvin Ryan, ed., *Newman and Gladstone: The Vatican Decrees*, (Notre Dame: University of Notre Dame Press, 1962), 12, 18, 69.

Dunkers fashioned no creeds; nor did they even commit their beliefs to paper, for perhaps tomorrow the Lord would afford them yet more light.[27]

On the other hand, it is a tradition well suited to beguile the faithful into taking the faith of many years for the faith of all the years—in obscuring for them the fact that there was a Christianity before there was an orthodoxy at all, before Fathers and Doctors of the Church, before a fixed canon of Scripture, indeed, even, for a few decades, before the name "Christian" itself arose at Antioch. (And might there one day be a Christianity *after* these things, just as there once was *before? Ab esse ad posse?*) It is an unhappy thought that might lend a somewhat new sense to the very first words of the *Provinciales* in which the author proclaims, "Nous étions bien abusés" (We were very much deceived).

[27] Benjamin Franklin, *Autobiography* in *Writings*, (New York: Library of America, 1987) 1416–17.

# PART THREE

## GOD IN *CHIAROSCURO*: THE *PENSÉES*

# 5

## PROOF IN THE *PENSÉES*: REASON AS RHETORIC, RHETORIC AS REASON

ἀλλὰ τὸ φαινόμενον πάντη σθένει οὗπερ ἂν ἔλθῃ.

But the apparent is omnipotent wherever it goes.[1]

> Timon of Phlius, *Indalmoi* (*Appearances*),
> in Diogenes Laertius, "Life of Pyrrho," 105

Harum sententiarum [quae vera sit deus aliqui viderit; quae veri simillima magna quaestio.]

Which of these opinions [is true, some god will have seen; even which is most like the truth is a difficult question.][2]

> Fr.S 111 [Cicero, *Disp. Tusc.* 1.11]

When Pascal died in 1662, he left behind a large number of written fragments of various lengths, texts whose proper arrangement and interpretation have mightily exercised editors and commentators ever since. Presented by editors under the title *Pensées*, the great majority of them contain a variety of themes that, directly or indirectly, contribute to a projected reasoned defense of the Christian religion—an Apology, though the word itself does not appear. In these fragments, we find many arguments and (at least one non-argument) that are explicitly offered as proofs (*preuves*).

But what notion of what constitutes a proof could underlie the very various, and sometimes eccentric, individual proofs that we find in the *Pensées*?

There are, I think, reasons for posing this question aside from a pedantic urge to ask any question that can be asked.

[1] R. D. Hicks, trans., Diogenes Laertius, *Lives of Eminent Philosophers* (Cambridge, Mass. and London: Harvard University Press, 1925), vol. 2, 517 (Loeb Classical Library).
[2] "De ces opinions quelle est la vraie? Un dieu le verra." Montaigne, *Essais,* II 12.

First of all, there is the matter of trying to clarify the historical record. Pascal's explicit comments on proof in the *Lettre au P. Noël* and in *De l'esprit géométrique* have, I think, given rise to a common, though mistaken, view that for him, "il n'est de bonne preuve que géométrique" (the only good proof is a geometrical proof).[3]

Second, many of the *Pensées'* proofs for the Christian faith are far from fulfilling the conditions for proofs laid down in the works just mentioned. Is it then with or without a grain of salt that we should take these proofs for Christianity?

Third, from the standpoint of the history of ideas, an enquiry into Pascal's ideas on proof reveals profound affinities with his master Saint Augustine. It also, as we shall see, makes for a revealing contrast with epistemological elements in his great contemporary Descartes. The same is true with respect to Cardinal Newman, another apologist with whom Pascal is often compared.

Last, and perhaps most important, reflection on these topics provides a natural lead-in to an issue in philosophy that is too easy to neglect. For implicit in the *Pensées* is an account of what reason is, what we might call a "logology." The stock and trade of the philosopher is to judge of views by their reasonableness. Traditionally, this has meant to hale them before an objective, impartial tribunal competent to hear all cases and to pronounce definitively upon them. But what is reason itself? What is *its* warrant? Just what does its endorsement really mean?

A look at Pascal on proof suggests paradoxical but powerful answers to these questions. In particular, it suggests that, at bottom, reason is a kind of rhetoric, a power that persuades us; that at times it persuades us irresistibly, as in the case of self-evident first principles; that, when all is said and done, we find rational argument to be probative, not merely because it observes certain formal rules, but because the observance of these rules invincibly convinces us of the truth of what follows from them; and that we cannot but account to be proof those things that do in fact convince us.

In sum, we encounter the notion that, fundamentally, reason is a power that persuades, and that persuasive power is proof.

That "proof" is a term of the first importance in the *Pensées* is undeniable. For therein Pascal alternatively mentions, sketches, and elaborates a wide variety of "proofs" of Christianity and its God. Most, though not all of these, are taken from or based upon the Scriptures. And, although Pascal tells us that his arrangement of his material will be new (fr.S 575), most of the proofs he offers are of long standing. They include the miracles

---

[3] This phrase is from Jean Prigent's fine "Pascal: pyrrhonien, géomètre, chrétien," in *Pascal Présent* (Clermont-Ferrand: Éd. G. de Bussac, 1962), 66.

wrought by Moses and Christ; the fulfillment in the New Testament of the prophecies of the Old; figures—the foreshadowing of persons and events in the New Testament by persons and events in the Old; and perpetuity— from the time of Adam to the present, the Messiah has always been believed in.

But even a brief inspection of the kinds of things Pascal calls "proof" suffices to reveal a bewildering multiplicity, and to highlight the term's uncertain logical force. For example, "zèle" and "aveuglement" (zeal and blindness) are proofs of "Dieu" (fr.S 195); so is "Jésus Christ" (fr.S 221), while the latter is proved by "Pourquoi *le livre de Ruth*, conservé" (Why the *Book of Ruth* [was] preserved, fr.S 335). Religion is proved not only by "Morale./Doctrine./Miracles./Prophéties./Figures" (fr.S 21), but by "la direc- tion," "le silence" and "la retraite" (retreat, fr.S 751). The last three proofs, like the argument for God's existence from the orderliness of nature, and like some of the figures, are effectively proofs for those who already have faith, but not for others. Even "la machine," the body, furnishes us with proof (fr.S 41). Its proof is essentially bound up with custom, "coutume." In fact, says Pascal, custom provides us with "nos preuves les plus fortes et les plus crues" (our strongest and best-believed proofs, fr.S 661)—a curious remark for anyone to make, but very curious coming from a great mathe- matician and physicist.

Of course, in the *Pensées* we are dealing, not with a work, but with fragments that were never fully developed or synthesized by their author, let alone seen through the press. But even when allowance is made for the highly elliptical and perhaps often provisional character of such a text, it is still far from obvious what theory or conception of proof might underlie and unify such a diversity of probative agents, pronouncements, qualities, events, and reasons for events.

To aid in unravelling the tangled semantic skein of "proof," and to bring into relief a latent theory of proof, one needs to proceed from analysis to synthesis. So let us begin with isolable and salient features of the term— prominent semantic and logical contours, if you will. There are many of these, notwithstanding the fact that Pascal allowed himself a freedom in his use of terms that poses at least some problems for any interpretation.

What, then, is remarkable about the proofs in Pascal's *Pensées?*

## PROOF NEED NOT BE DEMONSTRATION, NOR EVEN ARGUMENT

First and foremost, "preuve" is not simply equivalent to "démonstration" as defined in *De l'esprit géométrique* (c. 1657). That they are not the same is evi- dent once we contrast what are "preuves" in the *Pensées* with what is explained as "démonstration" in the latter work.

In *De l'esprit géométrique*, Pascal distinguishes between two methods of demonstration. The requirements of the first, an ideal method that would surpass even geometrical demonstrations, "consiste[nt] . . . à tout définir et à tout prouver" (consist . . . of defining everything and of proving everything). That is, all terms must be defined by others, and all propositions, premises included, must be deduced from others whose truth 'is already known. Obviously, this would lead to an infinite regress of definitions and inferences. Hence, this method, although it would be "certainement . . . belle," is "absolument impossible" (OC, III 394, 395).

The second method of demonstration is that of geometry, and it is the veritable paradigm of right reason. "[La géométrie] seule sait les véritables règles du raisonnement, et, sans s'arrêter aux règles des syllogismes qui sont tellement naturelles qu'on ne peut les ignorer, s'arrête et se fonde sur la véritable méthode de conduire le raisonnement en toutes choses" (Geometry alone knows the true rules of reasoning; it does not stop at the rules for syllogisms, which are so natural that no one can fail to be aware of them. It does not stop before arriving at the true method of conducting our reasoning in all things, on which method it bases itself, 391). This order of demonstration neither defines nor proves everything, "mais il ne suppose que des choses claires et constantes par la lumière naturelle, et c'est pourquoi il est parfaitement véritable, la nature le soutenant au défaut du discours" (but it supposes only things that are clear and constant according to the natural light, and this is why it is perfectly truthful, nature supporting it rather than speech, 395).

What is described as the second method is also discussed in Pascal's *Lettre au très révérend Père Noël* (1657). There, essentially the same requirements are put forward as "une règle universelle, que j'applique [variant: qui s'applique] à tous les sujets particuliers, où il s'agit de reconnaître la vérité" (a universal rule which I apply [is applicable] to all individual subjects wherein truth is to be recognized, OC, II 519).

Hence, it might seem reasonable to say that, according to Pascal, we should understand the universal rule for arriving at truth, viz., geometrical demonstration, to be the standard of proof in all areas save in what transcends "les sujets particuliers," for example, the Mysteries of the Faith. Indeed, in describing the universal rule Pascal says:

> [C]'est qu'on ne doit jamais porter un jugement décisif de la négative ou de l'affirmative d'une proposition, que ce que l'on affirme ou nie n'ait une de ces deux conditions, savoir, ou qu'il paraisse si clairement et si distinctement de lui-même aux sens ou à la raison, suivant qu'il est sujet à l'un ou à l'autre, que l'esprit n'ait aucun moyen de douter de sa certitude, et c'est que nous appelons *principes* ou *axiomes* . . . ou qu'il se déduise par des conséquences infaillibles et nécéssaires de tels principes ou axiomes . . . . (Ibid.)

One should never make a definitive judgment regarding the
negative or affirmative of a proposition unless what one affirms
or denies meets one of these two conditions: to wit, either it
appears so clearly and distinctly of itself to the senses or the reason, according as it is subject to one or to the other . . . that the
mind has no means of doubting its certainty, and this is what
we call a *principle* or *axiom* . . . or it is necessarily and infallibly deducible from principles or axioms of such a kind . . . .

In short, if we were to overlook the mention of the senses,[4] we might well
be tempted to say that, in truth, for Pascal "Il n'est de bonne preuve que
géométrique," and so that a good proof must be an argument from self-
evident premises whose conclusions follow deductively. But against this
view stands the fact that the *Pensées* abounds in explicitly designated
"proofs" that violate each and all of these conditions.

First of all, Pascal admits as proofs arguments proceeding from premises that are not at all self-evident, premises whose truth can indeed be
doubted, though it may seem reasonable to us to grant them as true. These
are premises that not everyone of good understanding would be *forced* to
grant. That is to say, he admits as good proof arguments that Aristotle in the
*Topics* called dialectical (though both Aristotle's dialectical and demonstrative arguments—the latter have self-evident premises, the former's are only
commonly conceded—must be, not only what we would call deductive, but
syllogistic in their form).

Thus, for Pascal, does the orderliness of nature, "le ciel et les oiseaux"
(the sky and the birds), prove that there is a God? Yes and No. "Car encore
que cela est vrai en un sens pour quelques âmes à qui Dieu donna cette
lumière, néanmoins cela est faux à l'égard de la plupart" (For notwithstanding that this is true in a sense for some souls to whom God has given this
light, nonetheless it is false with respect to most people, fr.S 38; cf. 222, 644).

---

[4] "Clairement et distinctement" evokes Descartes. However, Pascal's willingness to
take as a principle or axiom what is clear and distinct, not only to reason, but also
to the senses, is of course not compatible with Descartes, for whom only *a priori*
truths could be validated by clearness and distinctness. Nor is it compatible with
geometrical demonstration. Though the latter yields conclusions that are *true of*
experience, it cannot of course be *based on* experience. If it were, its conclusions
would be, in principle, falsifiable by subsequent experience, and so they would be
less than certain.
    Jean Khalfa helpfully contrasts Pascal and Descartes on first principles in
"Pascal's Theory of Knowledge" in *The Cambridge Companion to Pascal*, ed. Nicholas
Hammond (Cambridge: Cambridge University Press, 2003) 129–36. However, I am not
sure that Descartes's celebrated "je pense donc je suis" is so much founded on experience, though of a self-validating kind ("performative"), as on an *a priori* "clear and
distinct" awareness of the implications of having an experience.

Though some figurative meanings of Scripture are "claires" and (in a loose sense?) "démonstratives" as proofs of Christian belief, others are a bit strained ("qui semblent un peu tirées par les cheveux"), and "ne prouvent qu'à ceux qui sont persuadés d'ailleurs" (only prove to those who are already persuaded on other grounds, fr.S 250; cf. 751). And so, "il faut ouvrir son esprit aux preuves" (one must open one's mind to the proofs, fr.S 655). Otherwise, for lack of faith, grace, or just insight, one may not assent to all of the needed premises, and so the inferences from them will not be received as proofs.

Second, for Pascal, an argument can be a proof even if one who granted all of its evidential claims would not be forced to grant its conclusion. That is, nondeductive (inductive) and hence nondemonstrative arguments can be proofs.

> Les preuves que Jésus-Christ et les apôtres tirent de l'Écriture ne sont pas démonstratives. Car ils disent seulement que Moïse a dit qu'un prophète viendrait, mais ils ne prouvent pas par là que ce soit celui-là: et c'était toute la question. (fr.S 425)

> The proofs that Jesus Christ and the apostles draw from Scripture are not demonstrative, for they say only that Moses said that a prophet would come; but they do not thereby prove that this particular one is he, and in that lay the whole question.

> Les prophéties, les miracles mêmes et les preuves de notre religion ne sont pas de telle nature qu'on puisse dire qu'ils sont absolument convaincants, mais ils le sont aussi de telle sorte qu'on ne peut dire que ce soit être sans raison que de les croire. Ainsi il y a de l'évidence et de l'obscurité pour éclairer les uns et obscurcir les autres. Mais l'évidence est telle qu'elle surpasse ou égale pour le moins l'évidence du contraire, de sorte que ce n'est pas la raison qui puisse déterminer à ne la pas suivre. Et ainsi ce ne peut être que la concupiscence et la malice du cœur. (fr.S 423)

> The prophecies, even the miracles and proofs of our religion are not of their nature such that one can say that they are absolutely convincing, but they are also of such a kind that one cannot say that to believe them is to be without reason. Thus there is evidence and obscurity so as to enlighten some and benight others. But the evidence is such that it surpasses or at least equals the evidence for the contrary. So it is not reason that determines us not to follow the evidence, and thus it can only be concupiscence and malice in the heart.

Here, it is manifest that even if the evidential claims of the proofs in question be granted, one is not forced to acquiesce in their conclusions. Why, in fr.S 425, is the prophecy of Moses insufficient? It is because even if we grant that his prophecy is true prophecy, this will not *conclusively* establish the identity of the one who is to come, which is the point at issue in the conclusion. Hence, this proof is what we would call inductive. This accords with fr.S 423. There the proofs are explicitly described as not "absolument convaincants," and so their premises can hardly be such as to guarantee the truth of their conclusions.[5]

Third, Pascal calls something "proof" that is not an argument at all, let alone a demonstrative one. This is *coutume*, custom or habit, a means by which the body, "la machine" or "l'automate," can instill belief in us. If "Lettre qui marque l'utilité des preuves. Par la machine" (Letter which marks the usefulness of proofs. By the machine, fr.S 41) refers to the utility of *proofs by the machine*—as is all but certain, given that elsewhere Pascal explicitly calls belief induced by the body "proof" (fr.S 661)—then one kind of "proof by the machine" would involve habitually acting *as if* a certain belief were true until such time as one did *in fact* believe it.

The most notable instance of this occurs as a sort of codicil to the wager. If the correct answer to the theism/atheism question is beyond human ability to know, and if the issue is thus best to be decided by the potential benefits of the beliefs, then we should wager that a god exists who will infinitely reward those who believe in him and do his will. To the possible objection that one might be forced by reason to grant this conclusion, but yet be unable genuinely to believe in this god, Pascal offers the following advice: Go regularly to mass, take holy water, etc. In other words, behave *as if* you did believe, and in time you *will in fact* believe. "Cela vous fera croire et vous abêtira" (This will make you believe and will stupefy you [i.e., stupefy the passions that make you balk at believing], fr.S 680).[6] The behavioral regimen here prescribed is not called "proof"—in fact, it is explicitly offered as an alternative to the "augmentation des preuves de

---

[5] Perhaps one might object that the proofs in question were indeed demonstrative, and hence deductive (conclusive), but that "concupiscence" and "malice du cœur" keep some people from assenting to all of the needed premises; that in the case of the prophecies, for example, these defects blind some to the fact that the carnal goods foretold of the Messiah are but figures for spiritual ones. But though Pascal surely agrees that blindness is wrought by concupiscence, in fr.S 423 he is making a different point. There he insists that the proofs of Christian religion are by *their* nature not absolutely convincing ("les preuves de notre religion ne sont pas de telle nature qu'on puisse dire qu'ils sont absolument convaincants"). Thus, it cannot be *our* nature that keeps us from seeing them as demonstrative, though perhaps it might still keep us from seeing them as better arguments than the ones opposed to them.

[6] On the Cartesian view of beasts (*bêtes*) as mere machines, automata, "vous abêtira" implies "will make you an automaton," or, since our bodies are automata, "reduce you to your automaton level."

Dieu"—but if, as surely seems called for, we take the latter phrase to refer
to the *traditional metaphysical arguments* for God's existence, then the regimen for the body not only functions as a proof, but may be properly called
a proof.

In fact, in a similar epistemological context—one in which the body is
not acting, but, by receiving impressions, being acted upon—habitual
experience (a.k.a. custom) is explicitly labeled proof by Pascal. The
repeated experience of past events makes an impression on us which we
take to be proof that these events, or similar ones, will recur. Indeed,
Pascal goes so far as to call the proofs wrought by custom the strongest
proofs.

> Car il ne faut pas se méconnaître: nous sommes automate
> autant qu'esprit. Et de là vient que l'instrument par lequel la
> persuasion se fait n'est pas la seule démonstration. Combien
> y a-t-il peu de choses démontrées! Les preuves [sc. démon-
> strations] ne convainquent que l'esprit; la coutume fait nos
> preuves les plus fortes et les plus crues: elle incline l'automate
> qui entraîne l'esprit sans qu'il y pense. Qui a demontré
> qu'il sera demain jour, et que nous mourrons? Et qu'y a-t-il de
> plus cru? C'est donc la coutume qui nous en persuade . . . .
> (fr.S 661)

> For we must not misunderstand ourselves: we are automaton
> as much as mind. Hence it follows that the instrument through
> which persuasion is accomplished is not demonstration alone.
> How few things there are that have been demonstrated! Proofs
> [sc. demonstrations] only convince the mind; custom brings
> about our strongest and best believed proofs. It inclines the
> automaton, which drags mind along after it without the latter's
> thinking. Who has demonstrated that it will be day tomorrow
> and that we will die, and what is there that is better believed?
> It is thus custom which persuades us of these things . . . .

In fine, for Pascal, proof can hardly be equivalent to demonstration since
he is willing to call "proofs" arguments that are neither deductive nor
proceeding from indubitable premises as well as a probative agent, custom,
that is not an argument at all, but that bypasses reason and persuades the
mind through the body.

Now, at this point, it might be tempting to object by drawing a distinction between two kinds of Pascalian proof. One would be *de facto* proof,
such as the proofs by custom. Though we may in fact take the effects of
custom for proof, it is merely "the instrument through which persuasion is
accomplished." The other kind would be *de iure* proof, namely rational argument. It not only persuades us, but it is something that we are *right* to be persuaded by. And so we would understand fr.S 661 to mean: "Proofs—proper

ones—convince only the mind, but custom brings about our strongest and best believed 'proofs'."

I fear, however, that this interpretation, though tempting, is mistaken, and that latent in Pascal's use of the term "preuve" is a psychological, subject-oriented conception of the same that, at its deepest level, abolishes the *de iure/de facto* distinction.

## PERSUASION: THE ESSENCE OF PROOF

Implicit in the *Pensées* is a conception of proof as essentially a mode of persuasion, and of persuasion as in effect proof. On such a view, logical force is at bottom a kind of psychological force. For, in the final analysis, it is because rational arguments are *convincing*, the weaker ones inducing our mere assent, and the stronger ones extorting from us the conviction of certainty, that we account them to be proofs at all. In a formula: reason is a kind of rhetoric. And so is non-argumentative proof, proof by custom or habit; its essence too is persuasion, the fixation of belief.

As a result, if we are to speak strictly, we should say that, for Pascal, all proofs are proofs by virtue of their power. All proofs are at bottom *de facto* proofs, for when all is said and done, we know only that we cannot but account what does, in fact, persuade us of something's truth to be a proof of that thing.

Or, as the Pyrrhonist poet Timon of Phlius says in this chapter's epigraph, "The apparent is omnipotent wherever it goes." We cannot but take the overwhelmingly apparent for the real, coercive verisimilitude for truth. Indeed, it is only when something yet *more* persuasive convinces us that what we *formerly* took to be proven was false that we are able to speak of what first convinced us as *mere* "appearance," as having *only* "verisimilitude." In other words, some things are not "absolumment convaincant de la dernière conviction" (convincing to the point of final conviction, fr.S 141). But that the apparent and verisimilar impose on us *while we are under their spell* is the merest tautology.

That the view "persuasion is the essence of proof" is implicit in Pascal is strongly suggested by his common use of "convaincantes" to qualify good proofs and of "pas convaincantes" for bad ones (e.g., in frs.S 141, 164, 694, and 423). The phrases are of course idiomatic, but alternatives were available. Note, by the way, the veiled reference to force: by convincing, good proofs *vanquish* us ("vaincre"). Force is also explicitly linked with the notion of reason as a kind of rhetoric in his pronouncement that "il y a deux manières de persuader les vérités de notre religion; l'une par la force de la raison . . . ." (there are two ways of persuading to the truths of our religion; one by the force of reason . . . , fr.S 660).

The interpenetration of persuasion and proof clearly emerges in his critique of the dogmatic philosophers' insistence that we all conceive of things in the same way. He says that we have no (conclusive) proof of this ("nous n'en avons aucune preuve") because the reason given by the dogmatists—that we use the same words on the same occasions—"n'est pas absolument convaincant de la dernière conviction" (is not convincing to the point of final conviction, fr.S 141).

And, perhaps most importantly, given Pascal's views on what we would call intuitive reason, and he "sentiments" of the heart, *sentiments du cœur*,[7] it is apparent that even the most rigorous geometrical demonstration must ultimately rest on persuasion. For it is the heart, for Pascal a cognitive as well as an affective faculty, that is irresistibly persuaded by the overwhelming evidence of the first principles, the axioms that underlie our reasoning, to pronounce them true. Thus, "Tout notre raisonnement se réduit à céder au sentiment" (All our reasoning reduces to yielding to sentiment, fr.S 455). The heart's role as a persuader is particularly stressed in passages describing faith, itself a *sentiment du cœur*. The faithful who judge by the heart are, we are told, "très efficacement persuadés" [note again the veiled reference to force], and "bien légitimement persuadés" (very effectively and very legitimately persuaded, frs.S 414, 142).

The view that, for Pascal, reason is at bottom a kind of rhetoric and a yielding to force also finds support in the following analysis by Jean Mesnard.

> Mettant en parallèle la "puissance" et la "connaissance" [in the *Lettre à Christine de Suède* of June 1652], dont la savante reine de Suède réalise en sa personne l'union merveilleuse, Pascal déclare que les détenteurs de l'une et de l'autre peuvent également "passer pour des souverains". Le "droit de commander" qu'exercent les rois est une image du "droit de persuader" que possèdent les "génies". D'où la phrase capitale: "Ce second empire me paraît même d'un ordre d'autant plus élevé que les esprits sont d'un ordre plus élevé que les corps". Si la connaissance s'identifie ainsi au pouvoir de persuader, c'est, entre autres raisons, parce que la science se reconnaît pour Pascal à ce qu'elle impose à tous les esprits. Mais le rapport explicitement établi entre science et rhétorique constitue peut-être l'intérêt majeur de cette importante variation sur le thème.[8]

---

[7] A *sentiment du cœur* has a cognitive element, and is by no means a mere emotion. Cf. its Latin root, *sentire*, which means "to think," and "to perceive" as well as "to feel."

[8] Mesnard, "Le thème des trois ordres dans l'organisation des *Pensées*," in his *La Culture au XVIIe siècle* (Paris: Presses Universitaires de France, 1992), 472. For the Letter in question see OC, II 923–26.

Putting in parallel "power" and "knowledge," which marvel-
lous union the learned Queen of Sweden embodies in her
own person, Pascal declares that the possessors of both can
alike "pass for sovereigns." The "right of command" exercised
by kings is an image of the "right of persuasion" possessed by
"geniuses." Whence the capital sentence: "This second empire
even seems to me to be of an order as much higher [than the
empire of kingly command] as minds are of an order higher
than matter." If knowledge is thus identified with the power
to persuade it is because, among other reasons, for Pascal
knowledge is recognized by the fact that it forces itself on all
minds. But the relationship explicitly established between
knowledge and rhetoric furnishes perhaps the principal interest of this important variation on the theme.

Not only does proof rest on persuasion, but persuasion itself is effectively
proof. Hence, there can be nonrational proofs. Custom is called a proof,
and can only be one, precisely in the sense of "l'instrument par lequel la
persuasion se fait" (fr.S 661).

And in addition to custom, there is faith, likewise a persuasive instrument.
All things considered, I agree with Hugh Davidson's view that it is correct to
include faith among the Pascalian proofs.[9] It is, at the very least, quite defensible to make this claim, notwithstanding its apparently conclusive denial in
Pascal's well-known remark that "La foi est différente que la preuve" (fr.S 41).

Clearly the two are different in that one, faith, belongs to what Pascal
calls the order of charity, and the other, proof, to the order of mind.[10]
Moreover, they differ in provenance. Faith (or *inspiration*) is a certainty in
conviction that is a grace from God. But (rational) proof comes not from
without, but from within us: we reason from first principles pronounced
true by the heart (fr.S 142), and "nous les sentons naturellement en nous"
(fr.S 164). Then, too, faith and (rational) proof differ in that the former proceeds by steps whereas the latter is immediate.

But the preceding contrasts are between faith and rational proof, not
proof in the extended sense which would accommodate custom. Faith, custom, and reason all have a fundamental sameness as carriers of conviction,
bestowers of certainty—as kinds of rhetoric—that will clearly qualify them
as proofs in that extended sense.

---

[9] Hugh Davidson, *The Origins of Certainty* (Chicago: University of Chicago Press,
1983). See 146 n. 12 for Davidson's diagram of types of proof in the *Pensées*. It
includes *inspiration*, (cf. 26) which is effectively equivalent to *foi*. My own schema
of types of Pascalian proof appears on p. 89. See too the section on "Problems,"
pp. 83–88.
[10] For a magisterial account of Pascal's three orders, see the article by Mesnard cited
above (n. 8), "Le thème des trois ordres . . ."

## PASCAL OR DESCARTES?

The persuasive power of the heart in Pascal has its counterpart in the persuasive power of the natural light in Descartes, who influenced Pascal profoundly on the epistemological status of first principles, and who, in the following passage, concedes that their ultimate justification lies in their persuasive force.

> [A]ussitôt que nous pensons concevoir quelque vérité, nous sommes naturellement portés à la croire. Et si cette croyance est si forte que nous ne puissions jamais avoir aucune raison de douter de ce que nous croyons de la sorte, il n'y a rien à rechercher davantage: nous avons touchant cela toute la certitude qui se peut raisonnablement souhaiter.
>
> Car que nous importe, si peut-être quelqu'un feint que cela même, de la vérité duquel nous sommes si fortement persuadés, paraît faux aux yeux de Dieu ou des anges, et que partant, absolument parlant, il est faux? Qu'avons nous à faire de nous mettre en peine de cette fausseté absolue, puisque nous ne la croyons point du tout, et que nous n'en avons pas même le moindre soupçon? Car nous supposons une croyance ou une persuasion si ferme, qu'elle ne puisse être ôtée; laquelle par conséquent est en tout la même chose qu'une très parfaite certitude.[11]

> [A]s soon as we think we are conceiving some truth, we are naturally transported to belief in it. And if this belief is so strong that we can never have any reason to doubt what we believe in this way, there is nothing more to search for: we have concerning it all the certainty that can reasonably be wished for.
>
> For what is it to us if, perhaps, someone feigns that the very thing the truth of which we are so strongly persuaded appears false in the eyes of God or of the angels, and that hence, absolutely speaking, it is false? Why should we trouble ourselves about this absolute falsity, since we do not believe in it at all, nor have we the least suspicion of it? For we are supposing a belief or a persuasion so firm that it cannot be removed, which is thus, in all respects, the same thing as a very perfect certainty.[12]

[11] Descartes, "Réponses de l'auteur aux secondes objections," in *Œuvres de Descartes*, 2nd ed., eds. Charles Adam and Paul Tannery (Paris: Vrin, 1964–1974), IX-1, 113–14. Spelling modernized.

[12] Cf. "Au reste, de quelque preuve et argument que je me serve, il en faut toujours revenir là, qu'il n'y a que les choses que je conçois clairement et distinctement, qui aient la force de me persuader entièrement." Descartes, *Méditations* V in *Œuvres de Descartes*, IX-1, 54.

In this passage, certainty with respect to truth is clearly the result of force of persuasion. It is not a formal logical property, nor a consequence of such properties, but rather an effect on the mind of something apprehended by it. Or, more precisely, so far as we are concerned, certainty is an effect on the universal audience of human minds—of which one blithely considers oneself both an ideal and a typical representative.[13]

But Descartes is overbold, I think, in calling these certainties persuasions that can never be removed. Strictly speaking, we can know only that *at present* they appear to us to be indubitable, that is, that we cannot imagine how their persuasion could ever fail. But we have no guarantee that a certainty that seems irreversible to us at the moment is irreversible for us absolutely, that is, in principle and hence for all time.

In fact, given his uncompromising desire to avoid error at all costs, it is arguable that Descartes should hope that our certainties are *not* irreversible. For he admits that, in principle, our most overwhelming certainties *could be* mistaken; they could be false in the eyes of God, and hence false absolutely speaking. But then—to the effulgent glory of skepticism, the very position that Descartes is trying to overthrow—our irresistible belief in these absolute falsities would be incorrigible!

Thus, it is not surprising that Pascal should desire a certainty that is more than irresistible persuasion, one that would transcend conviction and

---

The same emphasis on persuasion and force as the ultimate warrants of our reasoning occurs in Nicole and Arnauld's *Port-Royal Logic* (1662), which draws very heavily from Pascal and Descartes. "Car ce que les Académiciens disoient, qu'il estoit impossible de trouver la vérité, si on n'en avoit des marques, comme on ne pourroit reconnoître un esclave fugitif qu'on chercheroit, si on n'avoit des signes pour le distinguer des autres au cas qu'on le rencontrast, n'est qu'une vaine subtilité. Comme il ne faut point d'autres marques pout distinguer la lumière des ténèbres que la lumière mesme qui se fait assés sentir; ainsi il n'en faut point d'autres pour reconnoître la vérité que la clarté mesme qui l'environne, et qui se soumet l'esprit et le persuade malgré qu'il en ait; et toutes les raisons des Philosophes ne sont pas plus capables d'empêcher l'âme de se rendre à la vérité, lors qu'elle en est fortement pénétrée, qu'elles sont capables d'empêcher les yeux de voir, lors qu'estants ouverst ils sont frappés par la lumière du Soleil." Antoine Arnauld and Pierre Nicole, *L'Art de penser: la logique de Port-Royal* (Stuttgart-Bad Canstatt, 1965), 12–13.

Nicole and Arnauld's insistence that no criterion of truth is necessary because the natural light is its own warrant is remarkable given their earlier insistence that the ability to discern the true from the false (*le bon sens*) is far from universal. Many suffer from "fausseté d'esprit"—in fact, there is an infinity of these "esprits grossiers et stupides" (8–9). Some modernization of spelling.

[13] For this and other reservations by rhetorical theorists about the "maximally efficacious rhetoric" of "compelling truth" and the "constraining force of reason," see Chaïm Perelman and Lucie Olbrechts-Tyteca, *The New Rhetoric: A Treatise on Argumentation*, trans. John Wilkinson and Purcell Weaver (Notre Dame: University of Notre Dame Press, 1969), 32–34.

guarantee *truth,* revelation of the real. The "démon méchant" and "Dieu bon" of the following passage show that he has Descartes very much in mind.

> Les principales forces des pyrrhoniens, je laisse les moindres, sont que nous n'avons aucune certitude de la vérité de ces principes—hors la foi et la revelation—sinon en [ce] que nous les sentons naturellement en nous. Or ce sentiment naturel n'est pas une preuve convaincante de leur vérité, puisque, n'y ayant point de certitude hors la foi si l'homme est créé par un Dieu bon, par un démon méchant ou à l'aventure, il est en doute si ces principes nous sont donnés ou véritables, ou faux, ou incertains, selon notre origine . . . . (fr.S 164)[14]

> The principal strengths of the Pyrrhonists (I pass over the lesser ones) lie in the fact that we have no certainty of the truth of these principles—outside of faith and revelation—save that in ourselves we naturally feel them [to be true]. But this natural feeling [*sentiment*] is not a convincing proof of their truth since, having no certainty outside of the Faith as to whether man has been created by a good God, a wicked demon, or by chance, it is doubtful, depending on our origin, whether these principles given to us are true, false, or uncertain . . . .

Like the skeptics, with whom he has a kind of spiritual consanguinity, Pascal cannot be content to call truth anything less than what is proof against *all* objection. He burns to know, not what we must in fact feel certain about, but what must absolutely be the case. "Nous brûlons du désir de trouver une assiete ferme" (We burn with the desire to find a firm seat, fr.S 230).[15] But no such firm seat can be found "hors la foi," outside an initial act of faith in (as opposed to a Cartesian proof of) a God who would

---

[14] Davidson seems to me to conflate conviction and truth for Pascal when he says "Any search for certainty is a search for a quality of a statement or a state of mind. Whether statement or attitude, it cannot be doubted, its validity is obvious, *its connection with reality is assured.*" Davidson, *The Origins of Certainty,* 101 (emphasis added).

[15] Although, on the face of it, this is an equestrian metaphor, it should be read in conjunction with frs.S 460 and 748 describing *les fleuves de Babylone.* "Malheureuse la terre de malédiction que ces trois fleuves de feu embrasent plutôt qu'ils n'arrosent! Heureux ceux qui, étant sur ces fleuves, non pas plongés, non pas entraînés, mais immobilement affermis sur ces fleuves, non pas debout, mais assis, dans une assiette basse et sûre, dont ils ne se relevent pas avant la lumière, mais après s'y être reposés en paix, tendent la main à celui qui les doit élever pour les faire tenir debout et fermes dans les porches de la sainte Jérusalem, où l'orgueil ne pourra plus les combattre et les abbattre!" (460). For an acute analysis of these fragments, whose theme is absolutely fundamental for Pascal, see Sellier, " 'Sur les fleuves de Babylone.' "

guarantee the veracity of our cognitive nature; a God who would ensure that only truth persuades us irresistibly.

But, unhappily, we have no infallibly manifest criterion of truth. Indeed, "trop de vérité nous étonne" (too much truth dumbfounds us), and thus "Les premiers principes ont trop d'évidence pour nous" (The first principles are too evident for us, fr.S 230). Moreover, imagination, "Cette superbe puissance ennemie de la raison, qui se plaît à la contrôler et à la dominer" (This proud power, enemy of reason, which is pleased to control and dominate it), bamboozles reason by making the true and the false look the same ("marquant du même caractère le vrai et le faux," fr.S 78). In short, "*l'homme est si heureusement fabriqué qu'il n'a aucun principe juste du vrai*" (Man is so happily constructed that he has no exact principle of truth; ibid).

But even so, Pascal would not have the readers of his Apology simply humble reason so as to make way for faith—this despite the fact that, if we speak but according to our natural lights, "le pyrrhonisme est le vrai" (Pyrrhonism is the truth, fr.S 570). Rather, he would have us choose between a view of the world on which, after an initial act of faith in God, absolute certainty in first principles can be ours—a view on which one of the deepest longings of our nature, the longing to know, can be *fully* satisfied—and a view that offers that longing no hope, a view on which only unshakable conviction, Cartesian certainty, can be ours. And where—despite Descartes's assurances that we can desire nothing more—we are left wondering if we possess mere coercive verisimilitude, truth's imposing counterfeit, or truth itself.

## PROBLEMS?

| | |
|---|---|
| *Christian.* | The wise man says, He that trusts his own heart is a fool. |
| *Ignorance.* | That is spoken of an evil heart, but mine is a good one. |
| *Christian.* | But how dost thou prove that? |
| *Ignorance.* | It comforts me in the hopes of Heaven. |
| *Christian.* | That may be through its deceitfulness, for a man's heart may minister comfort to him in the hopes of that thing for which he yet has no ground to hope. |
| *Ignorance.* | But my heart and life agree together, and therefore my hope is well grounded. |
| *Christian.* | Who told thee that thy heart and life agrees together? |
| *Ignorance.* | My heart tells me so. |

Bunyan, *The Pilgrim's Progress*

There are at least some *prima facie* problems with the interpretation, which indeed at first hearing must sound a bit extravagant, that implicit in the *Pensées* are the views that *au fond* proof is persuasion and persuasion proof. I should like briefly to consider three of them. The first is exegetical. Is Pascal really to be understood in this way? The last two are logical. Are the views themselves proof against some fairly obvious objections?

1. Are there not many passages in Pascal quite incompatible with what has been said so far? After all, Pascal would surely admit that we are, in fact, persuaded to believe by such *puissances trompeuses* (deceitful powers) as superstition, imagination, and *fantaisie*. But of course he does not consider these to be proofs.[16] And does he not, in the beginning of *De l'art de persuader* (the second part of *De l'esprit géometrique*), distinguish sharply between what does persuade us and what ought to, between proof *de iure* and *de facto*? With regard to natural truths "on ne devrait jamais consentir qu'aux vérités démontrées," he says, though "tout ce qu'il y a d'hommes sont presque toujours emportés à croire non pas par la preuve, mais par l'agrément. Cette voie est basse, indigne . . ." (One should consent only to demonstrated truths [though] All of mankind is nearly always carried away to believe, not by proof, but by what is agreeable. This way is low, unworthy . . ., OC, III 413).

There we have it. Only demonstration *should* convince us; it alone is *proper* proof. To believe by *l'agrément*—the essence of persuasion, when you come down to it—is "basse et indigne."

The contentions of this chapter would thus seem to be quite confounded, or at best reduced to the status of one strain among many in a not entirely harmonious epistemological chorus. But is either of these the case? I do not think so.

Certainly, we are capable of being persuaded—and deceived—by *les puissances trompeuses*, powers that impose on our susceptibilities to error. And, needless to say, we cannot help but be persuaded by *imagination*, *fantaisie*, etc., *while we are under their spell*. However, once rational argument has persuaded us to different belief, we reject the testimony of what we *only now* come to call *les puissances trompeuses*. We come to reject their testimony because we have found rational argument to be *in fact more convincing*. Were it not, it could never have dispelled prior conviction.

In short, one can consistently maintain that, for Pascal, all proof is in essence proof by power and *de facto* proof, but that inasmuch as reason,

---

[16] See Martin Warner, *Philosophical Finesse: Studies in the Art of Rational Persuasion* (Oxford: Oxford University Press, 1995), 165 ff., for the role of finesse in distinguishing between *fantaisie* and the good epistemological coin of *sentiment*.

when we can bring it to bear, persuades us more powerfully than the "proofs" wrought by *les puissances trompeuses*, we should rely on reason's testimony whenever there is a chance of soliciting it. If we are too ignorant or slothful to solicit it, if we are content to be persuaded by mere *l'agré-ment*—that is, by the will, the seat of *les puissances trompeuses*—then we have settled for proof that is not "convincing to the point of final conviction," proof that is weaker and liable to be overturned by a stronger. And this is wholly unacceptable, "basse, indigne," if, like the author of the *Provinciales*, "Je ne me contente pas du probable . . . je cherche le sûr" (I am not content with the probable . . . I seek the sure, V 84).

Of course, it is only with respect to naturally discernible truths that it is "basse" and "indigne" to believe by "l'agrément." Since "vérités divines" (divine truths) surpass reason (frs.S 656, 182), it is quite proper to admit them through the other of the "deux entrées par où les opinions sont reçues dans l'âme" (two entrances through which opinions are received in the soul, OC, III 413). That is, through the very seat of *l'agrément*, the will, which in the case of "vérités divines" acts through the heart. "Je sais que [Dieu] a voulu qu'elles entrent du cœur dans l'esprit, et non pas de l'esprit dans le cœur, pour humilier cette superbe puissance du raisonnement, qui prétend devoir être juge des choses que la volonté choisit . . . ." (I know that God has willed that they [divine truths] enter from the heart to the mind, and not from the mind to the heart, so as to humble this proud power of reasoning, which claims it ought to be the judge of the things the will chooses; ibid.).

And so, in sum, I think that we can interpret Pascal consistently. For him, persuasion and proof are fundamentally equivalent, and so all proof is really *de facto* proof, proof by power. But there is a hierarchy of types of proof since some are in fact more persuasive than others—indeed, reason exercises a kind of right of the strongest—and not all are competent in every domain.

2. When Pascal says that we cannot be assured of the truth of the heart's testimony on first principles without faith in "un Dieu bon" as its guarantor, is he not arguing in a circle? For, according to Pascal, faith itself is a revelation by the heart, a *sentiment du cœur*. "[V]oilà ce que c'est que la foi. Dieu sensible au cœur." (This is what faith is: the heart sensing God, fr.S 680). Thus, are we not being told that we can only know *les sentiments du cœur* to be true by taking one such *sentiment*, faith, to be a true one? In short, that we may trust the heart because we may trust the heart?

Is there then a "Pascalian Circle" analoguous to the one so often imputed to Descartes, who is taxed with vindicating God's veracity by our clear and distinct ideas and those same ideas by God's veracity?

I would reply, with Jean LaPorte,[17] that only if faith is a very special *sentiment du cœur* can the imputation of circularity be evaded.

So long as there exists a barrier between subject and object, between the knower and the known, faith itself would require yet a further guarantee. For, though the heart may be utterly and irresistibly convinced of God, how can we know that *this* conviction is correct, that "Rien ne donne l'assurance, que la vérité" (Nothing bestows assurance but truth, fr.S 496)? We cannot. But if faith, as an *inspiration* from God, were an encounter so intimate and immediate as to subvert the distinction between subject and object in a unique knowing experience, then no guarantee of harmony between the faculties of the knower and the being of the known would be needed. What need of harmony between subject and object if the barrier between them has been breached? If this barrier can be surmounted in the Beatific Vision, or perhaps in a *nuit de feu* bringing "certitude, certitude," why not also in the experience of faith itself? Although faith is a *sentiment du cœur*, is it *merely* that? As a kind of epistemological grace, its properties, like its status, might arguably be unique.

Indeed, the possibility of the falling of the barriers between man the subject and God the object is suggested not only by the language of mystics evoking the confounding of creature and creator in an *unitas mystica*, but by the nature of love itself. Its essence is to dissolve the barriers between subject and object, between lover and beloved, and it may be that Divine Love can and will annihilate them utterly. For that matter, unless God were able to surmount the barriers between subject and object, his certainty too would be a matter of mere conviction.

Of course, even should the preceding conjectures be on the mark—and they are many and bold—other limitations would remain inherent in the use of God as guarantor for the rectitude of *sentiment*. Even if faith should be a noncircular path to unconditional certainty, if we take it we can do so only at Another's instance and direction; and it is a path no man can make the eyes of another behold.

In fine, for Pascal, God functions very like his familiar analogue the sun (the Good) in Plato's Allegory of the Cave. God, like the sun, illumines Being and thus makes it knowable. And, as the poet says, who shall say that the sun lies—"solem quis dicere falsum audeat?"[18] But unless, and Plato does not tell us how, we can quit the cave and gaze *directly* on the sun's light, we will never know Being, only such of its shadows as may fall across our view. And without the sun, as without God, Being is dark.

---

[17] Jean Laporte, *Le Cœur et la raison selon Pascal* (Paris: Éditions Elzevir, 1957) 135–41.

[18] Virgil, *Georgics*, 1.463–64.

3. If we escape the circle, will we avoid the pendulum?

It is hopeless, one might object, to consider the *Christian* God as a guarantor of certainty, since belief in him is inextricably bound up with belief in Original Sin. Does not this doctrine of the profound corruption of our nature give us scant reason to trust *les sentiments du cœur*? Is it not, on the contrary, grounds for the profoundest skepticism, since it implies the corruption of our cognitive nature and powers?

One could well imagine an unbeliever, having been converted by Pascal's argumentation in the *Pensées*, who, on becoming a Christian, and hence affirming for the first time the doctrine of Original Sin, was immediately impelled to skepticism by the thought that this doctrine entailed the profound corruption of mankind's cognitive nature. It would then become logical for him to repudiate Christian belief inasmuch as he had come to embrace it through the guidance of that faulty nature. But, when he ceased to be a Christian, he ceased to be committed to the doctrine of Original Sin, so now he may confidently follow the dictates of his rational nature again. This means, of course, that he should now re-allow the cogency of Pascal's argumentation and become a Christian again, thus reaffirming Original Sin, renewing his distrust of his rational nature, repudiating Christianity again, etc. One might dub this to and fro "Pascal's Pendulum." [19]

It is an objection that is not without force, for Pascal did indeed believe that the Fall had impaired our cognitive nature. Hence "Ce n'est point ici le pays de la vérité" (This is not the land of truth, fr.S 425).

> Il y a sans doute des lois naturelles, mais cette belle raison corrompue a tout corrompu. (fr.S 94)

> There are undoubtedly natural laws [sc. in morals], but this fine, corrupt reason of ours has corrupted everything.

> Les casuistes soumettent la décision à la raison corrompue et le choix des décisions à la volonte corrompue, afin que tout ce qu'il y a de corrompu dans la nature de l'homme eût part à sa conduite. (fr.S 498)

> The casuists submit the decision to our corrupt reason and the choice of decisions to our corrupt will, so that all that is corrupt in the nature of man plays a part in his conduct.

Still, the belief that reason is a mischancy tool does not necessarily force one into a disavowal of reasoning, or into a Pyrrhonist suspension of

---

[19] Cf. "*Et ainsi, après bien des changements de jugement . . . j'ai connu que notre nature n'était qu'un continuel changement, et je n'ai plus change depuis. Et si je changeais, je confirmerais mon opinion. Le pyrrhonien Arcésilas qui redevient dogmatique*" (fr.S 453).

judgment. We may always believe as we list and at our own risk, trusting in such light as we have for want of a better. Or it might be, as Augustine reports, that one may come to a certainty about God than which there *could be* no better; one that, though it is indeed a psychological state, and hence a kind of proof *de facto*, is, like the Cartesian *cogito* that it fore-shadows, so overwhelmingly persuasively that doubt, even about what would be true from a God's-eye view, would be *in fact be annihilated.*

> intravi [in intima mea] et vidi qualicumque oculo animae meae supra eundem oculum animae meae, supra mentem meam lucem inconmutabilem [. . . .] nec ita erat supra mentem meam, sicut oleum super aquam nec sicut caelum super terram, sed superior, quia ipsa fecit me, et ego inferior, quia factus ab ea. qui novit veritatem, novit eam, et qui novit eam, novit aeternitatem. [. . . .] et clamasti de longinquo: ego sum qui sum. et audivi, sicut auditur in corde, et non erat prorsus, unde dubitarem, faciliusque dubitarem vivere me quam non esse veritatem . . . . (*Confessions* 7.10)

> I entered [into my deepest self] and by my soul's eye, of what-ever kind it was, I saw above that same eye of my soul, above my mind, an unchangeable Light . . . . Nor was It above my mind, as oil is above water or sky above earth. It was above me, because Its very self made me, and I was below It, because I was made by It. Who knows Truth knows It, and who knows It knows Eternity. [. . . .] And from afar you cried out, "I am who am." And I heard as one hears in the heart; and there was utterly nothing of which I might doubt. And it would have been easier to doubt that I am alive than to be in doubt whether Truth might not be . . . .

Is this a case of making a virtue out of the necessity of a belief? Or, as he who lived it would have it, is it necessity of belief bestowed by Virtue on our nature? Is it a mere assertion, possibly a mistaken one? We saw that Descartes asserts as much of our certainties while yet admitting that, absolutely speaking, they might be false. Or is it simply a report of utter epistemological fact?

## IN CONCLUSION

Guided by Pascal's mention of "preuves du dehors" (proofs from without) in fr.S 360, we might furnish the complementry rubric "preuves du dedans" (proofs from within) and so construct a schema of the types of Pascalian proof. Both of these terms have reference to the soul. Within it lie the fac-ulties of reasoning and of intuitive reason (*cœur*). Custom, since it is rooted in the body, derives from outside the soul.

In the diagram below, deduction and induction are, respectively, used in their modern senses. They are effectively present in Pascal, though not under their modern names. Deductions are thus arguments whose premises would, if true, constitute conclusive grounds for their conclusions, while an induction's premises, even if true, would yet be only inconclusive grounds for the same.

The two types of deduction in Pascal are represented below by the Aristotelian terms "demonstrative" and "dialectical" argument. Aristotle's classic distinction is between deductions from premises whose truth is known *per se*, and deductions from premises whose truth is merely a matter of common acceptance. But neither in Pascal—consider geometrical proofs—nor in the diagram are such arguments restricted, as they are in Aristotle, to arguments with syllogistic form.

| PROOF | Proof from within | reasoning | deduction | demonstrative argument |
|---|---|---|---|---|
| | | | | dialectical argument |
| | | | induction | non-conclusive argument |
| | | the heart | faith/ inspiration | Of God and from God, "un sentiment intérieur et IMMÉDIAT" (frS. 360, 680) |
| | | | intuition | Of first principles (fr.S 142) |
| | Proof from without | custom | habitual behavior | Turns custom into nature for us; diminishes passions that are obstacles to belief (frS. 680) |
| | | | our regular experience of nature | Is only custom though we take it for proof (frS. 661) |

Upon reflection, the view we have sketched of the interpenetration of reason and rhetoric, of persuasion and proof, should not seem very odd. Indeed, Furetière's *Dictionnaire universel* (1690) defines "preuve" as a means of persuasion ("Moyen dont on se sert pour persuader"). Nor is this very strange, given that among the meanings of the Latin *probo*, the ancestor of "preuve" and "proof," are many that imply persuasion—not only "to demonstrate," but "to win approval for," "to cause to be favorably regarded by" and (with *pro*) "to get accepted as."[20] The all-but-inescapable nexus of

---

[20] *Oxford Latin Dictionary*, s.v. "probo," 6a, b; 7c.

the ideas "proof, persuasion, and force" is likewise part of the overwhelm-ingly influential Aristotelian heritage. For example, Aristotle calls persua-sion (*pistis,* later the "faith" of the New Testament) a kind of demonstration (*apodeixis*), and demonstration a kind of persuasion (*Rhetoric* 1355a5). In fact, he continues, a particular kind of demonstration, the enthymeme—a somewhat informal syllogism, typically having one of its propositions unex-pressed—is reputed to be the most potent persuasion.[21]

None of these conceptual links should really surprise us, for it is clear that they are not the result of mere historical quirk or happenstance. We are all taught that to be a good reasoner is to insist upon the observance of certain logical rules, to have a certain formal structure in our argumen-tation. But why would we account the observance of these rules to consti-tute proof unless there were something about their observance, about the structure of the argument's formalism, that carried conviction with us? Is not the propriety of logical rules itself ultimately dependent upon self-evidence, or, in Pascal's terms, the heart, just as is the propriety of first principles? And when it comes to taking what does in fact persuade us to be a proof—and remember here the "track record" of the persuasive agent is important: have the convictions it brings often been overturned in the past?—how *could* we think or feel otherwise?

But what follows from all of this, aside from the obvious conclusion that we should refrain from saying that, for Pascal "The only good proofs are geometrical ones"?

## 1. A Twilight of Distinctions

Of course, twilight is not night, and in particular it is not a Hegelian "night in which all cows are black" wherein nothing can be distinguished from any-thing else. The fact remains, however, that persuasive power should be seen

---

[21] "Persuasion (*pistis*) is a kind of demonstration, for we are most persuaded when we think something to have been demonstrated; the demonstration of the rhetor is the enthymeme, and this is said to be the most powerful means of persuasion (*kuri-otaton ton pisteon*)." By extension from "persuasion," *pistis* can also signify "means of persuasion," and hence the roughly equivalent, quasi-technical sense of (proba-ble) proof or argument. The three senses are intertwined in the passage just cited.

That Aristotle's conception of argument is strongly connected to the reasoner is evident from the first page of the *Topics.* Demonstrative arguments' first princi-ples are propositions known *per se*: we cannot but assent to them as soon as their terms are understood. They bring about *pistis.* Dialectical arguments proceed from *endoxa.* That is, they are grounded in received opinion, or, more precisely, in prin-ciples accepted by all, by the majority, or by the most notable of a given group. From the fact that *endoxa* are called *ta dokounta* (things that appear to be so), it is clear that they gain currency by the persuasive force of their verisimilitude.

as a common essence underlying things commonly taken to be different in kind. Thus, rational argument, rhetoric, habit, mystical experience, and faith are at the deepest level alike: persuasive agents, fixators of belief. But, though Pascal seems to have been aware of this implication, clearly it was not always at the forefront of his mind, or perhaps not always central to the points he most wished to make. Otherwise, he would not have sometimes distinguished so sharply between intuitive reason (*le cœur*) and discursive reason (*le raisonnement*) as things of different orders. For though, like faith and proof, they do proceed "par différentes voies" (by different ways, fr.S 142), at bottom both are means or agents of persuasion.

## 2. PASCAL AND THE PROBLEM OF INDUCTION

From a philosophical perspective, the conflation of *de facto* and *de iure* proof has the consequence that it is defensible for us to hold as certain a conclusion for which the logical evidence is inconclusive if, in point of psychological fact, we cannot do otherwise.

Thus, on a view like Pascal's, the Humean problem of induction, which indeed he anticipates,[22] simply dissolves, much as it does in the title essay of Karl Popper's *Conjectures and Refutations*.

It is certain, says Pascal, though not demonstrated, that we will all die. But how can this conclusion be justified, let alone certain, founded only as it must be upon the evidence that hitherto *some* men have died—evidence that does not strictly justify a conclusion about *all* men, past, present, and future? An exponent of the view latent in Pascal that *de facto* and *de iure* proof are the same need only say what Luther said before the Diet of Worms: "Ich kann nicht anders." Or, much more fully: "In point of fact,

---

[22] "Quand nous voyons un effet arriver toujours de même, nous en concluons une nécessité naturelle, comme il sera demain jour, etc. Mais souvent la nature nous dément et ne s'assujetit pas à ses propres règles" (fr.S 544). This is clearly a special case of what was later termed the "problem of induction." In this passage, our past experience (the "coutume" of fr.S 661) of the conjunction of a "cause" and "effect" is shown to be inadequate grounds for the conclusion that in *all* of our experience we will find the two conjoined. This clearly shows a) that Pascal knew of the problem of induction itself, though not of course by name, and b) that, contrary to the view advanced by LaPorte, Pascal does not find scientific proof, or at least the part of it relying on induction, to be "sans replique." LaPorte, *Le Cœur et la raison selon Pascal*, 17.

On the other hand, though Pascal realized that the conclusions of what we call inductive arguments might turn out to be false, he clearly implies that we are justified in affirming them. The very conclusion instanced in fr.S 544 (that it will be daylight tomorrow) is, in fr.S 661, presented as vindicated by *coutume*, which is responsible for "nos preuves les plus fortes."

despite the admittedly partial evidence I have, given the power of customary experience over our ideas,[23] in truth 'I cannot do otherwise' than believe
that 'all men are mortal.' Though the logical support for this claim may not
be conclusive, the conviction of its certainty has been extorted in me. The
warrant of *induction* is *inducement*, not deduction." As in Popper, who
notes that even a single instance often impels us to generalize, the onus
then is on future experience to give the lie to our conclusion if it should
be mistaken.

That something like this is Pascal's view is suggested by the fact that
he does not see the "problem of induction" as much of a problem. In particular, he does not question the legitimacy of custom as a carrier of conviction. Of course, it helps if one's epistemology is fortified by faith in a
God who will guarantee, even though it is within strict limits, that "Rien
ne donne l'assurance, que la vérité" (Nothing bestows assurance but truth,
fr.S 496). "Gott helf mir, amen!" indeed!

And yet, perhaps fittingly, Pascal's stance on inconclusive evidence is
a topic on which the evidence is not quite conclusive. We saw above (in
fr.S 661) that, for him, it is not problematic for us to be certain about some
things, for instance, that we shall die, for which the logical evidence is
strictly speaking inconclusive. But in the earlier *Préface sur le traité du
vide* (1651) he states that, as a matter of logic, one cannot—and, more
importantly, we ought not—draw conclusions that go beyond their evidence. We may draw ones that seem to, but only if a tacit reservation is
understood.

> Car dans toutes les matières dont la preuve consiste en
> expériences et non en démonstrations, on ne peut faire
> aucune assertion universelle que par la générale énumeration
> de toutes les parties ou de tous les cas différents. C'est ainsi
> que, quand nous disons que le diamant est le plus dur de
> tous les corps, nous entendons de tous les corps que nous
> connaissons, et nous ne pouvons ni ne devons y comprendre
> ceux que nous ne connaissons point . . . . (OC II 784)

> In all matters wherein proof consists in experiments and not
> in demonstrations, we can make no universal assertion save
> on the basis of a complete enumeration of all the parts or of
> all the different cases. And so, when we say that the diamond
> is the hardest of all substances, we understand "of all sub-
> stances that we know." We cannot and must not include those
> that we do not know. . . .

---

[23] ". . . l'habitude, qui sans violence, sans art, sans argument, nous fait croire les
choses et incline toutes nos puissances à cette croyance en sorte que notre âme y
tombe naturellement" (fr.S 661).

Here he is saying that, by supplying a tacit proviso, what would otherwise be inconclusive inference can be made conclusive, that is, we may understand an induction as an elliptical deduction.

But is it in this sense that he is speaking in fr.S 661? Are we to take it as strictly proven, not that we are to die, or that tomorrow's sun will rise—these statements refer, after all, to *future* events, and hence go beyond of our experience of cases—but only that *in our past experience* others of our kind have died, and earlier suns have risen? In fr.S 661 it seems not.

This issue is clearly related to Filleau de la Chaise's claim[24] that Pascal believed that the human mind made a natural leap from strong, but incomplete, logical evidence to a certain conclusion—a position reminiscent of Newman's.[25] True, fr.S 661 seems to say this if we read it in light of fr.S 544 and take "nos preuves les plus fortes et les plus crues," proofs through custom about future events, to bestow *certainty*. But Filleau's claim that Pascal believed this to be the case of the sum of individually inconclusive "proofs" of Christianity has no support beyond his *ipse dixit*. Clearly, Pascal considered that the various considerations he adduced in favor of Christianity would coalesce into a powerful challenge to unbelief. But he never intimates that collectively they would or should bestow certainty. Indeed, this notion is belied by his explicit remark in fr.S 423, cited above, that the proofs of our religion are *not* absolutely convincing. There is always risk in arguing *ex silentio*, but if, as is possible, he was referring there to the proofs considered individually, how could he have failed to add that, collectively, they *were* "absolument convaincantes" if that was indeed his view?

---

[24] "[I]l sera visible qu'on pourrait faire voir une si grande accumulation de preuves pour notre religion, qu'il n'y a point de démonstration plus convaincante, et qu'il serait aussi difficile d'en douter que d'une proposition de géométrie, quand même on n'aurait que le seul secours de la raison." Filleau de la Chaise, "Traité où l'on fait voir qu'il y a des démonstrations d'une autre espèce et aussi certaines que celles de la géométrie," in his *Discours sur les Pensées se M. Pascal, etc.* (Paris: Éditions Brossard, 1922), 155–56. Filleau, one of the editors of the Port-Royal edition of the *Pensées* (1670), claims to be representing the views of Pascal here. LaPorte remarks this view of Pascal's apologetic proofs in Strowski, Chevalier and other commentators. *Le Cœur et la raison selon Pascal*, 147–58.

[25] "I consider that there is no such thing (in the province of facts) as a perfect logical demonstration; there is always a margin of objection . . . . Yet on the other hand it is a paradox to say there is not such a state of mind as certitude. [. . . .] I think it is *phronesis* which tells us *when* to discard the logical imperfection and to assent to the conclusion which ought to be drawn in order to demonstration, but it is not *quite*." *Letters and Diaries of John Henry Newman*, ed. Charles Dessain and Thomas Gornall (Oxford: Oxford University Press, 1978– ), vol. 24, 104–5.

3. PROOF AND PERSONS, FORCE AND WRETCHEDNESS

For Pascal, all proof relying on merely human powers should be seen as at bottom audience-relative. In the case of mathematics and the sciences, it may proceed from first principles whose verisimilitude is so imperious that we cannot deny it. But in other realms, the heart persuades us *all* to certainty on very few matters (fr.S 142). Outside of these, our arguments will perforce be grounded in principles that appear true to some but not to others. And so he says:

> Tous leurs principes sont vrais, des pyrrhoniens, des stoïques, des athées, etc. Mais leurs conclusions sont fausses, parce que les principes opposés sont vrais aussi. (fr.S 512)

> All of their principles are true, the Pyrrhonists', the Stoics', the atheists', etc. But their conclusions are false because the opposing principles are true too.

Hence, from Pascal's perspective, we are forced to conclude that, in most matters, rational proof, proceeding as it does from the variously perceived *vraisemblance* of beliefs not shared by all, is at bottom a somewhat private affair; that in many areas of the greatest concern to mankind there is not, and cannot be, a Great Tribunal of Reason before which all men of good-will and sound understanding can be hailed for decisive and impartial arbitrament of their disputes.

In other words, Pascal, like Newman, but unlike Descartes, did not believe that all of our conclusions could ultimately be founded on principles that any being with any pretense whatever to rationality would be compelled to grant. Like Newman's, Pascal's paradigm of rationality is very different. We can only, unless we would be disingenuous, argue from those principles that we do *in fact* grant. We can only steer by such light as in fact we have, and not, as Descartes would have it in the *Meditations*, by an ideal light that any being who is to count as rational ought to have. We can but say, if we may invoke Luther yet again, *Hier stehe ich*, "Here I stand."

Of course, if we rely on purely human resources, such light as we have is never really enough. To *know* that we can know, we must have faith in God as a guarantor of the heart's veracity. Our fallen nature, its cognitive powers vitiated by *les puissances trompeuses*, must receive his grace.

And so, in Pascal's epistemology we are drawn yet again to one of the poles of his apologetic argument. We confront yet another facet of his powerful portrait of the wretchedness of man without God, *la misère de l'homme sans Dieu*, the crucial Augustinian theme that nothing merely human and natural can ever really suffice us.

In the context of this theme, we find a strong parallel in the *Pensées* between the hollowness of what passes and must pass among mankind for justice, and what passes and must pass among us for proof. Fallen humanity, says Pascal, being unable to fortify justice simply justifies force (fr.S 135). We are reduced to saying that what rules among us in fact—force—rules by right. By the same token, without God we are reduced to taking what does in fact persuade us for proof that *ought* to persuade us. Once again, we have had to bow to force—to *preuves con VAINCANTES*—and, once again, we have had to pronounce force to be good. Once again, we have had to say that what is *de facto* is *de iure.*

In matters epistemological, we are all heirs of Descartes and Pascal. But those among us with Pascal's, not Descartes's, blood in our veins, who burn with the desire for a certainty that is more than irresistible constraint to conviction, invincible rhetoric, will feel the bitter truth of Nietzsche's remark that "Überzeugungen sind Gefängnisse" (convictions are prisons).

# 6

# THE FUNDAMENTAL ROLE OF JUSTICE IN PASCAL'S APOLOGETICS: THE HIDDEN GOD

Nec recuso, quod Caecilius adserere inter praecipua conisus est, hominem nosse se et circumspicere debere, quid sit, unde sit, quare sit . . . . Quod ipsum explorare et eruere sine universitatis inquisitione non possumus, cum ita cohaerentia, conexa, concatenata sint, ut nisi divinitatis rationem diligenter excusseris, nescias humanitatis . . . .

Unde autem vel quis ille aut ubi deus unicus, solitarius, destitutus, quem non gens libera, non regna, non saltem Romana superstitio noverunt?

. . . latebrosa et lucifuga natio [Christiana] . . . .

Nor do I object to what Caecilius has striven to advance among his chief points—that man ought to come to know himself, and to look around to see what he is, whence he is, why he is . . . . Which very thing we cannot examine and bring to light without an inquiry into all things, since they are so coherent, so connected, so chained together that, unless you carefully investigate the nature of divinity, you will not know that of mankind . . . .

But whence, who or where is this one and only god, solitary, alone, of whom no free peoples, no kingdoms, nor even any superstitions known to Rome have knowledge?

. . . the lying-hid and light-fleeing [Christian] tribe . . . .

Minucius Felix, *Octavius* (XVII, X, VIII)

Does the Christian religion genuinely explain the mysteries of the human condition? Does it *shed light* on our grandeur, wretchedness, powers, foibles, origin, duties, destiny? That is to say, does it give grounds and causes for the realities of our situation, "raisons des effets," that really advance our understanding? A considerable part of Pascal's apologetics consists in the effort to show that Christian revelation, in particular when taken in the sense of St. Augustine, does indeed illumine the enigmas that we face and that we are.

Moreover, this theme is conceptually related to two of the main prongs of Pascal's overall apologetic strategy as set forth in fr.S 46. The explicative power of Christian doctrine should make us wish that it were true, for it can allay many of the uncertainties that will inevitably baffle and vex the thinking person who does not know God. And its explicative power would enhance the case that the Faith is reasonable, for it will shed on the obscurities of our condition a light that is, if not effulgent,[1] at least sufficient to engender and to warrant conviction in those who desire and deserve to see.

Of course, even if Christianity does account for the mysteries of our condition—most notably our what, whence, whither, and why—that does not suffice to establish its truth, and Pascal knows this well.[2] But although explanation alone does not constitute an Apology, and although Pascal's apologetics are certainly not reducible to this, a demonstration of Christianity's explicative power is nonetheless indispensable to the rational persuasion of unbelievers to belief. At a minimum, the Faith must be able to account for what is manifest about our condition and situation—for example, the observable duality of human nature, and the conspicuous absence of any God there might be from the world of our experience. And, at a maximum, if Christianity is to emerge from an Apology as the best candidate for our belief, it must do better at accounting for these and other enigmas than Philosophy or other religions.

But, in the final analysis, does Christianity as Pascal presents it explain anything at all? For the God of Abraham, Isaac and Jacob is above all a hidden God. "Vere tu es deus absconditus" (Truly you are a hidden god, Isaiah 45: 15/fr.S 644).

---

[1] "La dernière démarche de la raison" (fr.S 220)—or perhaps, "de l'apologiste"—is to present the very impenetrability of Christian doctrine as itself a proof. Without the miraculous aid of Providence, so extravagant a set of beliefs could never have gained the wide currency and authority it enjoys! Hence Malebranche's "L'incompréhensibilité de nos mystères est une preuve certaine de leur vérité" (*Entretiens sur la métaphysique et sur la religion* in *Œuvres*, vol. 2, 947; cf. 948–49). This dead-pan anticipation of Hume's withering irony in the conclusion of his "Of Miracles"—the only real miracle attendant on Christianity is that anyone can believe it!—bears no real weight in Pascal's apologetics, though it does receive indirect recognition. "La seule science qui est contre le sens commun et la nature des hommes, est la seule qui ait toujours subsisté parmi les hommes" (fr.S 680).

[2] See Prigent, "Pascal: pyrrhonien, géomètre, Chrétien," 74. Though my study of Pascal's *enchaînement d'idées* was conceived, and its initial drafts written, independently of it, a part of my argument finds anticipation and confirmation in some lines on pp. 67–68 where Prigent makes some of the same textual and conceptual connections (notably the way, explained above on pp. 106–07, in which fr.S 656 provides a logical retort to objections almost sure to be raised to fr.S 164).

[Dieu] se cache ordinairement, et se découvre rarement à ceux qu'il veut engager dans son service. Cet étrange secret,[3] dans lequel Dieu s'est retiré, impénétrable à la vue des hommes, est une grande leçon pour nous porter à la solitude loin de la vue des hommes. Il est demeuré caché sous le voile de la nature qui nous le couvre jusques à l'Incarnation; et quand il a fallu qu'il ait paru, il s'est encore plus caché en se couvrant de l'humanité. Il était bien plus reconnaissable quand il était invisible, que non pas quand il s'est rendu visible. Et enfin quand il a voulu accomplir la promesse qu'il fit à ses Apôtres de demeurer avec les hommes jusques à son dernier avènement, il a choisi d'y demeurer dans le plus étrange et le plus obscur secret de tous, qui sont les espèces de l'Eucharistie. (Lettre aux Roannez [4] OC, III 1035–36)

[God] is ordinarily hidden, and discovers Himself but rarely to those that he wishes to engage in his service. This strange secret into which God has retired, impenetrable to human sight, is a great lesson for transporting us into solitude far from human sight. God has remained hidden under the veil of Nature which shielded Him from us up until the Incarnation; and when it was necessary that He appear, He hid Himself all the more by covering Himself with humanity. He was much more recognizable when He was invisible than He was when He made Himself visible. And finally, when He wished to fulfill the promise He made to the Apostles to remain with men until his final coming, He chose to remain with us within the strangest and most obscure secret of all, the species of the Eucharist.

And so, when Pascal grounds our existential situation in accounts of this God's volitions, motives, and actions, when all is said and done, does he shed light on it? Or, since a God who is not only transcendent but deliberately self-veiled is Himself a mystery, does not any attempt to explain that is founded on Him ultimately reduce to mystification rather than to explanation? It would seem to avail little if Pascal should dispel some of the darkness enshrouding our origin, nature, duty, and destiny only to it replace it straightaway with the darkness veiling a Hidden God.

Indeed, that might be a best-case scenario. For how could the immanent, natural groundings of philosophical, historical, or scientific explanation fail to

[3] So reads Louis Lafuma's text in *L'Intégrale* (267). That this reading is correct is suggested by the parallel expression in the last line cited. Mesnard gives "cet étranger secret" but without noting a variant reading. If it is the better, the *lectio difficilior* of Mesnard's text could perhaps be taken to imply that God's hiding from us is alien/foreign to him in that it is not his initial, natural relation to us but a consequence of the Fall of Adam and Eve.

be better known to us, in principle and in fact, than groundings of explanation in what is not only transcendent but wilfully inaccessible? In which case,
Pascal risks explaining the obscure by the more obscure—*obscura per obscuriora*, as the Scholastics used to say.[4]

Perhaps, one might retort, these issues would pose a significant problem
only if the explicative process went no further than we have supposed—only
if Pascal did not extend the process by in some measure revealing the
Hidden God himself. Indeed, is not the whole point of the Apology to show
the worldly and the "emancipated," free-thinking *libertins* who this God is
and why He is hidden?

The retort would seem a just one. However, the greater part of the
"proofs" offered in Pascal's apologetics—miracles, prophecies, the perpetuity of the Faith (the Messiah has always been believed in), the sublimity
of "une si divine morale" (fr.S 646)—are all intimately bound up with God's
justice.[5] And it is a justice that, at crucial, points, is ultimately impenetrable.

For example, "Dieu doit aux hommes de les point induire en erreur"
(God owes it to men not to lead them into error, fr.S 428).[6] It is thus, as
implied by the *obligation* not to mislead, on account of God's *justice* that
we may safely conclude that the original religion, faith in the Messiah
promised to our first ancestors, is the true one.

It is likewise justice that would oblige miracles, prophecies, and
prophecies' fulfillments to be sufficiently non-obscure for us to identify the
Messiah, whom they are intended by God to prove. Thus, miracles should
count as good epistemological coin only if they are in support of "une doctrine qui ne paraît pas visiblement faux aux lumières du sens commun, et si
un plus grand faiseur de miracles n'avait déjà averti de ne les pas croire"
(a doctrine that does not appear visibly false in the light of our common

---

[4] Pascal was, of course, keenly aware of the fact that a consideration advanced as
explicative (now commonly called an *explanans*) should be clearer, and hence
better knowable, than the phenomenon to be explained (the *explanandum*). "Car
on trouve toujours obscure la chose qu'on veut prouver et claire celle qu'on
emploie à la preuve. Car quand on propose une chose à prouver, d'abord on se
remplit de cette imagination qu'elle est donc obscure, et au contraire que celle qui
la doit prouver est claire . . ." (fr.S 454).

[5] Eduard Morot-Sir helpfully points out that, when "justice" in Pascal has reference
to God, it may indicate not (or not only) a value or virtue, but have an ontological
force. "La justice de Dieu" in Gérard Ferreyrolles, ed., *Justice et force: Actes du
colloque "Droit et pensée politique autour de Pascal." Clermont-Ferrand, 20–23
Septembre 1990* (Paris: Klincksieck, 1996), 286–87. (Cf. "Good" in the
Aristotelian/Thomistic tradition, where it can be a convertible term with "Being.")
In such cases it seems to me roughly synonymous with "l'ordre de Dieu" (as in
Morot-Sir's discussion of fr.S 653 [804 L'Intégrale], ibid., 287).

[6] Cf. fr.S 431, where this is glossed to mean *unavoidable* error.

conceptions, and if a greater worker of miracles had not already warned against believing them [sc. miracle-working preachers of false doctrine], fr.S 428). Were it not for such restrictions, we would unavoidably be led into error.

As for Christian morality, to be "si divine" it must of course be just. But to what conception of justice does it conform? And, if we take "Christian morality" to encompass God's own morality, we may ask, *inter alia*, some fundamental questions that might well occur to an Apology's unbelieving audience. Why should mankind have been tempted at all? Why was a Redeemer then necessary to reconcile God to fallen mankind? Why was it fitting that he should come in the veiled manner recounted in the Scriptures? Clearly, any account of the morality that is advanced by or embedded in Christian teaching must presuppose some explanation of what God considers right and just.[7]

Once brought to belief, Pascal's reader may well worship the Christian God despite any metaphysical mystery concerning his essence. But if the case for the Christian account of things should rest ultimately on moral mystery, on a conception of divine justice that is morally inaccessible, even repugnant, then, as Pascal implies in fr.S 428, should one not reject it as a doctrine "visiblement faux aux lumières du sens commun"?

And there would be other reasons, ones not so much moral as logical and prudential, why there would then be little likelihood of Pascal's reader ever coming to belief. Why should the *libertin* exchange his present darkness for Christian darkness? Moreover, the "wager" (fr.S 680), made in the hope of eternal reward for a correct leap in the dark, is of course to be a first step to belief in the *Christian* God. Yet, without supposing this God to observe a kind of justice that is intelligible to us, the reader would not be entitled to assume that He would pay off a bet!

Whence the *fundamental* importance of justice for Pascal's apologetics.

Here we might observe, in passing, that it is remarkable that Pascal seems so little vexed by a problem concerning divine justice that so troubled, even tormented his master, St. Augustine: the classical problem of evil.

For Augustine, as for all Christians, the universe is, in effect, a kingdom under the absolute rule of an all-good, all-wise, all-able monarch. But, if these assumptions are all true, how can there be evil at all, let alone so much of it? St. Augustine offers us a theodicy based on the view of evil's

[7] Pascal seems to me tacitly to affirm the centrality of divine justice to Christian revelation when he tells us that "Toute la foi consiste en Jésus-Christ et en Adam, et toute la morale en la concupiscence et en la grâce" (fr.S 258). Implied here is the justice of our testing in the persons of our first parents, of our subsequent punishment for their failure, of the awful and unique price set on our redemption, and the determinants that justly bring us to or keep us from salvation.

essential nullity. It is not a something, but a lack. Milton, Pope, Leibniz, and a host of others likewise strive to "justify the ways of God to Man." But Pascal does not. We shall see, I think, that there are good grounds for considering his silence on this score to stem from a conviction that such reasonings, which would vindicate God to man by means of metaphysical and moral principles rooted in *le sens commun*, are at bottom but vanity and presumption. But, be this as it may, an Apology bereft of theodicy remains wanting in a vital logical and rhetorical respect.

If one tries to demystify the Hidden God by explicating his justice, one soon confronts the obvious question of why He chooses to hide Himself from mankind. Of course, for the tradition embraced by Pascal and Augustine, the answer lies in the Fall, the ground of *our* self-inflicted unworthiness and willfull estrangement from Him. In the following passage, Pascal presents it as a matter of justice that God chose to be hidden from us even in the Incarnation, which was a sort of theophany in *chiaroscuro*. Needless to say, a God who clothes himself in human flesh remains hidden behind that veil. But even that the Incarnation occured at all is willed by God to be hidden from some.

> [T]ant d'hommes se rendant indignes de sa clémence il a voulu les laisser dans la privation du bien qu'ils ne veulent pas. Il n'était donc pas juste qu'il parût d'une manière manifestement divine et absolument capable de convaincre tous les hommes. Mais il n'était pas juste aussi qu'il vînt d'une manière si cachée qu'il ne pût être reconnu de ceux qui le chercheraient sincèrement. (fr.S 182)

> So many having made themselves unworthy of his mercy, He wished to leave them deprived of the good they did not desire. Hence it was not just that He should have appeared in a manner manifestly divine and absolutely capable of convincing all men. But neither was it just that He should have come in a manner so hidden that He could not have been recognized by those who would be sincerely searching for Him.

Perhaps this contention will suffice for those who are already believers. After all, it is not for mere man to reproach the divine justice—to "Snatch from his hand the balance and the rod/Re-judge his justice, be the God of God!"—especially when it has seen fit to include him within the luminous circle of a saving revelation for want of which so many others err in darkness. "Cease then, nor Order Imperfection name/Our proper bliss depends on what we blame."[8] But from the point of view of

---

[8] Alexander Pope, *Essay on Man*, I 281–82, 121–22.

the unbeliever, to whom perforce all apologetics must be addressed, will this divine justice seem reasonable or fantastical? An illumination or a veil? Or even a stone of stumbling? In a word, is the divine justice fundamentally explicable or not?

On Pascal's view, what do we know of it?

We know of course that God must be just. "Il y a un devoir réciproque entre Dieu et les hommes [. . . .] Dieu doit accomplir ses promesses [. . . .] Dieu doit aux hommes de ne les point induire en erreur" (There is a reciprocal duty between God and men . . . . God must keep his promises . . . . God owes it to men not to lead them into error, fr.S 428).

But the duties or obligations of God are in no sense the constraints of a justice independent of Him whose value He does but acknowledge. Quite to the contrary: the justice of God, Pascal affirms, is at bottom nothing but his will.

> Changeons la règle que nous avons prise jusqu'ici pour juger de ce qui est bon. Nous en avions pour règle notre volonté, prenons maintenant la volonté de Dieu: tout ce qu'il veut nous est bon et juste; tout ce qu'il ne veut pas, mauvais et injuste. [. . . .] [L]a volonté de Dieu . . . est seule toute la bonté et toute la justice . . . . (fr.S 769)

> Let us change the rule we have had up till now for judging of what is good. Our rule was our will; now let us take God's will. All He wills is good and just for us, all that He does not will, bad and unjust. [. . . .] The will of God alone . . . is all goodness and all justice . . . .

The fragment concludes by adding to an obvious inference—that something directly contrary to God's will is a sin—a less obvious and more severe one: in the cases wherein events, which are themselves a manifestation of God's will, show that God did not mean us to have a thing, "l'absence de la volonté de Dieu . . . la rend injuste et mauvaise" (the absence of God's will makes it unjust and wicked).

Thus, the justice of God is established by a tautology: God wills what is just because He wills what He wills.

But although, after the manner of its kind, the tautology is clear, the justice of God remains an enigma. "S'il y a un Dieu," says Pascal, who in a kind of preamble to his celebrated wager is speaking "selon les lumières naturelles" (according to the natural light), "il est infiniment incompréhensible, puisque, n'ayant ni parties ni bornes, il n'a nul rapport à nous. [. . . .] Le fini s'anéantit en présence de l'infini et devient un pur néant. Ainsi notre esprit devant Dieu, ainsi notre justice devant la justice divine." (If there is a God, He is infinitely incomprehensible, since, having neither parts nor limits, He has no relation to us. [. . . .] The finite is annihilated in the presence of the infinite and becomes a pure nothing. So it is with our mind before God, so it is with our justice faced with the divine justice, fr.S 680).

In fact, Revelation aside, even "our justice" eludes our understanding.

> *J'ai passé longtemps de ma vie en croyant qu'il y avait une justice, et en cela je ne me trompais pas, car il y en a, selon que Dieu l'a voulu nous révéler. Mais je ne le prenais pas ainsi, et c'est en quoi je me trompais, car je croyais que notre justice était essentiellement juste et que j'avais de quoi la connaître et en juger. (fr.S 453)*
>
> La justice et la vérité sont deux pointes si subtiles que nos instruments sont trop mousses pour y toucher exactement. S'ils y arrivent, ils en écachent la pointe et appuient tout autour plus sur le faux que sur le vrai.   (fr.S 78)
>
> *I spent much of my life believing that there was such a thing as justice, and in that I was not mistaken, for there is, according as God has willed to reveal it to us. But I did not take it so, in which I was mistaken, for I believed that our justice was essentially just, and that I was able to know it and to judge of it.*
>
> Justice and truth are two points so fine that our [mental] instruments are too blunt to touch them exactly. If they happen to touch them, they flatten the point and come to rest all around it, more on the false than on the true.

If anything, our natural ignorance of justice is overdetermined. For it is a consequence not only of the corruption of our reason resulting from the Fall ("cette belle raison corrompue a tout corrompu," this fine, corrupt reason of ours has corrupted everything, fr.S 94), but of the fact that Adam's sin left us tainted with injustice at our very core ("les vertus nous sont étrangères, et nos péchés nous sont propres," the virtues are foreign to us, and our sins are proper to us, fr.S 769).

Hence, it should go without saying that we cannot explain divine justice by analogy to our own. In point of fact, our justice is but an inevitable concession to force. Like Plato, Pascal sees clearly that the central problem of politics is to put force in the service of justice. And, again like Plato— who shows in his *Republic* that to do this would require means that are impossible or all but—Pascal sees clearly that the task is beyond us. "Et ainsi ne pouvant faire que ce qui est juste fût fort, on a fait que ce qui est fort fût juste" (And so, as we could not bring it about that what is just should be strong, we have contrived that what is strong should be "just," fr.S 135).

And yet, as Erich Auerbach pointed out in a paradoxical reversal that is a truly Pascalian *renversement du pour au contre*, given that fallen mankind is radically unjust, it is in a sense very just that injustice—namely, the force which enables the strong to enthrone their desires and interests as custom and law—should reign over us in lieu of the true justice that, since we are unjust, we do not deserve.[9]

And, one might add, the justification of force tends obliquely to right in still another way. For even if, being at bottom but force, our justice is unjust, still our subservience to its power enables us to avoid civil war, for Pascal as for Hobbes the worst of the ills to which the body politic is subject.

In short, although we cannot recognize (true) justice, we can readily recognize injustice, to which our conceptions are only too conformable. Hence, in the *Écrits sur la grâce* Pascal would have it that we can clearly see the injustice of the "épouvantable" (frightful) doctrine of Calvin, which is "injurieuse à Dieu et insupportable aux hommes" (insulting to God and intolerable to man), while the fact that the radically contrary doctrine of Molina "flatte le sens commun" (flatters our common understanding[s]) by no means suffices to prove its truth (OC, III 786; cf. 767).

And so, at the last, far from being luminous, the justice of God remains an enigma. For not only does it fail to flatter *le sens commun*, it contradicts it, affronting it with blatant paradox. The following passage could hardly be more forceful on this point.

> Chose étonnante cependant que le mystère le plus éloigné de notre connaissance, qui est celui de la transmission du péché, soit une chose sans laquelle nous ne pouvons avoir aucune connaissance de nous même!
> Car il est sans doute qu'il n'y a rien qui choque plus notre raison que de dire que le péché du premier homme ait rendu coupables ceux qui, étant si éloignés de cette source, semblent incapables d'y participer. Cet écoulement ne nous paraît pas seulement impossible, il nous semble même très injuste. Car qu'y a-t-il de plus contraire aux règles de notre misérable justice que de damner éternellement un enfant incapable de volonté pour un péché où il paraît avoir si peu de part qu'il est commis six mille ans avant qu'il fût en être. Certainement rien ne nous heurte plus rudement que cette doctrine. Et cependant, sans ce mystère le plus incompréhensible de tous nous sommes incompréhensibles à nous mêmes. (fr.S 164)

> It is, however, an astounding thing that the mystery the furthest removed from our knowledge, which is that of the transmission of sin, is a thing without which we can have no knowledge of ourselves!
> For there is no doubt that there is nothing which shocks our reason more than to say that the sin of the first man has

---

[9] Erich Auerbach, "On the Political Theory of Pascal," in his *Scenes from the Drama of European Literature* (Minneapolis: University of Minnesota Press, 1984), 101–33.

rendered guilty those who are so far from that source that they seem incapable of sharing in it. This flow of guilt seems to us to be, not only impossible, but even most unjust. For what is there more contrary to the rules of our miserable justice than eternally damning an infant incapable of will for a sin in which he seems to have so little part, one committed six thousand years before he existed. Certainly nothing jolts us more forcibly than this doctrine. And yet without this mystery, the most incomprehensible of all, we are incomprehensible to ourselves.

Here Pascal candidly avows that, in offering this cornerstone of the Christian revelation as an explanation of the human condition, he is explaining mystery by mystery—worse still, *obscura per obscuriora*—whence it would follow that, considered as explanation, his apologetic is technically deficient. Now, he immediately adds:

Le nœud de notre condition prend ses replis et ses tours dans cet abîme. De sorte que l'homme est plus inconcevable sans ce mystère, que ce mystère n'est inconcevable à l'homme.

The knot of our condition has its twists and turns in this abyss. So it is that man is more inconceivable without this mystery than this mystery is inconceivable to man.

But, if one were to be so bold as to use an expression of Pascal's to contradict him, one might say that this last affirmation is not "absolument convaincant de la dernière conviction" (absolutely convincing to the point of utmost conviction, fr.S 141). Is it possible that "l'homme est plus inconcevable sans ce mystère, que ce mystère n'est inconcevable à l'homme" if the transmission of Adam's sin is "le mystère le plus éloigné de notre connaissance"? If "il n'y a rien qui choque plus notre raison"? If it seems to us not only "impossible" and "très injuste" but utterly "contraire aux règles de notre misérable justice"? (Can "épouvantable aux hommes" be far behind?) If, to say it all, it is of all mysteries "le plus incompréhensible de tous"?

In fine, it is clear that Pascal's intended explication of human nature and the human condition is shot through with mystery. What then remains for a Pascalian to say, unless it be piously to echo Augustine and to affirm that, though it is a mystery, yet it is so: "Mysterium, non mendacium est"?

In the *Pensées* there are two responses to this question: one from the perspective of faith, the other from that of the unbeliever.

From the vantage point of faith, "*Tout tourne en bien pour les élus* [Rom. 2:28]. Jusqu'aux obscurités de l'Écriture, car ils les honorent à cause des clartés divines. Et tout tourne en mal pour les autres, jusqu'aux clartés, car ils les blasphèment, à cause des obscurités qu'ils n'entendent pas" (*Everything turns to good for the elect.* Even including the obscurities of Scripture, for they honor them on account of what is clearly divine. And everything turns to ill for the others, for they blaspheme what is clear on account of the obscurities that they do not understand, fr.S 472). Nor, as we have been noting, is it at all astonishing that "les clartés divines" should elude the "autres," embedded as the former are in accounts that presuppose a darkling divine justice.

What then remains to say to the unbelieving "others," save that they are blind—in fact, blinded, inasmuch as the impenetrable justice of God has not ordained that they perceive the divine clarities which would persuade them to accept the divine obscurities?

Obviously, the only other option for Pascal is to speak to the unbeliever according to the perspective which is properly apologetic, that of the natural light. But it, too, is a vantage from which our view is quenched in darkness at every attempt to see to the bottom of things. Whether we would deepen our knowledge of Supreme Being or of our own, we end balked by mystery on every side.

> Incompréhensible que Dieu soit, et incompréhensible qu'il ne soit pas; que l'âme soit avec le corps, que nous n'ayons point d'âme; que le monde soit créé, qu'il ne le soit pas; etc.; que le péché originel soit, et qu'il ne soit pas. (fr.S 656; cf. 230)

> Incomprehensible that God should exist, and incomprehensible that He should not exist; that there should be a soul with the body, that we should have no soul; that the world should be created, that it should not; etc. That Original Sin should exist, and that it should not.

At first glance, the contradictions presented in this passage, the theses and antitheses, if you will, seem obvious prototypes of the Kantian antinomies. But in lieu of presenting opposed affirmations on each hand, as does Kant, Pascal on each hand points to mystery and incomprehensibility. Certainly, we read here, the great theses of the Christian religion are incomprehensible. *But the antitheses of the freethinkers, of the atheists and materialists, are likewise incomprehensible.* And so, when he encounters a Christian apologetic which, as explanation, is rooted in darkness, the unbeliever should consider that the opposing explanations also end in mystery, *and that thus the mere fact of mystery can be discounted as an objection, for it will count no more against the Faith than against its alternative.*

But there is another emphasis that is no less helpful for Pascal.

On the philosophical level, Pascal is no less dismissive of dogmatic rationalism than he is of skepticism on the human level, to say nothing of the Christian plane. It is a fact, even if it is incomprehensible, that though dogmatism and skepticism are exhaustively complementary—for either knowledge is possible for us, or it is not; there can be no other option— nonetheless, both elements of the opposed pair must appear to us as false. For reason confutes the one, and our nature the other (fr.S 164). Analogously, both elements in the exhaustive oppositions of God's existence and nonexistence; of the union and interaction of soul with body or, if we have no soul, their absence; of creation of the universe (a begin- ning in time) and its eternity (no beginning in time); and of corrupt and incorrupt human nature, appear to us as fundamentally incomprehensible, inexplicable. But, by logic, one element of each pair of exhaustive oppo- sites must be true. *Thus, in each case, something incomprehensible to us must be true. Why not then the element that is proclaimed by the Faith?* For, at its depths, reality is opaque.

Indeed, part of the likelihood of Christianity comes from the fact that it not only teaches this truth, but accounts for it. For as soon as one accepts the Faith, says Pascal, the cornerstone mysteries of our nature and predica- ment receive some light. They are not illumined as such—the enigma of the transmission of Adam's sin continues to affront our reason. But light is directed to the *fact* of their existence, and to the existence (though not to the understanding) of a reason for that fact. Such a reason is the enigmatic justice of the Hidden God, a justice that, by its nature, at crucial points is just not susceptible of a theodicy grounded in *le sens commun*.

So, when all is said and done, Pascal in his apologetics will offer the unbe- liever less an explanation of his nature and condition than a demonstra- tion—both in the sense of "argument" and of "pointing out"—that, at bottom, reality defies explanation.[10] He will offer him less an illumination than a choice—a choice between the obscurities that both reason and faith must finally confront, and to one of which each must thus submit. If the unbeliever should trust in Revelation, he will have, not the reasons *within*, but the reasons *for the existence of* its fundamental obscurity, and so he may feel entitled to leave off being troubled by this. But if he does not

---

[10] This is a defining feature of Christian belief, and arguably a major reason for its success. On this score, one may recall that the young Augustine was beguiled into Manicheism in no small part by the promise that Mani would banish all mystery (*De utilitate credendi* 2; cf. *Contra Faustum* 15.6), and that he left the Manichees when he realized, after his long-awaited but fruitless interview with Faustus, that this promissory note would never be paid. "Dogmatic" philosophy often peddled a like epistemological optimism, as in, for example, Lucretius's famous praise of Epicurus: "O tenebris tantis tam clarum extollere lumen qui primus potuisti . . ." (*De rerum naturae*, 3.1–2). At the very least, the epistemological pessimism of Christianity carried with it the rhetorical and logical advantantage of not overpromising.

accept Revelation—for example, if, following the natural light to its end in contradictions, he finds Pyrrhonism to be the truth, and so takes refuge in doubt—he will have nothing but mystery. For Pascal, as Jean Prigent has well said, the choice always comes down to Christianity or nothing, "le christianisme ou le néant."[11]

We are now in a good position to see why, according to the entwining of apologetic themes presented in fr.S 182, Pascal intended to begin only "Après avoir expliqué l'incompréhensibilité" (After having explained incomprehensibility).[12] To do otherwise would be in vain. For Pascal was as fully persuaded of the exactitude of these words of St. Paul, "Nunc videmus per speculum in ænigmate" (Now we see but in a glass and darkly) as he was of the affirmation that follows: "tunc autem facie ad faciem" (but thereafter, face to face, 1 Cor. 13:12).

[11] Certainly, Pascal has not shown that there is no third option. But if and when, as per titles in the *Pensées'* Table, Pascal will have led the unbeliever to a realization of the bankruptcy of the "Philosophes" and of the "Fausseté des autres religions," he might consider himself entitled to consider the unbeliever to have renounced the *search* for a third option (even though its mere logical possibility remains open). The judgment of Prigent that here Pascal offers Revelation to the unbeliever only as a *vraisemblance* is perhaps too modest. See Prigent, "Pascal: pyrrhonien, géomètre, chrétien," 74.

[12] The sequence of titles of *liasses* in the Table to the Copies of the *Pensées* clearly cannot reflect the precise order in which Pascal meant to treat his apologetic themes—a fact whose hard learning has contributed much to the confusion of commentators over the years. Still, it may not be accidental that the themes of clarity, obscurity and blindness are conspicuous in the *liasse* entitled "Fondements," which precedes the *liasses* titled after individual proofs of Christianity. Absent prior consent to his accounts of "l'incompréhensibilité" et "l'aveuglement," Pascal would be hard pressed to make effective use of the inconclusive, though, at their least, not unreasonable, proofs destined for the following *liasses* (viz. miracles, prophecies, et al.). Cf. for example frs.S 423, 425.

# 7

## MYSTIC/ANTI-MYSTIC: ON SPEECH AND SILENCE IN PASCAL'S MÉMORIAL

Père juste le monde ne t'a point connu, mais je t'ai connu.

Just Father, the world has not known you; but I have known you.

> Pascal, the Mémorial (fr.S 742)

[N]eque enim aut paucis aut multis verbis indicari potest quod indicari verbis non potest.

Neither with few nor with many words can you make known what words cannot reveal.

> Saint Augustine, *Letters* (CCXXXI, 1)

The *Pensées* of Pascal consists not only of fragments but of lacunae, and so it is well worth the attentive reader's while to reflect on both. For what is true of every text—that in it lie both the said and the unsaid—is especially true of a fragmentary text, and even truer of one that is both fragmentary and unfinished. For the nonce, let us pass over what is said in Pascal, and instead linger briefly over the much less often plumbed unsaid. In the eternal silences of his lacunae's infinite spaces, is there any absence that makes its presence particularly felt?

One of what we might call the *Pensées'* speaking silences was briefly adverted to in chapter 6, on God's justice. Why is there in Pascal's apologetics no vindication of the ways of God to man proceeding from principles conformable to *le sens commun*? After all, in a universe *sub deo iusto*, evil—according to Augustine's neo-Platonic metaphysics, itself an absence (of being) that makes its presence very much felt!—can be a prodigious stone of stumbling athwart the path to belief, or even block the way entirely, like the boulder athwart Hannibal's alpine pass. A paradigmatic illustration of this evident verity is provided in the chapter "Rebellion" in Dostoyevsky's *Brothers Karamazov*. There, Ivan's recoil at the horrific sufferings of little children is not only famously stark and gripping in itself, but is a key premise to a powerful argument against philosophical theodicy of the kind found in Augustine, and, later, systematized by Leibniz—a kind of theodicy that Pascal conspicuously foregoes. For even if one affirms that evil must be tolerated by God so as to allow the achievement of greater universal good— in effect, Machiavelli's "look to the results," *si guarda al fine*, though restricted here from commission to permission—still, it is far from evident that any result, no matter how fine or fair, would be worth being procured at the price of the agonies of innocents. (When, for Augustine, it comes to rationalizing the sufferings of children, he can only suggest their possibly salutary effect upon sinful parents.)

But to my way of thinking, the *Pensées'* most surprising silence is the one covering the mystic[1] experience that brought Pascal himself "certitude, certitude" in faith: his celebrated encounter of November 23, 1654, with the God of Abraham, Isaac, and Jacob, the "nuit de feu" of which he left so eloquent a "Mémorial" (the term derives from his sister, Gilberte, and her friends).[2]

---

[1] The mystical character of the text, and of Pascal's experience, has been denied or attenuated by some commentators. This issue will be taken up in the text below.

[2] According to a commentary on the text by le Père Guerrier (*Troisième manuscrit Guerrier*, OC, III 56), "Tous convinrent qu'on ne pouvait pas douter que ce parchemin, écrit avec tant de soin et avec des caractères si remarquables, ne fût une espèce de mémorial . . . ." L. Brunschvicg is considered the first to take the term as a title for the document, a choice followed by criticism since. (Sellier, however, in a note to his edition [fr.S 742, n. 2], cites the above passage of Guerrier with the term as already a title: *Mémorial*.) Though the term does not derive from Pascal, it is just. The acts of writing a document, and of keeping it always on one's person, certainly imply a desire to commemorate the experience to which the document refers.

As Mesnard says (ibid., 45), "Suscité par une experience mystique, le *Mémorial* a été composé dans un état d'extrême lucidité. C'est une veritable *monument*, au sens étymologique du terme, édifié par Pascal pour éterniser l'unique." Its character as a monument (i.e., memento) does not, however, exclude its having some of the characteristics of an aide-mémoire, whose humble status may be misleadingly repellent when brought forward here. These are revealed in the fixing of the date and time; in the indication of the Other who was present (specifying the attendance, so to speak); in the report of feelings evoked in Pascal; and (in the parchment text) in the resolution he makes of "Soumission totale à Jesus-Christ et à mon directeur." In short, the document seems to aim both to celebrate and to evoke memory.

For a bibliography, a magisterial analysis of the document, and its double text, see Mesnard in OC, III19–53. His edition should also be consulted for the abbreviations, figures, and textual layout of both the paper and the parchment. See also Henri Gouhier, "À propos du Mémorial de Pascal," *Revue d'histoire et de philosophie religeuses* 35 (1955):147–58.

A paper and a parchment copy, the latter now lost, both autographs though not identical, were found in the lining of the deceased Pascal's *doublure.* Its importance for him was such that, when he changed garments, it was resewn into the lining of the new one so that it would be always on his person. As Jean Mesnard justly remarks,

> L'écrit le plus extraordinaire qui soit sorti de la plume de Pascal est aussi celui qui lance au commentateur le défi le plus redoutable. Tout langage semble dérisoire, appliqué à cet incomparable langage, déroutant par sa hardiesse comme par sa simplicité; et, devant l'expression d'une intimité secrète brutalement dévoilée par la mort, le silence aurait une sorte de convenance suprême. Mais cet écrit est en même temps de ceux qui excitent le plus vivement notre désir de savoir. (OC, III 19)

> The most extraordinary piece of writing from Pascal's pen is the one that presents the commentator with the stiffest challenge. All language seems risible when applied to this incomparable language, language apt to mislead by virtue of its boldness and its simplicity alike; and, in the presence of this expression of a secret intimacy brutally unveiled by death, silence would seem to be supremely fit. But at the same time, this piece of writing is among those that most excite our desire to know.

In Pascal's day, mystical writings ran considerable risk of appearing in a censored version, or even on the Index of Forbidden Books. As accounts of private revelations, they could easily seem to be manifestations of a Protestant spirit. And, as they were typically couched in language that, taken literally, overflowed or contradicted orthodox formulas—at least in the eyes of the unmystical tribe of scholastically trained theologians—they could easily seem heretical. But it is hard to believe that these considerations would weigh heavily upon the author who, in the *Provinciales,* not only entered, but stoked, the fiercest controversy of his day. Why then is Pascal silent on the *nuit de feu* in those *pensées*[3] that he destined for an Apology for the Christian faith, a venue where, above all, speech would seem so needful for the parting of veils and the imparting of "certitude, certitude"? For in the apologetic fragments, Pascal shows a willingness to turn all kinds of arguments and insights to his purpose—as the saying goes, "faire flèche de tout bois" (make an arrow out of any kind of wood)—so that the weaving together of very varied "proofs," though they are individually nondemonstrative, may nonetheless engender conviction in the reader.

---

[3] First published in 1740, seventy years after Port-Royal edition of the *Pensées*, the Memorial was not collected into the *Pensées* until later still.

We may concede that the experience of the 23 November was unique, private and irreproducible. But even so, it is hardly likely that the apologist would remain silent if he thought that speech might be of any avail for the salvation of his readers. Why then does Pascal forego any allusion to evidence (if only in its root sense of "seeing," *vue*) that brought him personally "certitude, certitude"?[4]

The question becomes even more forceful if again we reflect that, for Pascal, humankind's need for "certitude" is as desperate as its achievement is uncertain. For, as noted in the two preceding essays, on Pascal's reckoning we are simply awash in doubt and mystery. In this world we are, as it were, caught in the flux of a rushing torrent—the "rivers of Babylon"—whose depths soon defeat our sight, plunge where we will.

On the principle that what is fine is well met with twice, or even thrice—*Dis kai tris ta kala*, as the Greeks used to say—the following texts,[5] though they appeared earlier, in chapter 6, are so central to Pascal's view of our condition (or predicament) as to be well worth recalling.

> Incompréhensible que Dieu soit, et incompréhensible qu'il ne soit pas; que l'âme soit avec le corps, que nous n'ayons point d'âme; que le monde soit créé, qu'il ne le soit pas; etc.; que le péché originel soit, et qu'il ne soit pas.

> Incomprehensible that God should exist, and that He should not exist; that there should be a soul with the body, that we should have no soul; that the world should be created, that it should not; etc. That Original Sin should exist, and that it should not.

---

[4] It goes without saying that an Apology must be founded on reason rather than on what surpasses or bypasses it. Still, in its discussion of the Apostles and the risen Christ ("l'hypothèse des apôtres fourbes est bien absurde," fr.S 341), the *argumentation* of Pascalian apologetics has recourse to an analysis of *witnesses to a miraculous event*—which, though taken at the interior level, is a plausible if not unavoidable description of the author of the Memorial. Mesnard (OC, III 38–41) sees the document as the memento of an enthusiasm that, though mystical, is the continuation and culmination of a long process, one wholly interior but lacking "tout élément merveilleux" (40). This reservation seems to me unnecessary, whether by "merveilleux" is meant "natural but most extraordinary" or even "miraculous." For, as Mesnard points out elsewhere, the initiative in a mystical encounter is with the divine. See *Les Pensées de Pascal* (Paris: SEDES, 1976; revised 1993), 323. The exercise of that initiative on the part of the hidden God is certainly marvelous in the weaker sense; arguably it is even miraculous, for it would be a supernatural abrogation of one of nature's regularities, viz., the uniform presence of the divine absence. Cf. André Bord (for whom the experience is "bien de l'ordre de la charité, surnaturel"), "Pascal: Essai de biographie spirituelle," in Dominique Descotes, Antony McKenna, and Laurent Thirouin, eds., *Le Rayonnement de Port-Royal* (Paris: Honoré Champion, 2001), 266.
[5] From frs.S 656, 164, and the fourth of the *Lettres aux Roannez*.

Chose étonnante cependant que le mystère le plus
éloigné de notre connaissance, qui est celui de la transmission du péché, soit une chose sans laquelle nous ne pouvons
avoir aucune connaissance de nous même!

Car il est sans doute qu'il n'y a rien qui choque plus notre
raison que de dire que le péché du premier homme ait rendu
coupables ceux qui, étant si éloignés de cette source, semblent
incapables d'y participer. Cet écoulement ne nous paraît pas
seulement impossible, il nous semble même très injuste. Car
qu'y a-t-il de plus contraire aux règles de notre misérable justice que de damner éternellement un enfant incapable de
volonté pour un péché où il paraît avoir si peu de part qu'il est
commis six mille ans avant qu'il fût en être. Certainement rien
ne nous heurte plus rudement que cette doctrine. Et cependant
sans ce mystère le plus incompréhensible de tous nous
sommes incompréhensibles à nous mêmes.

It is however an astounding thing that the mystery the
furthest removed from our knowledge, which is that of the
transmission of sin, is a thing without which we can have no
knowledge of ourselves!

For there is no doubt that there is nothing that shocks our
reason more than to say that the sin of the first man has rendered guilty those who are so far from that source that they
seem incapable of sharing in it. This flow of guilt seems to us
to be, not only impossible, but even most unjust. For what is
there more contrary to the rules of our miserable justice than
eternally damning an infant incapable of will for a sin in which
he seems to have so little part, one committed six thousand
years before he existed. Certainly nothing jolts us more forcibly
than this doctrine. And yet without this mystery, the most
incomprehensible of all, we are incomprehensible to ourselves.

[Dieu] se cache ordinairement, et se découvre rarement à ceux
qu'il veut engager dans son service. Cet étrange secret, dans
lequel Dieu s'est retiré, impénétrable à la vue des hommes, est
une grande leçon pour nous porter à la solitude loin de la vue
des hommes. Il est demeuré caché sous le voile de la nature
qui nous le couvre jusques à l'Incarnation; et quand il a fallu
qu'il ait paru, il s'est encore plus caché en se couvrant de
l'humanité. Il était bien plus reconnaissable quand il était
invisible, que non pas quand il s'est rendu visible. Et enfin
quand il a voulu accomplir la promesse qu'il fit à ses Apôtres
de demeurer avec les hommes jusques à son dernier avènement, il a choisi d'y demeurer dans le plus étrange et le plus
obscur secret de tous, qui sont les espèces de l'Eucharistie. [6]

---

[6] In an illuminating study, Hélène Michon remarks on this passage that, for Pascal,
the obscurity of God's presence in the Eucharist is "en lien avec sa démarche

> [God] is ordinarily hidden, and reveals himself but rarely to those that he wishes to engage in his service. This strange secret into which God has retired, impenetrable to human sight, is a great lesson for transporting us into solitude far from human sight. God has remained hidden under the veil of Nature which shielded Him from us up until the Incarnation; and when it was necessary that He appear, He hid Himself all the more by covering Himself with humanity. He was much more recognizable when He was invisible than He was when He made Himself visible. And finally, when He wished to fulfill the promise He made to the Apostles to remain with men until his final coming, He chose to remain with us within the strangest and most obscure secret of all, the species of the Eucharist.

But although God is well and truly hidden, and although, in his apologetics, Pascal relies very heavily on revelations, notably miracles and prophecies, that we can know only by report, and that of their nature blind some and enlighten others, he declines to make use of the revelation of his *nuit de feu*. Perhaps the Memorial itself, and especially its silences, will tell us why.

What is most striking about this precious document, whether by virtue of its presence or its absence?

One may well be taken aback by its very first words, for they show that it is a decidedly scientific spirit that informs this Memorial of an apparently mystical encounter. Like the good scientist he was, Pascal begins by specifying the time, date, and duration of his experience—a proceeding whose objective detachment seems strangely at odds with the passionate interiority of what follows.[7] Here are the initial lines (text of the parchment).[8]

---

apologétique: Dieu se cache pour être mieux connu . . : ." Michon, "Le Chapelet secret du saint-sacrement," in Descotes et al., *Le Rayonnement de Port-Royal*, 54. But even if one concedes this to be so, "mieux connu" is still "dans le plus étrange et le plus obscur secret de tous"!

[7] Though surprising, the sober and detached spirit of the opening lines is far from unparalleled. St. John of the Cross offers the reader an explicative Prologue, and the "chapelet secret" of Port-Royal's Mère Angélique Arnauld has a jurisprudential motif (the restoration of rights God has foregone by virtue of entering into the Eucharist), and is written in the form of a commentary on sixteen attributes! See Michon, "Le Chapelet secret du saint-sacrament," for a discussion of both.

[8] For ease of reference, the balance of the parchment text in Mesnard's edition follows. Again, for figures, abbreviations, and precise details of layout (e.g., indents) of both the parchment and paper texts, see OC, III 50–1.

> Dieu d'Abraham, Dieu d'Isaac, Dieu de Jacob,
> non des philosophes et savants.

L'an de grâce 1654.
Lundi 23 novembre jour de saint Clément
pape et martyr et autres au martyrologe romain
Veille de saint Chrysogone martyr et autres etc.
Depuis environ dix heures et demie du soir
jusques environ minuit et demi.

*FEU*

The year of grace 1654.
Monday 23 November feast of Saint Clement
pope and martyr and others of the Roman martyrology
Eve of Saint Chrysogonous martyr and others etc.
from about ten thirty in the evening
until about half past midnight.

*FIRE*

    The ecclesiastical emphasis of this avant-propos—it recurs at the end of the document, where Pascal vows "Soumission totale à Jesus-Christ et à mon directeur" (Complete submission to Jesus-Christ and to my spiritual director)—is also quite surprising. For, is it not of the essence of a mystical

Certitude, joie, certitude, sentiment, vue, joie
Dieu de Jesus-Christ.
*Deum meum et deum vestrum.* Jean 20, 17.
Ton Dieu sera mon Dieu. Ruth.
Oubli du monde et de tout hormis DIEU.
Il ne se trouve que par les voies enseignées
    dans l'Évangile. Grandeur de l'âme humaine.
Père juste, le monde ne t'a point
    connu, mais je t'ai connu. Jean, 17.
Joie, Joie, Joie, et pleurs de joie.
Je m'en suis séparé.
*Dereliquerunt me fontem.*
Mon Dieu, me quitterez-vous?
Que je n'en sois pas séparé éternellement.
Cette est la vie éternelle qu'ils te connaissent
    seul vrai Dieu et celui que tu as envoyé
Jésus-Christ
Jésus-Christ
Je m'en suis séparé. Je l'ai fui, renoncé, crucifié.
Que je n'en sois jamais séparé!
Il ne se conserve que par les voies enseignées
    dans l'Évangile.
Renonciation totale et douce.
Soumission totale à Jésus-Christ et à mon directeur.
Éternellement en joie pour un jour d'exercice sur la terre.
*Non obliviscar sermones tuos. Amen.*

encounter, if such this be, that it dispense with intermediaries? Such an encounter presupposes a *direct* confrontation with the heart and first principle of the real. However, in the Memorial, Pascal displays a continual preoccupation with mediators divine and human. At the very beginning, as we have seen, he invokes saints and martyrs Clement and Chrysogonous. (Though in a way this is fitting, given that in what follows Pascal, himself, is a martyr in the term's root sense of "witness.") He names "Jésus-Christ" four times; he names "L'Évangile" (Scripture) twice, and cites or echoes it nine times; and in Louis Périer's decipherment of the parchment copy's last three lines, his "spiritual director" is mentioned once. (One of the mentions of "Jésus-Christ" is also found here). All of these are intermediaries between the hidden God and man.

When one reflects on the sobriety and detachment of a document that begins by fixing the date and time, and by integrating the experience it memorializes into the ecclesiastical calendar, and when one reflects on the importance the document accords to intermediaries, it becomes a bit less difficult to understand how it has often been viewed as without mystical import at all—for example, by Sainte-Beuve (an "action de grâce"), and Condorcet (an "amulette")[9]—or viewed as not "mystical" in the term's highest and most proper sense, for example by Henri Gouhier.[10] And if one reflects on the absence in the document of a number of mystical commonplaces—for example, of expressions of harmony between the self and the totality of things, or of pantheism, or of the annihilation of self in the presence of or in union with the infinite—the conviction grows apace that whatever mysticism may indwell is not of the mere common garden variety.

Yet, given the text of the document, and the varieties of mystical experience, it is hard to see how the qualifier "mystical" can be fairly denied. The document commemorates an event, not a ratiocination; a summit of religious experience, not merely religious thought. And the event is, as the root sense of "mystical" suggests, a revelation/initiation not accorded to all ("le monde ne t'a point connu, mais je t'ai connu," the world has not known you, but I have known you). The emotion of the experience commemorated is evident, not only in the fervor of the language, for instance, "FEU," "pleurs de joie" (FIRE, tears of joy), but in the handwriting (paper). The profound intimacy of the experience, and its cardinal importance, are

[9] See F. T. H. Fletcher, *Pascal and the Mystical Tradition* (New York: Philosophical Library, 1954), 7, 11.

[10] See Gouhier's influential "Le Mémorial est-il un texte mystique?" in *Blaise Pascal, Commentaires* (Paris: Vrin, 1966), 49–65. But see also Mesnard's discussion in *Les Pensées de Pascal*, 321–26, where he argues for the document's mystical character while taking the term in a wider sense than Gouhier. Cf. also Harding Meyer, *"Pascals "Memorial," ein ekstatisches Dokument?" Kirkengeschichte* 68 (1957): 335–41.

vouchsafed both by the document's language and by its continual closeness
to Pascal's physical person. Jean Mesnard's appreciation of the matter is
surely the inescapable one.

> L'enthousiasme qui saisit Pascal dans la nuit du 23
> novembre 1654 était bien, à notre avis, une sorte d'état mys-
> tique, comme il découle du sens profond du mot.
> L'expérience a été faite par lui, dans la certitude et dans la
> joie, dans le "feu" d'une grâce souveraine, de la présence
> immédiate d'un Dieu qui est devenu *son* Dieu. Une révélation
> personelle lui a été donnée, terme d'une longue attente, mais
> aussi commencement d'une nouvelle vie. (OC, III 41)

> The enthusiasm that gripped Pascal on the night of
> 23 November 1654 was, in our view, well and truly a kind of
> mystical state in the profound sense of the term. In certainty,
> in joy, in the "fire" of a sovereign grace, he has had experi-
> ence of the immediate presence of a God who has become
> *his* God. A personal revelation was accorded him, the end of
> a long wait, but also the beginning of a new life.[11]

But perhaps the most surprising characteristic of Pascal's Memorial is
the nearly complete lack of a common if not constitutive element of what
could fairly be called "mystical language," namely, the neglect of attempts
to *describe* either the experience undergone or the object of that experience—topics on which, contrariwise, the commonality of mystics can be
positively verbose, for the temptation to conjure the ineffable into speech
is a powerful one. In striving to relate their encounter, to describe the
encountered, or, at the least, to awaken in the reader some sympathetic
echo of what they felt, mystics have left little undone by way of inventing
striking metaphors, strident paradoxes, soaring hyperboles, and breathtak-
ing contradictions.[12] Consider, as a fairly typical specimen of a common
kind of mystical discourse, the following texts taken almost at random from
that *fons et origo* of Western mysticism, the Pseudo-Dionysius (*Mystical
Theology* chs. 1, 2).[13]

---

[11] See also note 4 above.

[12] Whether these devices are reflective of an overflow of meaning, or of the defect
of the same, and whether they end in intimations of what surpasses speech, or in
the nullity of empty abstraction, are of course crucial questions. In Michon's discussion of the quarrel of the "chapelet secret," antithetical judgments of this kind
are treated as closely tied to readers' assumptions and expectations about language,
and about the amount of free play or uncertainty in meaning that one is prepared
to tolerate. Michon, "Le Chapelet secret du saint-sacrament," 58–73.

[13] The translation that follows is essentially a rendering of the one that appears in
Pseudo-Denys, *La théologie mystique/Lettres* (Paris: Migne, 1991), 21, 29. For a fine

Super-essential Trinity,
You who are above Divinity,
Above the Good,
You who maintain Christians in the knowledge of things
   divine,
Conduct us, beyond Unknowing,
Towards the most-high and most-luminous peaks of the
   mystic scriptures.
There where lie veiled the simple, insoluble, immovable
   mysteries of Theology
In the trans-luminous Dark of Silence
Wherein one becomes initiate in the secrets of that radiant
and resplendent Dark in its utter obscurity . . . .

Into that most-luminous Darkness
May we ourselves enter
And, by Unseeing and Unknowing,
May we see and know
What is beyond all vision and knowledge
By the very fact of seeing nothing and knowing nothing.
For there one truly sees and knows,
And super-essentially celebrates the Super-Essential
When one abstracts from all that exists.

Such discourse has a kind of fitness if only by being a singular way of speaking of the Singular. It bears witness to the mystic's determination to communicate something unique by means of a (suitably?) unique way of speaking and describing. At a minimum, language, and by implication thought, is made to reveal its own incapacity for signifying by signaling how greatly its object (or would-be object) surpasses it. For, if it is to convey sense, such radically oxymoronic and hyperbolic mystical language must be read as transcending, and hence in a manner denying, correspondence between word and object.

Thus, faced with epistemological impasse, mystical language, even if its tone is rhapsodic, is a *pis-aller*. How can one render the transcendent without falsifying and betraying it with speech, which is meaningful to us only by virtue of its relationship to the immanent? For the mystic, just as the *sui generis* escapes all categories, so words must be made to escape the categories of their meaning. Whence *aporia*—or more precisely, dilemma. For words about what is Beyond Category carry sense only in the measure they are unfit to their object, and any words are fit for such an Object only to the degree that their meaning evaporates.

discussion of the modes of signifying of the many tropes of mystical language ("langage d'amour"), see Michon, "Le Chapelet secret du saint-sacrament," 58 ff. It is based on St. John of the Cross's Prologue. For a sympathetic analytical view see H. Gene Blocker, "The Language of Mysticism," *The Monist* 59:4 (October 1976): 551–62.

But Pascal, in the Memorial, pointedly foregoes recourse to the sort of language we have been discussing. In fact, with a few possible exceptions, he makes no effort at all to describe the object of his experience.

One possible exception is the word "FEU" (fire), which precedes the famous formula that *names* (rather than describes) what is encountered, and then gives an anti-description by proclaiming what it is *not*. "Dieu d'Abraham, Dieu d'Isaac, Dieu de Jacob, non des philosophes et savants" (God of Abraham, God of Isaac, God of Jacob, not of philosophers and scholars). Of course, "FEU" is a recurring element in biblical visions of God,[14] and the uppercase letters make it tempting to read it so here. But fire is also a figurative commonplace for religious ardor, in which case it would be descriptive, not of the thing experienced, but of the one experiencing.

Other candidates for description lie in the apostrophe "Père juste" and in the biblical citation (paper text) "Dereliquerunt me fontem aquae vivae" (They have forsaken me, the fountain of living water, Jer. 2:13). But does the citation aim to describe God, albeit figuratively, along with the fact of our abandonment of Him? For *fontem aquae vivae* can easily be read, not as a figurative description of the divine, but as a figure of the divine *role* of dispenser of grace through baptism. As for the apostrophe, the first element in "Père juste" is, strictly speaking, principally the signaling of a relationship rather a description; likewise, "juste" signals the kinds of things one does more than the kind of thing one is.

In fine, in the Memorial Pascal chose to name, to indicate, and to address the God he encountered rather than to try to describe Him, save perhaps by biblical reference and, obliquely, by negations and relations. In it, one encounters, at best, a kind of demi- or even quasi-descriptive semantic *chiaroscuro* blanketing (or blanking?) an experience that it memorializes, but does not relate or describe. In it, one will look in vain if he seeks the strident figures and tropes that abound in the more "descriptive" discourse of a Dionysius. It is as if FEU had consumed them all, or perhaps flooded the text with Dionysian "inaccessible light." The semantic field that we call the Memorial is perennially budding, *joliment en herbe*, but the figures of common mystical speech do not figure there. They are conspicuously absent from Pascal's haunting mélange of quotation, apostrophe, pronouncement, question, sigh, lament, rapture, and resolve.

Why then, at the last, does a writer so variously able and eminently resourceful as Pascal forego the attempt to describe or to relate to the readers of the Apology, and in large measure even to himself, his experience and encounter on that night of nights?[15]

---

[14] Cf. for example Exodus 19:18 and 24:17; also Deut. 4:11–36, and 5:4–26.

[15] It might be tempting to aver that, in the case of the Memorial, Pascal foregoes description (and with it, narration) because what he experienced that night was

Or, consider a not unrelated question. If we narrow the issue to the intended audience of the Memorial, that is to say, to Pascal himself, how are we to explain what, on reflection, is arguably its most cryptic phrase? That is, why does Pascal say that "Il ne se trouve que par les voies enseignées dans l'Évangile" (He is only found by the ways taught in Scripture) when, to all appearances, he himself has just found Him ablaze in a mystic night?

If we restrict the issue to the Apology, then, given the prominence accorded to mediators in the Memorial, the extension of Pascal's descriptive and narrative silences from that document to his apologetic project becomes even harder to understand. For the apologist himself is a mediator between the mysteries of the Faith and his readers, who are thus mystics in the ancient and etymological sense of the term—that is, people who present themselves as candidates for guidance/initiation into mysteries. The apologist is thus a mystagogue in the sense of a guide/initiator of novices who have at least some interest in becoming initiates or adepts. An Apology is an Eleusis. But Pascal's silences show him to be a mystagogue to whom the revelation of mysteries is not wholly pleasing.

Unless, perhaps, his reticence may stem rather from the side of the One Encountered. Perhaps one can attain "joie," "certitude," even "vue" without experiencing clarity, the Obscure remaining even now obscure, anything remotely analogous to a Beatific Vision being still reserved for the world to come. Perhaps, as that "naturally Christian soul" Seneca put it, "Eleusis servat quod ostendat revisentibus" (Eleusis keeps back some things it will show to those who return to look again, *Naturales Quaestiones,* VII 30).

Or then again, we may take Pascal's silence as his revelation. For in fact, it is very eloquent. It serves as a sign of the sincerity with which he adjudged the strainings and flailings of "mystical language" to be unavailing, and of the depths of his conviction that, in his essence, the Hidden God escapes not only our sight, but our thought and our speech. It powerfully suggests that, even in the Memorial, a document meant for his eyes only, Pascal despaired of presenting in speech the perception ("vue") and awareness ("sentiment") experienced in his *nuit de feu.* And that thus, *à plus forte raison,* he had scant hope of communicating to others the source of his "certitude, certitude, sentiment, joie" (paper text).

---

indelibly imprinted on his heart and mind, and so, though he might well have considered description or narration possible, they were superfluous in a document intended for himself alone. But in this case, why compose and bear with one a monument/aide mémoire of any sort? In any event, we are hardly entitled to pronounce *a priori* that the experience was ineffaceable. If, say, dreams provide something resembling an analogue, it would be sobering to reflect how the memory of even dreams that are, when experienced, vivid, gripping, and penetrating to the last degree, may evanesce within hours if not minutes of waking.

Small wonder, in short, that even though he is deeply aware that his role as apologist demands a willingness to make good use of all the resources of language—for nothing less than his reader's all is at stake—Pascal remains silent where many another mystic would not. Even his numerous quotations and echoes of Scripture are a kind of silence, for in them it is not Pascal who speaks, but God. In the Memorial, as in the Apology, the one who can speak well of God is God. "Dieu parle bien de Dieu" (fr.S 334).

As here we are arguing *ex silentio*, we can only say that it is very much *as if* Pascal is keenly conscious of the ludicrous situation produced when speech, or even the act of speaking itself, contradicts the very attempt of language to signify.

As when the Academic skeptics, the "académiciens" of fr.S 141, aver that "Nothing is known."

Or when the ancient sophist (Gorgias) says that "Nothing is, and if it were it could not be said."

Or, to take an instance that forcibly struck Unamuno, when the pessimist speaks out or writes books, for true pessimism would be mute in its despair, seeing no good in an effort to enlighten or to enlist sympathy.[16]

Or, when the mystic babbles about the ineffable, ignorant or disdainful of Saint Augustine's dictum, sage even though it is tautologous, that Pascal so scrupulously observes: "neque enim aut paucis aut multis verbis indicari potest quod indicari verbis non potest."[17]

Arrant impossibility—and arrant betrayal—to put the unspeakable into speech! All considered, the silence of Pascal is far more eloquent, and bids fair to be far more revealing, than the metaphoric and paradoxical loquacity of the common run of mystics. Where they speak, Pascal adores.

---

[16] "If there were in the world a sincere and total pessimism, it would of necessity be silent. The despair which finds a voice is a social mood, it is the cry of misery which brother utters to brother when both are stumbling through a valley of shadows which is peopled with—comrades. In its anguish it bears witness to something that is good in life, for it presupposes sympathy . . . . The real gloom, the sincere despair, is dumb and blind; it writes no books, and feels no impulse to burden an intolerable universe with a monument more lasting than brass." From "A Dramatic Inferno," *Nation*, 6 July 1912, cited by Miguel de Unamuno in *The Tragic Sense of Life* (New York: Dover, 1952) 264–65.

[17] Letter 231, 1. Though, ever the rhetorician, a few lines further Augustine cannot resist following a flower of rhetoric—unable to say perpetually how pleased I was with your letter, I must content myself with merely repeating it—with "sic enim fortasse dici potest quod dici non potest." A tome detailing the confusions that Rhetoric has visited upon Philosophy, whether out of playfulness or out of a grim determination to make meanings fit the Procrustean bed of a figure or trope, would be a telling instance of that oh-so-long recital of woes, the proverbial "Iliad of ills."

# PART FOUR

## AFTERWORD

# 8

# "WATCHMAN, WHAT OF THE NIGHT?"

Multis enim sensi mirabile videri eam nobis potissimum pro-
batam esse philosophiam quae lucem eriperet et quasi
noctem quandam rebus offunderet . . . .

Indeed, I have noticed that to many it seems a wonder that
I have approved above all a philosophy that would seem to
snatch the light away and to flood the world with a darkness
as if of night . . . .

Cicero, *De natura deorum*, I 3

When, in 1902, J. B. Bury succeeded Lord Acton as Regius Professor of
Modern History at Cambridge, he certainly interpreted "modern" rather
largely, for he continued to focus his research and writing on the later
Roman Empire—"even if he did not go so far as to say, with a German
authority, that 'Modern History begins with the call of Abraham.'"[1] There is
a real sense, though, in which even the more expansive estimate of the
"German authority," whether facetious or not, is both shrewd and just.

Stories are like houses. We build them, move into them, and proceed
to live in them, passing them down through the generations until it seems
they will no longer serve. The story of the one God, the Fall, and the
Messiah is arguably, as proclaimed by no less an authority than the cinema,
the Greatest Story Ever Told. It is, to vary the house motif, the story in
which and by which the West, both at home and in the many lands it has
shaped, ended up telling itself to itself. So considered, it is, or at the least
has been, not merely a story that we tell, but a story that we are. It is less
like a narrative structure or frame than a narrative loom on which patterns
and borders are woven into the fabric of even nonbelievers' identities

---

[1] F. J. C. Hearnshaw, preface (1927) to *Invasion of Europe by the Barbarians* by
J. B. Bury (New York: Norton 1967), v.

(whence the rage of a Nietzsche). As such, it distinguishes us from people shaped by different narratives—including all of those who, *pace* Pascal and others on the "perpetuity" of the Faith, preceded the story by as much as a hundred thousand or more years.

Paradoxically, what is, on the face of it, one of the story's greatest weaknesses—that the metaphysical mysteries with which it enshrouds the Deity have a correlate in the mysteries of his morals—is arguably one of its greatest strengths, perhaps even the prime reason for its appeal to so many and its hold for so long. For, in its dark, the sprawling Christian story has, throughout the long years of its telling, mirrored all of the moral anomalies, paradoxes, and irresolvables—the latter we may call "surds"—that our world has. And that we have.

All-powerful, all-knowing, and wholly benevolent, nonetheless the Deity anomalously tolerates the foreseen cancer of evil throughout his natural, angelic, and human creation. Even though, in the light of *le sens commun* and reasonings therefrom, evil's coexistence with the All-Good and All-Able is *inexplicatum et inexplicabile*, nonetheless it is clearly a necessary feature of any belief-system that would account for what is observable ("save the phenomena") of our world and of ourselves. An intellectual indigestible, evil is a kind of a moral surd, resembling those values in the number system that exist notwithstanding that they have an inevitable residuum that numbers cannot fully resolve and express.

Indeed, the surds in the Christian story, far from being incidentals at its periphery, are rooted in the divine nature itself. If his love is infinite, it is also commanded,[2] and his punishments too are infinite for his finite creatures who, whether by choice or accident, fail to love Him as they ought. He would have us know Him, but He hides Himself. He would have us follow Him, but what church, council, pope or anti-pope, preacher or theologian, text writ or spoken, what shifting view of our own conscience and under-standing shows us the way? He would gladly suffer the little children to come unto Him, but his justice excludes the unbaptized ones, for they are stained with the guilt of their first ancestors. He is so mild that repentance (contrition), or maybe mere fear of punishment (attrition), will reconcile the sinner to him at any time. But he is so draconian as to visit the same, supreme penalty of damnation not only on the perpetrators of genocide but on the practitioners of "solitary vice"; on lovers who don't wait for the preacher; and, in the Catholic confession, on reprobates who neglect Mass of a Sunday, or on the impious "whose god is their belly," *cuius deus ven-ter est*, gluttons who wantonly consume a hamburger on a day prescribed for abstinence from meat.

[2] Cf. Augustine, *Confessions*, I 5. "Quid tibi sum ipse, ut amari te iubeas a me et, nisi faciam, irascaris mihi et mineris ingentes miserias?"

Viewed in the "natural light," such contrasts are very liable to provoke, as did an earlier story-system in Virgil, an exclamation of indignant incredulity. Can such rancor really dwell in a divine mind? "Tantaene animis caelestibus irae?" And, perhaps, provoke as well its no-less-famous Virgilian answer. Given on the authority of a goddess no less, and backed by ocular demonstration, it is that the divine power can be merciless even to the guilt-less, a point the poet drives home with a repetition like a hammer blow: "divum inclementia, divum."[3]

Earlier times saw in Virgil's query a reprehension of paganism, and thus an index of a "naturally Christian soul" in the poet. But his answer is an index of just plain nature, the nature that, though driven out with the proverbial pitchfork, always comes running back. Although they are affronts to divine perfection in the light of *le sens commun*, contrasts of the sort instanced above cannot be *fundamentally* baffling to pagan piety. For it was a piety directed toward gods who did not create the world, who were not all or always good, who did not love us, and who certainly did not expect us to love them.[4] Their arbitrary and capricious deeds and decrees could well be a source of fear. "The gods terrify me and Jupiter is my enemy!"— *Di me terrent et Iuppiter hostis*! The Greeks called this feeling *deisidaimonia*, dread of the divine, though for Lucretius it is the essence of just plain *religio*. But whether they were part of *religio* or *superstitio*, our pieties or our pathologies, the classical gods' actions, though they might be wayward and wild, and often even wicked, were nonetheless in character for beings with no pretense to perfection, and so they did not have an ineliminable residue of the inexplicable.

Though in our day philosophers and theologians still essay theodicies with metaphysical and moral roots in *le sens commun*, the surds in the Christian story itself are, as a rule, politely ignored by the pious.

Of course, the moral sensibilities embodied in *le sens commun* evolve, and so, it may come to balk where once it found no paradox, as in the notions of hereditary guilt and blood revenge. Consider, in this connection,

---

[3] *Aeneid*, 1.11 and 2.602.
[4] As the pseudo-Aristotelian author of the *Magna Moralia* observes (II, xi 6), it would be an absurdity (*atopon*) to love Zeus—a view that anti-Christian polemicists, particularly in the seventeenth and eighteenth centuries, have not been slow to apply to the sometimes fierce and self-willed God depicted in the Old Testament. Easily accessible examples of such moralistic critiques of God are to be found or readily implied in the famous article "David" in Bayle's *Dictionnaire historique et critique*, in Thomas Paine's *Age of Reason* and in Voltaire's rather neglected *Examen important de Milord Bolingbroke* (included in his *Mélanges*). It is a tradition that Mark Twain continues in his posthumous *Letters from the Earth*. Much of this material is strongly reminiscent of the moral critiques of pagan deities by Christian writers such as Augustine.

not only doctrinally rooted challenges to justice as humanly understood, such as those instanced above, but those challenges (or affronts) detailed in the Scriptural narrative itself. Almost universally, the Sunday pulpit maintains a well-bred, discreet silence on, say, the Lord's vengeance on King Ahab through his children (II Kings 10:1–11). Orchestrated by his prophet Jehu, it results in seventy children's heads being placed before the holy man in two large heaps. Thus "The Lord has accomplished all that he foretold through his servant Elijah." [Cf. I Kings 21:20–24. Through Elijah, the Lord will requite evil for evil. Ahab's male line, free or slave, will be exterminated like Jeroboam's and Baasha's.] Gilding the lily, "Thereupon Jehu slew all who were left of the family of Ahab in Jezreel, as well as all his powerful supporters, intimates, and priests, leaving him no survivor." Subsequently, "The Lord said to Jehu, 'Because you have done well what I deem right, and have treated the house of Ahab as I desire, your sons to the fourth generation shall sit on the throne of Israel'" (II Kings 10:30).

Nor does the psalmist's blessing on anyone who dashes out the brains of a Babylonian baby much exercise pulpit eloquence (Ps. 137:9). Nor do the Deity's sanguinary war-instructions to the Israelites in Numbers (31:1–47) and Deuteronomy (20:10–13, 16), e.g., "Thou shalt save alive nothing that breatheth"—though they are bitterly mocked in Mark Twain's *Letters from the Earth*. Notwithstanding such draconic injunctions, which are quite in the spirit of the psalmist's "and of thy goodness, slay mine enemies" (143:12), to much of contemporary Christian piety God is a virtual pacifist! He is, also on humane grounds, opposed to capital punishment (though not, strange to say, to eternal fire!).

To our day, unpalatable or even shocking elements of traditional orthodoxy are, in effect, just so many "crazy aunts in the attic." Though, alas, they are incontestably there—and not always quiet—they are as irrelevant as they would be embarrassing if they were brought into the room.

It is the strength of the long tradition shared by Pascal and Augustine that it does not try to marginalize or to compartmentalize the surd element, the ultimately-unresolvable-at-least-by-us, whether it appears in the Faith, in the world, or in ourselves. This is so much so that, for Augustine, the paradox of evil's existence, nay flourishing *sub deo iusto* is a near-obsession. At the last, though, it is a paradox that he can "resolve" only by recourse to heroic measures. That is to say, only at the price of embracing a further paradox, evil's essential non-existence, and a conundrum, the creature's ability to act independently of a God from whom it has derived all aspects of its being. (In other words, the will is free even though, in the light of *le sens commun*, "doing follows from being," *operari sequitur esse*.)

In this tradition, God is not, as often in our day, a medicine for anxiety. Indeed, a judge so inscrutable and exigent is powerful grounds for it!

"Toutes conditions et même les martyrs ont à craindre: par l'Écriture" (People of all conditions, even the martyrs, have cause for fear: from Scripture, fr.S 752). Still, as the universal *fons et origo*, God functions as the anchor of all explanation, or at least of the best that we may hope for, and so He spares us the supreme anxiety of utterly unplumbed circumambient dark.

"Watchman, what of the night?" Such darkling answers as the believer is vouchsafed to Isaiah's query (21:11) at least have the authority of coming from the dark.

Still, the tradition shared by Pascal and Augustine is one of vast resource, not only imaginative but logical, when it comes to supplying accounts for what we observe of ourselves and the world—including observed absence—which ability is no small part of its power of attraction. For example, its linchpin concepts of a hidden and inscrutable Deity, and of a fallen mankind, can be inferences from observation. For we can observe our frailty, his absence, and a world that we cannot imagine as divine handiwork throughout. ("Who trusted God was love indeed/ . . . Tho' Nature, red in tooth and claw/With ravine, shriek'd against his creed."[5]) But these same linchpin concepts can, as axioms of faith, just as easily be upheld as the *grounds* for what we observe. As such, they will then appear as confirmed by observation instead of inferred from it. And if the tradition should sometimes offer accounts that lie somewhere between explanation's reality and similitude, this is, as it were, merely a confirmation of its dark views on how little light there is at reality's depths. On this score, the Faith, having not overpromised, keeps faith by being as good as its word.

Above all, when it comes to rendering an account that "saves the phenomena," it is a tradition that, after a certain initial naïveté concerning God and evil—"Wilt thou not slay the wicked, O God?" (Ps. 139:19)—has learned not to be afraid of a manifest truth that is potentially the most appalling of all.[6] It has learned to face the fact that *the existence of a God who thinks, judges, and acts only in accord with principles whose justice we can recognize is impossible.* It has learned to admit that, if there were such a Being, his providence would be utterly incompatible with the stark facts

---

[5] These famous lines are from Tennyson's "In Memoriam," §56.

[6] But fear is not far; it soon bubbles to the surface with Pierre Bayle. "[L]e tragique pascalien est celui d'un Dieu caché, il est de l'ordre d'une insondable nostalgie de Dieu; celui de Bayle est l'ombre portée d'un Dieu méchant, il est de l'ordre du désespoir. Et même si cette hypothèse d'une toute-puissance méchante est sans doute de l'ordre d'une tentation vite repoussée, il rest que, face au dilemme soulevé par Pascal—'Il faut que nous naissions coupables ou Dieu serait injuste' [fr.S 237]—Bayle n'a plus de réponse assurée." Jean-Michel Gros, "L'Apologie de Pascal et le fidéisme de Bayle," in *Pierre Bayle, citoyen du monde*, eds. Hubert Bost and Philippe de Robert (Paris: Honoré Champion, 1999), 252–53.

of a natural world replete with disaster, an animal world "red in tooth and claw," and a moral world shot through with sin. It has, in short, come to the tacit realization that theodicy rooted in *le sens commun*, notwithstanding that it may satisfy the vanity of the philosophers who confect it, or that expressed in consolatory platitudes it may serve in the pulpit, is in fact—a mirage.

> Ah Love! Could thou and I with Fate conspire
> To grasp this sorry Scheme of Things entire,
> Would we not shatter it to bits—and then
> Re-mould it nearer to the Heart's Desire!

So speaks Omar (lxxiii). But Virgil's word is the last. And his word is that the last word is with the gods, who would have things far otherwise than would we. *Dis aliter visum.*[7]

For, in the final reckoning, if what we take as evident principles of moral judgment are right, God and creation are wrong. In fact, God would be evil—and to the extent that it is conceivable, "inclementia divum, divum" is the most terrifying and unlivable conclusion of all. *Hence,* according to the tradition Pascal and Augustine share, our principles of judgment must be as askew, as corrupt, as fallen as is the human understanding which finds them to be so evident. Otherwise the all, *to pan,* the scheme of things entire, and its Framer, must be askew and corrupt.

And yet, so unstable is our knowledge that the very judgment that condemns our judgment is insecure, and not only on account of the self-reinforcing dynamic of "Pascal's Pendulum" sketched in chapter 5.

For if our natural depravity were as great as the tradition would have it, would mankind have reacted to the Good News of the Gospel like the thane in Bede—or in a manner like Grendel in *Beowulf*? Grendel, a monster wearing God's curse, lurking joyless in the dark without, maddened at hearing the scop's harp in Heorot sing the Creation, man's place therein, and the lights of heaven. Though he does not present it as such, it is arguable that the strongest of Pascal's arguments for human greatness, for his great complementary theme of *la grandeur de l'homme,* lies in the *Pensées'* very first words in the order of the First Copy: "Les psaumes chantés par toute la terre" (The Psalms are sung throughout the earth, fr.S 37/L'Intégrale 1). But, ironically, these words of Pascal, when considered in light of our strange refusal to be Grendels, form one of the strongest arguments *against* the conceptual framework whose linch-pin is

---

[7] So speaks *le sens commun. Di melius* is the more hopeful commentary of religious or philosophical piety. Cf. Seneca, *Epistulae morales,* 98.5.

our thoroughgoing[8] natural depravity—against the very Faith whose champion Pascal is, and which bids the Psalms be sung.[9]

In Genesis, before the light, there was the dark. But though driven back, it still veils the face of the deep. Even such light as the Faith affords trickles from a sort of dark lantern casting light and shadow. But what of that? If, before creation, God suffered the dark to be roundabout, shall we do less?

Indeed, from the standpoint of the faith that imbued Pascal, the dark (*l'obscurité*) is not terrible, nor is it properly a *problem* save in the false light of our pride and our importunate desire to know (*libido cognoscendi*). His celebrated account of the three orders includes the order of the mind; in it the highest good is truth. But above this order is another, the order of charity, and therein the highest good is love. When all is said and done, for Pascal and his tradition we are not in this world to know it, or even to know God. Our highest task is not to know Truth—not even Truth about Him who is highest—it is to love. Not to love Truth. Nor even Darkness. (For therein our *libido cognoscendi* cannot distract, nor corrupt reason mislead, and faith alone must guide.) Both are but idols. Our task is to love Him.

> On se fait une idole de la vérité même, car la vérité hors de la charité n'est pas Dieu et est son image et une idole qu'il ne faut point aimer ni adorer. Et encore moins faut-il aimer ou adorer son contraire, qui est le mensonge.

---

[8] Thoroughgoing because it is a corruption that, if unredeemed and unremedied, in fact separates us from God so thoroughly that by right we are unquestionably worthy of eternal separation from Him. That is to say, according to the tradition, natural man both does and deserves to "lurk joyless in the dark without."

In the last of his *Lettres philosophiques*, Voltaire famously taxes Pascal with being a "misanthrope sublime, qui s'acharne à peindre l'homme dans son plus mauvais jour." But Pascal, like orthodoxy itself, and even its Augustinian strain, seems at times to feel compelled to soften its account of what, given the theology of the Fall, might in its upshot fairly be called the Grendel-like state of natural man. Cf. for example fr.S 164 wherein, despite the Fall, we remain good enough to recognize our corruption and to have an idea of "la vérité" and "la béatitude" that we lack. (The latter point might consort ill with his view, discussed above in chapter 5, that our corrupted moral vision does not allow us to see what is truly just.) But it is no big step from the orthodox view that, in the domain of moral action, unaided natural man will persistently reject the good—a rejection profoundly rooted in his nature—to the view that such a being would rage Grendel-like at the good, finding it alien and hostile. But, even if he fell short of Grendel-like rage, would natural, as-yet unbaptized man, being *ex hypothesi* corrupt and an enemy of God, embrace the Gospel *en masse* and fill the world with psalms?

[9] Perhaps, if pushed to its limit, it is even an argument for a famous judgment, eminently un-Augustinian, of that Augustinian favorite Sallust: "Falso queritur de natura sua genus humanum." *Bellum Iugurthinum*, 1.1.

> Je puis bien aimer l'obscurité totale; mais si Dieu m'en-
> gage dans un état à demi obscur, ce peu d'obscurité qui y est
> me déplaît, et parce que je n'y vois pas le mérite d'une entière
> obscurité, il ne me plaît pas. C'est un défaut, et une marque
> que je me fais une idole de l'obscurité, séparée de l'ordre de
> Dieu. Or il ne faut adorer que dans son ordre. (fr.S 755)

> We make an idol for ourselves out of truth itself, for truth
> apart from charity is not God; it is his image, and an idol that
> must not be loved or adored. And still less must one love or
> adore its contrary, which is the lie.
>     I can readily love total darkness; but if God engages me
> in a state of half-darkness, the small dark in it displeases me;
> and because I fail to see in it the merit of total darkness, it
> does not please me. This is a fault, and a mark that I am mak-
> ing darkness, separated from the order of God, into an idol for
> myself. However, one must only adore according to his order.

Here Pascal finds our environing *chiaroscuro* displeasing even though—or
rather, because—it is but a half-dark. But what of those whose experience
of dark is the least luminous of all—those who have sought, but not found?
Those who, at the last, are like Tolkien's Gollum, who went into the deeps
under the Misty Mountains to learn their secrets but found no secrets, only
dark.

Sainte-Beuve, who spent thirty years in the research and writing of his
masterpiece *Port-Royal*, seems to have had a somewhat analogous experience. In entering the world of the Augustinians, he had initially sought to
penetrate the mystery of those pious souls and to collect the poetry latent
in their inner depths ("je voulais surtout, à l'origine, en pénétrant le mystère de ces âmes pieuses, de ces existences intérieures, y recueillir la poésie
intime et profonde qui s'en exhalait"). But the severity of their creed soon
dispelled this mirage, repelled the seeker, and drastically altered his search.
"Mais à peine avais-je fait quelques pas, que cette poésie s'est évanouie ou
a fait place a des aspects plus sévères: la religion seule s'est montrée dans
sa rigueur, et le Christianisme dans sa nudité" (But I had scarcely advanced
a few steps before this poetry evaporated or gave way to aspects more
severe: religion without mix or alloy, Christianity unclad stood before me
in its rigor).

His burgeoning resistance to Augustinianism's properly religious allure
then led him to hope to seize and to depict, though not to be seized by,
the Augustinians' "fleeting spark they call divine," a spark whose illumination leaves the mind as free, cool, and impartial after as it was before
("[L]'étincelle, celle même qu'on appelle divine, mais une étincelle toujours
passagère, et qui laisse l'esprit aussi libre, aussi serein dans sa froideur,
aussi impartial après que devant").

But it seems that, at the last, whatever fleeting spark of illumination he may have found cast more of a flicker on zoology than on divinity. For he ended, as he continues in his remarkable Conclusion, simply by observing his subjects as part of the remarkable variety of the forms the human species could take ("les variétés de l'espèce, les diverses formes de l'organisation humaine"), forms whose moral make-up is strangely modified by their society and by the artificial maze of their doctrines ("étrangement modifiée au moral dans la société et dans le dédale artificiel des doctrines"). If his subjects were to return to life, he would pay them a visit or two by way of duty, seeking to verify "l'exactitude de mes tableaux" (the accuracy of my depictions), but he is emphatically not of their company. What doctrine is there more artificial than yours! "Et quelle doctrine plus artificielle que la vôtre!"

> [J]'ai été à ma manière un homme de vérité, aussi avant que je l'ai pu atteindre.
> Mais cela même, que c'est peu! Que notre regard est borne! qu'il s'arrête vite! qu'il ressemble à un pale flambeau allumé un moment au milieu d'une nuit immense! et comme celui qui avait le plus au cœur de connaître son objet, qui mettait le plus d'ambition à le saisir et le plus d'orgeuil à le peindre, se sent impuissant et au-dessous de sa tâche, le jour où la voyant à peu près terminée, et le résultat obtenu, l'ivresse de la force s'apaise, où la défaillance finale et l'inévitable dégoût le gagnent, et où il s'aperçoit à son tour qu'il n'est qu'une illusion des plus fugitives au sein de l'Illusion infinie![10]

> I have been, in my way, a man of truth, as far in the van as I was able to be.
> But how little a way that is! How limited is our view! How quickly it comes to a halt! How like it is to a pale candle lit for a moment in the midst of a vast night! And how the man whose heart was the most committed to knowing his object, who put the most ambition into seizing it, and the most pride into depicting it, feels powerless and below the level of his task on the day when, seeing it almost finished, and the result obtained, the intoxication of his strength is calmed—on the day when final failure and the inevitable revulsion claim him, and when he perceives in his turn that he is only an illusion of the most fugitive kind in the bosom of the infinite Illusion!

*Vanitas vanitatum?* Final *débâcle?* Certainly so, according to Augustine and the age-old orthodoxy proclaiming that outside the Church there is no salvation, *extra ecclesiam nulla salus!* But there is, maybe, even in this tradition a glimmer of light (will o' the wisp?) at the heart of the darkness—one

---

[10] Sainte-Beuve, *Port-Royal* , vol. 3, 674–75.

to which, on the assumption that Dante speaks aright of their anomalous sal-vation, Trajan and Ripheus might bear witness.[11]

Does the "inaccessible light" of the divine darkness veil all eyes save those of the Augustinian and orthodox? Steeped though he is in the spirit of the *Confessions*, Pascal puts into the mouth of Jesus words that, whether he will it or no, go beyond Augustine's great theme that to seek after God is to respond to God's call to seek Him.[12] Strictly construed, these words, among Pascal's most famous, hint that when all is said and done, God might be a worse theologian than many another. "Console-toi, tu ne me chercherais pas si tu ne m'avais trouvé" (Be consoled; you would not seek me unless you had already found me, fr.S 751).[13] Some mildness too may dwell in mystery, in a sightless dark wherein, if a venerable tradition has sensed or dreamt aright, we shall, like the eyeless Oedipus, at last see clearly, blinded no longer by the illusion that our eyes were able to see.

---

[11] Cf. Dante, *Purgatorio* X 70–90, *Paradiso* XX 43–48; *Purgatorio* XXVI 43, *Paradiso* XX 68.

[12] E.g., Augustine, *Confessions*, XIII 1. "Invoco te, deus meus, misericordia mea, qui fecisti me et oblitum tui non oblitus es. Invoco te in animam meam, quam praeparas ad capiendum te ex desiderio, quod inspirasti: nunc invocantem te ne deseras, qui priusquam invocarem praevenisti et institisti crebescens multimodis vocibus, ut audirem de longinquo et converterer et vocantem me invocarem te."

[13] Cf. "Rien ne donne l'assurance, que la vérité. Rien ne donne le repos, que la recherche sincère de la vérité" (fr.S 496).

# SELECT BIBLIOGRAPHY

Auerbach, Erich. "On the Political Theory of Pascal." In *Scenes from the Drama of European Literature*, 101–33. Minneapolis: University of Minnesota Press, 1984.

Bord, André. "Pascal: essai de biographie spirituelle." In *Le Rayonnement de Port-Royal. Mélanges en l'honneur de Philippe Sellier*, ed. Dominique Descotes, Antony McKenna, and Laurent Thirouin, 259–70. Paris: Honoré Champion, 2001.

Brown, Peter. *Augustine of Hippo: A Biography*. 2nd edition. Berkeley and London: University of California Press, 2000.

Bunyan, John. *Grace Abounding to the Chief of Sinners*. Harmondsworth: Penguin, 1987.

Davidson, Hugh. *The Origins of Certainty*. Chicago: University of Chicago Press, 1979.

Descotes, Dominique. *L'Argumentation chez Pascal*. Paris: Presses Universitaires de France, 1993.

———. "La Responsabilité collective dans les *Provinciales*." In Roger Duchêne, *L'Imposture littéraire dans les* Provinciales *de Pascal. Suivie des actes du colloque tenu à Marseilles le 10 mars 1984*, 350–62. 2nd ed. Aix-en-Provence: Université de Provence, 1985.

Descotes, Dominique, Antony McKenna, and Laurent Thirouin, eds. *Le rayonnement de Port-Royal. Mélanges en l'honneur de Philippe Sellier*. Paris: Honoré Champion, 2001.

Duchêne, Roger. *L'Imposture littéraire dans les* Provinciales *de Pascal. Suivie des actes du colloque tenu à Marseilles le 10 mars 1984*. 2nd ed. Aix-en-Provence: Université de Provence, 1985.

Faudemay, Alain. *Le Clair et l'obscur à l'âge classique*. Geneva: Slatkine, 2001.

Fénelon, François. *Œuvres*. Vols. 1–2. Paris: Gallimard (Pléiade), 1983–1997.

Ferreyrolles, Gérard. *Blaise Pascal: Les Provinciales*. Paris: PUF, 1984.

———, ed. *Justice et force: Politiques au temps de Pascal. Actes du colloque de Clermont-Ferrand 20–23 septembre 1990*. Paris: Klincksieck, 1996.

Fletcher, F. T. H. *Pascal and the Mystical Tradition*. New York: Philosophical Library, 1954.

Fontaine, Nicolas. *Mémoires ou histoire des solitaires de Port-Royal*. Paris: Honoré Champion, 2001.

Force, Pierre. *Le Problème herméneutique chez Pascal*. Paris: Vrin, 1989.

Gallucci, John. "Pascal poeta-theologus." *Papers on French Seventeenth Century Literature* 17, no. 32. (1990): 151–70.

Gouhier, Henri. "À propos du Mémorial de Pascal." *Revue d'histoire et de philosophie religeuses* 35 (1955): 147–58.

———. *Blaise Pascal, Commentaires*. Paris: Vrin, 1966.

———. *Blaise Pascal: Conversion et apologétique*. Paris: Vrin, 1986.

———. "Le Mémorial est-il un texte mystique?" In Henri Gouhier, *Blaise Pascal, Commentaires*, 49–64. Paris: Vrin, 1966.

Gros, Jean-Michel. "L'Apologie de Pascal et le fidéisme de Pierre Bayle." In *Pierre Bayle, Citoyen du Monde. De l'enfant de Carla à l'auteur du* Dictionnaire. *Actes du Colloque de Carla-Bayle (13–15 septembre 1996)*, ed. Hubert Bost and Philippe de Robert, 243–56. Paris: Honoré Champion, 1999.

Hammond, Nicholas, ed. *The Cambridge Companion to Pascal*. Cambridge: Cambridge University Press, 2003.

Howells, Robin. "Polemical Stupidity in the *Lettres provinciales*." In *Pascal/New Trends in Port-Royal Studies. Actes du 33e congrès annuel de la North American Society for Seventeenth-Century French Literature. Tome I. Arizona State University (Tempe) May 2001*, ed. David Wetsel and Frédéric Canovas, 231–37. Tübingen: Gunter Narr, 2002.

Jonsen, Albert R., and Stephen Toulmin. *The Abuse of Casuistry: A History of Moral Reasoning*. Berkeley and London: University of California Press, 1984.

Khalfa, Jean. "Pascal's Theory of Knowledge." In *The Cambridge Companion to Pascal*, ed. Nicholas Hammond, 122–43. Cambridge University Press, 2003.

Koch, Erec. *Pascal and Rhetoric: Figural and Persuasive Language in the Scientific Treatises, the* Provinciales *and the* Pensées. Charlottesville: Rockwood Press, 1997.

Kolakowski, Leszek. *God Owes Us Nothing: A Brief Remark on Pascal's Religion and on the Spirit of Jansenism*. Chicago: University of Chicago Press, 1995.

Krailsheimer, A. J. *Pascal*. New York: Hill and Wang/Farrar, 1980.

———, trans. *Pensées*. Harmondsworth: Penguin, 1966; revised 1995.

———, trans. *The Provincial Letters*. Harmondsworth: Penguin, 1967.

LaPorte, Jean. *Le Cœur et la raison selon Pascal*. Paris: Elzévir, 1950.

LeGuern, Michel. "Les *Provinciales* ou les excès d'un polémiste abusé." In Roger Duchêne, *L'Imposture littéraire dans les* Provinciales *de Pascal. Suivie des actes du colloque tenu à Marseilles le 10 mars 1984*. 2nd ed. 309–14. Aix-en Provence: Université de Provence, 1985.

LeGuern, Michel and Marie-Rose. *Les* Pensées *de Pascal: De l'anthropologie à la théologie*. Paris: Larousse, 1972.

Levi, Honor, trans. *Pensées and Other Writings*. Edited by Anthony Levi. Oxford: Oxford University Press (Oxford World's Classics), 1995.

MacKenzie, Louis A., Jr. *Pascal's* Lettres Provinciales: *The Motif and Practice of Fragmentation*. Birmingham, Ala.: Summa, 1988.

Malebranche, Nicholas. *Œuvres*. Vols. 1–2. Paris: Gallimard (Pléiade), 1979–92.

Martz, Louis. *Thomas More: The Search for the Inner Man*. New Haven: Yale, 1990.

Melzer, Sara E. *Discourses of the Fall: A Study of Pascal's* Pensées. Berkeley and London: University of California Press, 1986.

Mesnard, Jean. "Aux origines de l'édition des *Pensées*: Les deux copies." In *Les «Pensées» de Pascal ont trois cents ans*, 1–29. Clermont-Ferrand: G. de Bussac, 1971.

———. *La Culture au XVIIe siècle. Enquêtes et syntheses.* Paris: Presses Universitaires de France, 1992.

———. *Pascal.* Paris: Desclée de Brouwer, 1965.

———. *Les* Pensées *de Pascal.* Paris: SEDES, 1976; rev. ed. 1993.

———. "Le thème des trois ordres dans l'organisation des *Pensées*." In Jean Mesnard, *La Culture au XVIIe siècle*, 462–86. Paris: Presses Universitaires de France, 1992.

———. ed. *Blaise Pascal. Œvres complètes.* Paris: Desclée de Brouwer, 1964–. Vols. 1–4 to date. (The *Provinciales* will appear in vol. 5 and the *Pensées* in vol. 6.)

Meyer, Harding. "Pascals Memorial, ein ekstatisches Dokument?" *Zur Kirchengeschichte* 68 (1957): 335–41.

Michon, Hélène. "Le Chapelet secret du Saint-Sacrement: la question de l'écriture mystique." In *Le Rayonnement de Port-Royal. Mélanges en l'honneur de Philippe Sellier*, ed. Dominique Descotes, Antony McKenna, and Laurent Thirouin, 51–74. Paris: Honoré Champion, 2001.

Miel, Jan. *Pascal and Theology.* Baltimore and London: Johns Hopkins University Press, 1969.

More, Thomas. *The Complete Works of Thomas More.* Vols. 1–15; in 19. New Haven: Yale University Press, 1963–97.

Morot-Sir, Eduard. "La justice de Dieu selon Pascal." In *Justice et Force. Actes du colloque «Droit et pensée politique autour de Pascal». Clermont-Ferrand, 20–23 septembre 1990*, ed. Gérard Ferreyrolles, 281–96. Paris: Éditions Klincksieck, 1996.

Natoli, Charles. "L'importance fondamentale de la justice dans l'apologétique de Pascal: le Dieu caché." In *Justice et Force. Actes du colloque «Droit et pensée politique autour de Pascal». Clermont-Ferrand, 20–23 septembre 1990*, ed. Gérard Ferreyrolles, 297–305. Paris: Éditions Klincksieck, 1996.

———. *Nietzsche and Pascal on Christianity.* Berne: Peter Lang, 1985.

———. "Pascal: mystique/anti-mystique." *Cahiers du dix-septième: An Interdisciplinary Journal* 6, no. 1 (1992): 113–24.

———. "Proof in Pascal's *Pensées*: Reason as Rhetoric." In *Meaning, Structure and History in the* Pensées *of Pascal: A Colloquium Organized by the University Honors Program of Portland State University (April 5–6, 1989)*, ed. David Wetsel, 19–32. Paris-Seattle-Tübingen: Biblio 17, 1990.

———. "Les *Provinciales*: ruse contre ruse, force contre force?" In *Le rayonnement de Port-Royal. Mélanges en l'honneur de Philippe Sellier*, ed. Dominique Descotes, Antony McKenna, and Laurent Thirouin, 289–99. Paris: Honoré Champion, 2001.

———. "Révélation/Révolution: une réflexion sur la nouveauté dans les *Provinciales* de Pascal." In *Le savoir au XVIIe siècle. Actes du 34e congrès annuel de la North American Society for Seventeenth Century French Literature*, ed. John D. Lyons and Cara Welch, 243–53. Tübingen: Gunter Narr, 2003.

———. "The Role of the Wager in Pascal's Apologetics." In *The New Scholasticism* 57, no.1 (1983): 98–106.

———. "S'aimer mieux dans un tronc d'arbre: The *Provinciales* as *Heauton timoroumenos*." In *Philosophies of Classical France/Philosophies au siècle classique en France*, ed. Ziad Elmarsafy, 149–60. Berlin: Weidler, 2001.

Nicole, Pierre. *Traité de la comédie, et autres pièces d'un procès du théâtre.* Paris: Honoré Champion, 1998.

O'Connell, Marvin R. *Blaise Pascal: Reasons of the Heart.* Grand Rapids: Eerdman, 1997.

Parish, Richard. *Pascal's* Lettres Provinciales: *A Study in Polemic.* Oxford: Clarendon Press, 1989.

Pascal. Blaise. *Œuvres complètes.* Edited by Louis Lafuma. Paris: Éditions du Seuil, 1963.

———. *Œuvres complètes.* Edited by Jean Mesnard. Paris: Desclée de Brouwer, 1964- . 487–799. Vols. 1–4 so far.

———. *Pensées.* Edited by Philippe Sellier. Paris: Garnier (Classiques Garnier), 1991.

———. *Les Provinciales.* Edited by Louis Cognet and Gérard Ferreyrolles. Paris: Bordas (Classiques Garnier), 1992.

Pugh, Anthony R. *The Composition of Pascal's Apologia.* Toronto: University of Toronto Press, 1984.

Prigent, Jean. "Pascal: pyrrhonien, géomètre et chrétien." In *Pascal Présent.* No editor given, 59–76. Clermont-Ferrand: Éditions G. Bussac, 1962.

Racine, Jean. *Abrégé de l'histoire de Port-Royal.* In Jean Racine, *Œuvres Complètes*, 315–60.

———. "Lettre aux deux apologistes de l'auteur des 'Hérésies imaginaires'." In Jean Racine, *Œuvres Complètes*, 311–14.

———. *Œuvres Complètes.* Paris: Éditions du Seuil, 1962.

Rex, Walter. *Pascal's* Provincial Letters*: An Introduction.* New York: Holmes & Meier; Sevenoaks: Hodder and Stoughton, 1977.

Sainte-Beuve, Charles. *Port-Royal.* Vols. 1–3. Paris: Gallimard (Pléiade), 1953.

Sellier, Philippe. "Des *Confessions* aux *Pensées*." In Philipe Sellier, *Port-Royal et la littérature*. Vol. 1, *Pascal*, 195–222. Paris: Honoré Champion, 1999.

———. *Essais sur l'imaginaire classique. Pascal — Racine — Précieuses et Moralistes—Fénelon.* Paris: Honoré Champion, 2003.

———. *Pascal et saint Augustin.* Paris: Colin, 1970.

———. "Pascal et saint Augustin: théologie et anthropologie." In Philipe Sellier, *Port-Royal et la littérature*. Vol. 1, *Pascal*, 249–62. Paris: Honoré Champion, 1999.

———. *Port-Royal et la littérature.* Vol. 1, *Pascal.* Paris: Honoré Champion, 1999.

Sellier, Philippe. *Port-Royal et la littérature.* Vol. 2, *Le siècle de saint Augustin, La Rochefoucauld, Mme de Lafayette, Sacy, Racine.* Paris: Honoré Champion, 2000.

———. "Port-Royal: littérature et théologie." In Philipe Sellier, *Port-Royal et la littérature.* Vol. 2, *Le siècle de saint Augustin, La Rochefoucauld, Mme de Lafayette, Sacy, Racine,* 11–30. Paris: Honoré Champion, 2000.

———. "Les premières *Provinciales* et le dialogue des idées au XVIIᵉ siècle. In Philipe Sellier, *Port-Royal et la littérature.* Vol. 1, *Pascal,* 143–55. Paris: Honoré Champion, 1999.

———. "Qu'est-ce que la jansénisme (1640–1713)?" In Philipe Sellier, *Port-Royal et la littérature.* Vol. 2, *Le siècle de saint Augustin, La Rochefoucauld, Mme de Lafayette, Sacy, Racine,* 43–76. Paris: Honoré Champion, 2000.

———. " 'Sur les fleuves de Babylone': la fluidité du monde et la recherche de la permanence dans les *Pensées.*" In Philipe Sellier, *Port-Royal et la littérature.* Vol. 1, *Pascal,* 239–48. Paris: Honoré Champion, 1999.

———. "Vers l'invention d'une rhétorique: les *Provinciales.*" In Philipe Sellier, *Port-Royal et la littérature.* Vol. 1, *Pascal,* 169–85. Paris: Honoré Champion, 1999.

Thirouin, Laurent. *Le Hasard et les règles: le modèle du jeu dans la pensée de Pascal.* Paris: Vrin, 1991.

———. *L'Aveuglement salutaire. Le réquisitoire contre le théâtre dans la France classique.* Paris: Honoré Champion, 1997.

Topliss, Patricia. *The Rhetoric of Pascal: A Study of His Art of Persuasion in the* Provinciales *and the* Pensées. Amsterdam: Leicester University Press, 1966.

Voltaire. *Mélanges.* Paris: Gallimard (Pléiade), 1961.

Warner, Martin. *Philosophical Finesse: Studies in the Art of Rational Persuasion.* Oxford: Oxford University Press, 1995.

Wetsel, David. *L'Ecriture et le Reste: The "Pensées" of Pascal in the Exegetical Tradition of Port-Royal.* Columbus: Ohio State University Press, 1981.

———. *Pascal and Disbelief: Catechesis and Conversion in the* Pensées. Washington, D.C.: Catholic University of America Press, 1994.

———. ed. *Meaning, Structure and History in the* Pensées *of Pascal: A Colloquium Organized by the University Honors Program of Portland State University (April 5–6, 1989).* Paris-Seattle-Tübingen: Biblio 17, 1990.

Wetsel, David, and Fréderic Canovas, eds. *Pascal/New Trends in Port-Royal Studies. Actes du 33e congrès annuel de la North American Society for Seventeenth-Century French Literature. Tome I. Arizona State University (Tempe) May 2001.* Tübingen: Gunter Narr, 2002.

Zola, Émile. *Les Rougon-Macquart.* Vols. 1–5. Paris: Gallimard (Pléiade), 1960–67.

# NAME INDEX

## A

Acton, Lord, 125
Adams, John, 55n3
Aeschines, 61
Ahab, 128
Aquinas, Thomas, 16n18
Ariew, Roger, xiii
Aristophanes, 30, 39–40, 62
Aristotle, 43, 73, 89, 90
Arnauld, Angélique, 42n2
Arnauld, Antoine, xi, 24n33, 30–36, 44;
 Pascal's collaboration with, 36–38; on
 proof, 81n12
attrition (vs. contrition), 48
Auerbach, Erich, 103–4
Augustine of Canterbury (saint), 17
Augustine of Hippo (saint), xii, 4,
 21–24, 62–63, 128–30; and Arnauld,
 30; on common sense, 44;
 *Confessions*, 13, 22–24, 88, 126n2,
 133–34; on evil, 100–101, 109–10; on
 grace, 13–17, 23–24, 51–52, 63; and
 Jerome, 20; and More vs. Luther, 56;
 on mystery, 105, 107n30; and
 Pelagian heresy, 15n7, 65; on
 revelation, 97; on words and the
 ineffable, 109, 121
Augustinianism, xi–xii, 12–23, 42, 59,
 62–64, 131n8, 132–34

## B

Bacon, Francis, 54n1
Balzac, Honoré de, 29
baptism, 15, 17–20
Barry, Fr. Paul de, 50
Bayle, Pierre, 41, 57n8, 63, 127n4,
 129n6

Beatific Vision, 86
Beccaria, Cesare, 17n19
Bede (saint), 6–7, 17n19, 130
Benedictine rule, 42n2
Blair, Lawrence, 23n32
Blocker, H. Gene, 118n13
Bord, André, 112n4
Borneo, 23n32
Bossuet, Jacques Bénigne, 59
Brown, Peter, 63n20
Brunschvicg, L., 110n2
Bunyan, John, 48, 83
Bury, J. B., 125

## C

Calvin, John, 16n18, 44, 51, 104
Canada, 20, 23–24
capital punishment, 128
casuistry, xii, 30–49, 55–62, 87
Cato, xi
Chaucer, Geoffrey, x
*chiaroscuro*, 5, 36, 101, 119, 132
Chrysogonous (saint), 115–16
Chrysostom, John (saint), 30
Cicero, xi n2, 53n11, 55n3, 69, 125
civil war, 104
Clement (saint), 115–16
Cognet, Louis, 33n10
Condorcet, Marquis de, 116
conversion, 59–60
corporate guilt, 14
Cyprian (saint), 20n28, 56

## D

Dante Alighieri, 20–21, 134
Davidson, Hugh, 79, 82n14
deductive reasoning, 72–74, 76, 89